Production Editor: Judith D. Cohen

Excerpt from *The Interpretation of Cultures* by Clifford Gertz. Copyright ©
1973 by Basic Books, Inc. Reprinted by permission of BasicBooks, a division
of HarperCollins Publishers, Inc., and Harper Collins Publishers, London.

"A Choice of Weapons," copyright © 1954 by Phyllis McGinley, renewed ©
1982 by Phyllis Hayden Blake, from *Times Three* by Phyllis McGinley. Used
by permission of Viking Penguin, a division of Penguin Books USA Inc.

This book was set in 10 pt. Bookman by Lind Graphics of Upper Saddle
River, New Jersey, and printed and bound by Haddon Craftsmen of Scran-
ton, Pennsylvania.

Library of Congress Cataloging-in-Publication Data

Warme, Gordon.
    Reluctant treasures : the practice of analytic psychotherapy /
Gordon Warme.
        p. cm.
    Includes bibliographical references and index.
    ISBN 1-56821-217-8
    1. Psychoanalysis. I. Title.
    [DNLM: 1. Psychoanalytic Theory. 2. Psychoanalytic Therapy—
methods.   WM 460 W277a 1994]
RC504.W29 1994
616.89'17—dc20
DNLM/DLC
for Library of Congress   93-47136

Manufactured in the United States of America. Jason Aronson Inc. offers
books and cassettes. For information and catalog write to Jason Aronson
Inc., 230 Livingston Street, Northvale, New Jersey 07647.

Reluctant Treasures

The Practice of Analytic Psychotherapy

Gordon Warme, M.D.

JASON ARONSON INC.
Northvale, New Jersey
London

I will listen to your tale, though the fumes of life it exhales will come nigh to choke me. Word for word will I listen to it, for no one will ever tax me with lack of courage. So come with me, you life reeking mortals of both sexes, come with me to my hollow tree and tell me of life's manifold uncleanlinesses. Tell me as much as you like and I will listen to them.

Thomas Mann

He belonged to that great school . . . of philosophical practitioners . . . Disdainful of honors, of titles, and of academies . . . and practicing virtue without believing in it.

Gustave Flaubert

Contents

Acknowledgments

Frankly, I wrote this book without deciding to do so ahead of time—I just sat down to write and this is what came out. The ideas have been brewing for a long time, but listening to patients was undoubtedly the constant stimulus that kept me thinking about why people live as they do. Since the book is about the suffering of the many people who come to us for help, it has been written with great earnestness. Yet as I put my thoughts upon the page it became apparent that a certain irony was infusing everything that I wrote. Rather than being troubled by the levity that appeared I decided that by being simultaneously earnest and ironic, I was acting in the best analytic tradition, and in the ambiguous manner called for by my title.

I was also stimulated by literature, sometimes more by literature than by clinical articles. Thomas Mann (Warme 1987) led me to an awareness of ironic truths that sharply illuminated my patients' lives for me and, at the very same time, made those same patients more trying and enigmatic. The study of Thomas Mann induced me to read literary criticism and, in turn, those critics induced me to reread and rethink Shakespeare in particular, and the writers of the Western literary tradition in general. All of these influences fed upon and invigorated one another and, for me, much of the psychoanalytic literature woke up—although other parts of that literature grew pallid and became unimportant.

Naturally, my students and teachers have also played a role in the development of my thinking. In particular I offer my thanks to Norman Doidge and to Howard Gorman, each of whom criticized the manuscript and whose suggestions I have probably ignored more than I should have. Both are former students whose influence on me goes far beyond their association with this book.

The former has major theoretical disagreements with me and, in his inevitable conscientious and intellectually rigorous way, belabored me mercilessly. Why, he wanted to know, did I so often quote authorities if I am so certain that no person has privileged knowledge of the truth? The only answer I could give to him is that I *like* the quotes and that the felicitous language of such "authorities" is merely intended to *enrich* my way of putting things. If you believe that this response was convincing to Dr. Doidge, then you do not know him very well! To add insult to injury, this colleague speculated that I could not possibly believe all that I have written and that I have exaggerated my arguments for rhetorical ends. Finally, when he read yet another assertion of mine about the impossibility of having solid knowledge of any substantial facts, Dr. Doidge retorted as follows: "Does this mean I won't see you at work on Monday mornings any more?"

Dr. Gorman, on the other hand, feels that I have all too often failed to draw all possible conclusions from the agreeable theoretical positions that I espouse. Again and again, he says, I slip into positivistic statements that tarnish the analytic edifice that I am trying to construct. First I was exaggerating and now I have not gone far enough. What can I say? I've done my best.

I have loved and been loved on many occasions in my life. To those persons—those loves—I owe an unmeasurable debt.

All have given me the personal experience of life—of the pains and the satisfactions of life—which, I hope, have made a better person of me. Without them I could not do my work.

I owe warm thanks to Judith Cohen, my editor, who guided me through the publishing process. She, Diana Hartmann, and my anonymous copy editor helped worry my text into an acceptable form and thereby became involved in what is, after all, a precious piece of my life.

Jason Aronson, my publisher, willingly offered me his editorial advice. He plucked words out of my manuscript and correctly prophesied that they would make a good title. I am grateful for his enthusiastic encouragement of my work.

Introduction

This book is about the complexities of psychoanalytic practice. It aims to instruct students and practitioners in the ambiguities and contradictoriness that make analytic work difficult—if not infuriatingly difficult—and, at the very same time, make such work an activity of consuming interest.

One of my goals is to correct what I consider to be a disturbing tendency in psychoanalytic thinking. Many theoreticians and practitioners seem to be intent on reverting to preanalytic explanatory modes and, *pari passu*, to advocating nonanalytic therapeutic methods. Those who have, as I am inclined to put it, fallen into error, do so because they rely on nonanalytic axiomatic underpinnings or on confused and contradictory axiomatic underpinnings. Such frameworks are, of course, the philosophical models by way of which we make sense of our patients and by way of which we can construct our psychological theories.

This book is intended to supplement, and probably to dispute, what has often been explicated in existing manuals. It is needed, I suspect, because theoretical ideas change but, even more so, it is needed because the theory of technique is at risk of being derailed. Students, as they talk to me of what they are being taught, seem inclined to wander away from what I think to be key analytic notions. Often they do not see patients as conflicted, guilty, and as self-deceiving but, rather, they are inclined to see patients as victims of neglectful parents. Neglectful parents there surely are, and respectful recognition of that fact is the natural response of any person with a serious interest in the field of psychoanalytic psychotherapy. Nevertheless, as I will argue again and again in this book, the theoretical model of psychoanalysis is based on a definition of persons as conflicted, guilt-ridden, and self-deceiving. The theory also takes as a definitional starting ground the pervasively desirous nature of persons. This axiomatic starting point, I might point out, is very similar to that used by Shakespeare, Chekhov, Proust, and any number of other literary giants. My debt to them will become clear to the reader as I struggle to establish a coherent theory of psychoanalytic change.

Freud's position was clear. Patients present themselves to us in particular ways and, he said, in our curiously skeptical analytic way, we must realize that they resolutely reside in their own rigidly preferred psychological worlds. Those worlds cunningly serve to deny any other possible worlds. All other possible realities are thereby rendered impossible and nonexistent or, in other words, are repressed. In the language of Wittgenstein, the "states of affairs" that the patient announces to us are his vehemently adhered to and precious realities, and all other states of affairs are denied any existence or plausibility. Nietzsche (1873) explained how difficult it is for any of us to ever know the truth about ourselves:

> How can a human being know himself? He is a dark and shrouded thing; and if a hare has seven skins, a human being could strip off seven times seventy and would still be unable to say, "now this is really you, this is no longer a rind." Moreover it is a tortuous, dangerous undertaking to dig into oneself like this and to descend. . . .[p. 129]

I argue in the book that many contributors prefer to ground the theory and practice of psychoanalysis on pre-modern philosophical assumptions. These assumptions all have something to do with substantial realities that are thought to be "realer" than is any psychological world or any announced state of affairs. Psychoanalytic theory is at great pains to deny this and to assert that every reality is both relevant *and* arbitrary, both understandable *and* refutable. In the psychoanalytic situation, what is contained within the human soul comes to be more important than what happens to that soul. Life, reality, and psychology take on a subjective cast that only psychoanalytic psychology can adequately capture.

The bulk of the book spells out the oddly ambiguous technical consequences of the analytic position. I spell this out as didactically as I can, even though I suspect that analysts are born and not made. It is quite possible that the main task of teachers is to discover tender shoots that are already destined to evolve into the oddly reflective and introspective persons that we call psychoanalysts. Despite having written a book that purports to explain how to do it, I am not sure that we have many concrete facts to teach to our students.

> And this is the secret of education: it does not give us artificial limbs, wax noses, or eyes with spectacles, and whatever could offer such gifts is merely a travesty of education. Real education is liberation, clearing away all weeds, rubble and vermin. . . .[Nietzsche 1873, p. 130]

The ambiguity of the analytic method is located in the fact that the practicing psychoanalyst forever finds herself "in between." She is not, I hasten to add, caught between paralyzing and arbitrary forces as is the obsessional; instead, she discovers herself to analytically reside in between swarms of mutually contradictory worlds. To her, realities are *psychic realities*, that is to say, she acknowledges only that every person lives in a multitude of psychological realities. The analytic practitioner/theorist knows the value of conventional realities but denies them any ultimate truth status. She is a psychologist pure and simple.

In the hope that the reader is not yet jaded by what may well appear to be a daunting assignment, I will, in Chapter 1, define the area of concern of the psychoanalytic theorist. In Chapter 2, I venture into an exercise in psychoanalytic theory building. For those who have had enough of theory for now, the reading of Chapter 2 can be deferred. Some will find it refreshing to go on to the clinical issues that I begin to address in Chapter 3. In that chapter, I spell out in considerable detail how the analytic psychotherapist sets up the contract between herself and the patient. Some may feel that such a simple matter does not warrant so much attention but, as I will point out in that chapter, the contract constitutes a vital pole in a dynamic tension that pervades the whole analytic treatment process.

All of us think a great deal about how we can establish for the patient a setting in which all of his madness, and all of his genius, and all of his artistry, at least in principle, can come into view. This freeing up, and welcoming of what, to the patient, is unconventional—this atmosphere of "anything goes" (or, more exactly, anything can be heard)—is extremely precious since it is the window through which the patient's hidden worlds can enter for reclamation into his psychological life.

The one-sided welcoming of the unconscious does not take place in a vacuum. In an unobtrusive manner there is, in the background, the therapeutic contract that, as quietly as possible, stands for another set of values. Quiet though it is, the contract constitutes the second pole in the therapeutic tension arc. In the contract is exemplified professionalism and prudence, not to speak of an explicit acknowledgment by the analytic therapist that she values time and money. Not only that, but, by way of the contract, the analyst establishes that she has a definite therapeutic task and that the patient, just as definitely, attends because he needs help. This acknowledgment is important because, as will be referred to repeatedly, on a day-to-day basis, she fights shy of seeing her patient as being unwell. I have therefore spelled out the quiet importance of the therapeutic contract in some detail. As Nietzsche (1878) said, "If one has a strong faith, then one can afford the beautiful luxury of skepticism" (I, p. 18). And if one has a contract, one can afford the beautiful luxury of tolerance and neutrality.

In Chapters 4 to 6 and Chapter 10, I emphasize precisely the opposite, that is to say, I argue that, during the treatment process per se, the analytic therapist silently takes for granted the constraints of the therapeutic contract. These chapters describe the psychological shifts that take place in the patient and the attitude to be adopted by the analyst. Therein I spell out how I believe the self-revelations of the patient can be facilitated. In keeping with the practice of earlier books on technique, I originally intended to include a chapter on the topic of regression but, after a lot of worrying, decided that the term may mislead more than it enlightens. I have therefore dropped the word regression as an explicit explanatory term. In its place I have substituted the more neutral term *psychological shifts,* discussed in detail in Chapters 4 to 6.

In Chapter 7, "Transference and Countertransference," I address a core observational focus that analytic psychotherapists must never neglect. I attempt, in that chapter, to critique a definition of transference that I once considered to be a good one and submit to the reader a definition of my own. I hope my definition, like a new vaccine, will immunize analysts against errors better than have earlier definitions/ vaccines. That chapter also addresses what I consider to be an enduring and troubling problem in our field, a problem that is summed up by calling it the problem of institutionalized countertransference. By this I mean a rhetoric that claims that certain patients are not to be offered the benefits of an analytic treatment approach. What I argue is that debarment of these patients is a straightforward countertransference problem that has come to be institutionalized as an exclusion category for analytic treatment.

Chapters 8 and 9 are the occasion for me to announce and to remind the reader that interpretation is the key intervention in all analytic therapies and that withholding it from patients, except on tactical grounds, is never warranted. I use the term *tactical* in the sense that our ultimate goal is that all interventions eventually prepare us to make interpretations. It follows that, in that chapter, I attempt to cast doubt on the division of psychological distress into the categories of oedipal and preoedipal pathology, a division that excludes certain patients from the analytic experience, and that is identical to the countertransference exclusion category that I have already mentioned.

I use Chapter 11 to reflect upon the temptations placed in the path of the analytic practitioner by the demands of the clinical situation, that is to say, the many temptations to deviate from the standard analytic method. In Chapter 12, in analogous fashion, I take note of a host of theoretical modifications that also tempt us to deviate from our arduous analytic stance. Chapter 13 attempts to give a more coherent explication of the theoretical ideas that have infused all of the previous chapters, with a particular emphasis on the theory of psychoanalytic change. I hope my attempts at wit will prevent these chapters from being too theoretically dry.

I deny in these chapters that analytic change is analogous to, or identical with, developmental change. Instead, I claim that analytic psychotherapists view their patients as motivated, desirous, and guilty inhabitors of a personal moral order—a moral order that, first, is modeled on the oedipal-cultural law and, second, is more or less arbitrarily self-designed. Change depends on shifts in the balance between the imperatives of personal desire on the one hand, and the imperatives of the personal and cultural law on the other.

1

The Ironic Science

... what happened, is happening and will happen to us all, from the very beginning until the end of human life upon this earth.

John Cowper Powys, 1962

Before the nature of psychoanalytic practice can be ordained, the student must be clear about the frame of mind in which she will approach her patients—that is to say, what her theoretical stance will be. And before setting out on advanced exercises in psychoanalytic theory building, the theorist must determine what it is that she is theorizing about. This introductory chapter aims to establish more precisely (or all too often, I fear, more imprecisely) what that quixotic something is.

The desire of the beginning analyst is to help and to cure. A common hope is that she, in keeping with her therapeutic idealism, will be able to give to her patients that care and determined attention that they have never had before. Cer-

1

tainly, as a young psychoanalyst, I myself was convinced that patients had been cheated by life and that I, determined analyst that I thought myself to be, would give them what they had missed out on. It may be true that (some) patients have been shortchanged by life, and that we, the analysts, give something precious and worthy to them. But these truths, as we all eventually learn, are only a few among many truths about patients and about what happens in psychotherapy. Furthermore, many of the other truths that we eventually discover demonstrate to us that we can never give what we had hoped to give; indeed we, the analysts, discover to our chagrin that, since we are self-deceiving and self-serving like all persons, we bring to the therapeutic task vanities and varieties of self-interest of which we have never dreamed.

It is ironic that, despite our best intentions, and despite the self-reflective skills that our professions train us in, we must be forever circumspect and skeptical about how much we can do, about why and how patients change, and about our own motivations. Freud's (1893–1895) ironic comment to a hypothetical patient illustrates my point:

> No doubt fate would find it easier than I do to relieve you of your illness. But you will be able to convince yourself that much will have been gained if we succeed in transforming your hysterical misery into common unhappiness. [p. 305]

If I ask myself why this comment of Freud's has been so often quoted, I can only conclude that many have recognized the irony that "cure" is a paradoxical notion since, insofar as he who is cured is a polysemous creature—in other words, an ordinary mortal—he also lives a life of "common unhappiness." This wry remark, made when Freud was not yet 40 years old, points to the most fundamental of analytic ideas. So much is not what it seems to be, according to Freud, that we cannot afford to be naive about even basic presumptions and goals, including presumptions about the nature of the cure itself. Sometimes such ideas are unpalatable to us but, more often, they turn out to be the very things that make patients so extraordinarily and endlessly fascinating. Furthermore, these ideas direct us toward an awareness of the bewildering complexity and uniqueness of every person.

The psychoanalytic idea offers to the analytic therapist no ready answers and its technical and therapeutic rewards are yielded up reluctantly. The theorist and the practitioner must defer their immediate therapeutic satisfactions for more difficult pleasures. Like great literature and great music, the theory and practice of analytic psychotherapy yield ambiguous and reluctant treasures. I am tempted to invoke the word *sublime* for the hesitant dividends that we eventually earn but, for fear of slipping (yet again) into a romantic totalization of my own, will not do so.

Philip Rieff (1966) exhorts us to remember this central analytic idea. All persons are, he points out, at great pains to console themselves for the misery of living. In the service of such consolation, we all seek ultimate explanations, set up imagined solutions for those miseries, and anticipate cures and whatever other future utopias we can dreamily or urgently contrive. In this book Rieff hammers home how, in violation of the analytic idea, revisionist theoreticians seem repeatedly to set up concrete solutions for the misery of living. The particular objects of his critique are Jung, Reich, and D. H. Lawrence.

Barnaby Barrett (1984) calls such theoretical self-consolations "totalizations," that is to say, grand and unitary reductionisms. We make this error when we say things such as "her assertiveness will modulate when she works through her penis envy" or when we say that "patients recover when they achieve insight [full genital orgasm, individuation, integrity of self, ego autonomy]." The notion of ego autonomy, for example, suggests that wellness consists of some version of free will. One need only think of unwilled but nevertheless attractive states of mind to realize how impoverished our lives would be were we fully free or autonomous. Do we not all savor being driven by creative energy, or overwhelmed by beauty or by love and desire? Later I will argue that these so-called achievements, either individually or in concert, have less to do with analytic cure and, indeed, with the analytic enterprise in general than is sometimes thought.

At its best, analytic theory is able to apprehend these paradoxical qualities of persons. But, all too often, changes in the theory and practice of psychoanalytic theory turn out to be unwitting attempts to escape from this global complexity and doubt. Consequently, theoretical innovations all too often take the form of reductionistic enthusiasms or, as Nietzsche called them, "intoxications." The intoxications of love, of religious faith, of scientific discovery, and of political truths tempt us all. But the analytic theorist-therapist, even though herself tempted and enthralled at times, ultimately reacts by acknowledging her desire to find a solid theoretical footing and yet, despite that desire, reluctantly declining to demand such a surefooted theory.

The analytic theorist is well aware of the all-too-human longing for romantic opiates. Tears come to her eyes when she thinks of the traditional ending of fairy tales: ". . . and they lived happily ever after." But she also is fascinated by the darker German version of this ending: ". . . and if they have not died, they live there still."

Ultimately, all scientific theories share the quixotic nature of psychoanalytic theory. If, for example, we opt to interpret the world in terms of objectivism, we can understand our observational powers as reliable, and thereby conclude that we can reach true conclusions about the world. But it must be remembered that objectivism is only possible after a decision has been made—an *interpretation* of the world has been made—that, for purposes of the inquiry in question, the world is to be understood in objectivistic terms. In other words, there is necessarily an interpretive occasion anterior to any particular way of studying the world. Analytic theory is peculiar insofar as its focus is on the interpretive act itself. Since interpretation is both subjective and infinitely various, the unfortunate analytic theorist is forever tentative, sees many sides to every question, and is, to put it mildly, infuriatingly difficult to pin down.

Those who essay to contribute to psychoanalytic theory

ought to be exquisitely aware that the English translations of Freud that most of us use are liable to lead us astray on many fronts. Darius Ornston's (1985) work can be of great help in this regard. He carefully demonstrates how the best-known English translations that we use are theoretically charged— charged, that is, with language choices that modify Freud's intent far more than we usually realize. What he emphasizes is that translators have typically preferred a Latinized language rather than a plain English that would be more faithful to Freud's plain German and more faithful to the original theoretical intent. Freud's German descriptions are earthy and immanent. Persons, when portrayed in such language, are more immediately revealed in all their brutality, kindness, vulnerability, and civility. Scientistic and Latinized language is more liable to lack the compelling force and lucidity of ordinary German or, for that matter, of ordinary English.

The reluctance to know the plain facts about persons is nothing new. One need only think of the enormous fears and resistance that accompanied translations of the Bible into the vernacular. Luther, Tyndale, and Erasmus alike were seen as subversive and dangerous. Such fears of knowing are the province of psychoanalytic study and of psychoanalytic theory.

I would like to compare Freud to the biblical author "J," who was brought to my attention by the extraordinary writings of the literary critic Harold Bloom (Bloom and Rosenberg 1990). "J" is an early recorder of the stories of the Pentateuch (the Torah, the five books of Moses). Bloom's argument is that "J," a literary genius, tells us these biblical stories with unrivaled poignancy, drama, and, most important of all, with unrivaled psychological genius. Her (Bloom argues that "J" was a woman) portrayal of Yahweh is known to us all but, to a certain extent, few of us have let ourselves realize what an odd portrait of God she has painted for us. Her Yahweh is, along with his Godly powers and Godly expectations, capricious, foolish, and brutal. Think only of Yahweh's demand that Abraham kill Isaac, his unprovoked attempt to murder

Moses, and his offense at the sensible derision of the aged Sarah when Yahweh prophesies the birth of Isaac. The Yahweh portrayed to us by "J" is, as Bloom and Rosenberg point out repeatedly, weird, uncanny, and impish.

My point here is that "J" has portrayed for us an image of God that is an urgent reminder to us of the nature of man. We who study the psychological nature of man are reminded by this image that man, too, is brutal, impish, and weird—hence my characterization of our work as theorizing about the quixotic. These truths about persons—truths both brutal and amusing—must be the vital focus of analytic theorizing and of therapeutic analytic work.

The crucial recognition that we must make is of a fundamental irony. The irony is that, for every person, *"absolutely incommensurate realities collide and cannot be resolved"* (Bloom and Rosenberg 1990, p. 25). That irony is (and the reader will be repeatedly reminded of my quirky resolve to attend to such ironies) the informing premise of this entire book. It is, I affirm, the informing premise of psychoanalytic theory per se and is traditionally referred to as the problem of *conflict.*

Study of the Bible helps us maintain our theoretical focus in another important respect. Biblical redactors have mutilated the scriptures, a mutilation that has consistently led us away from the extraordinary image of Yahweh given to us by the magnificent "J." Later writers, possessed of less powerful minds than was she, have gutted the splendidly steamy and colorful portrait—not to speak of the psychologically compelling portrait—of God that has been bequeathed to us by "J." Here is where my comparison with Freud comes in. Later psychoanalytic writers have been eternally at risk of redrawing persons in a normative mold. Like the misty, halo-clad, God-above-the-clouds of the popular imagination, the psychological person who we study is repeatedly redrawn in terms that forget weirdness, impishness, cowardice, and the credulous enthusiasms of real persons.

A more mundane example of this point was given to me by Dr. S., an analysand:

"Do you remember *Fanny and Alexander?*" Dr. S. began
yet another of his stories. A wonderful Swedish family is
celebrating Christmas. The extended family is large and
wealthy, there are many children and many servants, and
all are happy. The Christmas scene—decorations, meals,
greetings of one another—refreshes the observer's spirit.
Not only is this a wonderfully happy family that was being
described, but it is also a *good* family. In preparation for
what was to follow, Dr. S. added that this is not a *virtuous*
family. As one reads the book or watches the film, one
comes to realize that, as well as being good people and
happy people, they are also sinners. Sinners? Yes, he said,
they are sinners. The grandmother is having (dare he say
it?) an affair with a Rabbi. A preadolescent boy (outrage,
outrage) periodically sleeps with one of the maids (and not
for purposes of sleep), and an uncle sleeps, whenever he
can, with that same maid. Perhaps worst of all, another
uncle takes the children from the Christmas dinner table,
leads them to a secluded stairwell and there, for their
education and enlightenment, farts magnificently.

"Aha, you say, my anal fixation, my preoccupation
with farts has appeared yet again! In response and self-
defense I would say that only an (excuse me) asshole would
make such a banal reductionistic interpretation."

I am sorry to say that Dr. S. was right in thinking that this
might be said of him, especially by those who fear the
complexity and self-deception that is focused on by psychoanalysis. This family, rife with mischief, with wickedness
and with sin, is a good family and a happy family. In an
unorthodox way, Dr. S. was trying to argue that mischief,
wickedness, and sin are not evil and are, perhaps, good. Like
Yahweh, these people are weird, impish, and paradoxical.
The happy mischief that Dr. S. saw in *Fanny and Alexander*
was, to him, a statement on behalf of tolerance and generos-
ity. In addition, it was a rejection of virtue. Fathers, Dr. S.
declared, *do* fart for their children, and mothers, in response,
cry out "Father, don't *do* that!" But the objections of the
mothers are shrewdly psychological just as are the windy
noises made by the fathers. They rebuke the fathers, I
suspect, in order to illustrate that wickedness is problematic

and complex, that the paradoxical affirmation and denial of wickedness leads to wisdom and patience and decency. In this interpretation of the story sin is not bad. Rather, Dr. S. said, evil (as distinct from sin) is bad, and virtue (as distinct from goodness) is bad. And here is how the story of *Fanny and Alexander* goes on to make Dr. S.'s point.

The father of the family dies and the mother remarries—in fact, marries the Calvinistic minister who had conducted the father's funeral service. He is very different from the first father of that "wholesome, happy family," for he is, in every respect, a *virtuous* man. He is moralistic, judgmental, and punitive—indeed, he is a monster. He, this virtuous man, is like the judgmental conscience-superego of my patient, Dr. S. "One should never trust oneself," he argued, "when one becomes virtuous. Virtue is the sin of pride— the first of the seven deadly sins."

Dr. S. told a patient his interpretation of *Fanny and Alexander,* including the story of the windy uncle. "Because of my dignified office, my dignified business suit, and my dignified four-in-hand necktie, my patient was a bit nonplused by my earthy language. I hasten to reassure you that the telling of the tale was not done idly but was part of my interpretive strategy!"

Dr. S.'s patient did not lose her composure for very long and informed him that she knew exactly what he was talking about. Years before, she had been engaged to the son of a prominent Canadian politician. In conversation her betrothed revealed that he had never heard his father fart, a revelation that made her uneasy. The uneasy thought was that, perhaps, she should think twice about marrying a man whose father did not fart. To her, she said, this reflected an uptightness, a prissiness, a lack of humor that she feared might have malodorously affected his son, her fiancé. Ultimately, that engagement was broken and, some years later, she heard that the father had died of a heart attack. This she did not believe. He had died, she assumed, of a strangulated fart.

In later chapters of this book I will put forward extended discussions of psychoanalytic writers who, wittingly or unwittingly, have been redactors of the psychoanalytic idea. I can, however, illustrate what I mean by briefly identifying a number of well-known psychoanalytic redactors. Melanie Klein (and these comments apply as well to her close theoretical ally, Jacques Lacan) creates a psychological person who is born in madness but, through parenting or through analytic treatment, can achieve a romanticized state of wholeness or integration. No fundamental weirdness or acknowledgment of the irreconcilable are to be found.

Anna Freud (1981) and Heinz Hartmann (Schafer 1976, Chapter 4, "An Overview of Heinz Hartmann's Contributions to Psychoanalysis"), authors who are usually thought of as bulwarks of the psychoanalytic idea, are the proponents of a similar romantic hope. Their version of romanticism points to a variety of corruptions of the ego—analogous to Klein's infantile psychosis—that can be healed in the service of a normative stability or mental health.

A variety of ethological theorists, notably Bowlby (1969–1980), Kohut (1984), and others of the object relations schools, promote similar views. Authors as sophisticated as these would not, obviously, be so naive as to suggest that an infant is without its moments of unhappiness—infants cry, of course—but just the same, many in this group of theorists tend to view psychological disquiet as due to disturbance (presumably environmental disturbance) of an infantile utopia that, with proper analytic intervention, can be reattained. Insofar as they believe this, the ethologists remind me of the Renaissance enthusiasts who believed in the utopian ideal of ancient Greece, and in the possibility of reestablishing that spurious ideal. This strain within ethology clings to the hope that the child is born in glory, is corrupted, and should be freed. A golden age of creativity and joy is nonironically possible.

Normative redactors share two further characteristics: hierarchical thinking and a historicist belief in "progress."

The redactor typically, perhaps always, structures the world in hierarchical terms. Psychoanalysis typically has shied away from such thinking, and has embodied that reluctance in the psychoanalytic notion of *neutrality*. The term is used mainly in a technical way, indicating that the practitioner qua practitioner declines to judge the patient's behavior, to take a position regarding what is to count as improvement, or to legislate what is to count as a goal of the analytic treatment.

As will become clear in the chapter on the psychoanalytic contract, the analyst holds to this notion as a theoretical principle but, at the very same time, is acutely aware that all persons, at all times, live within hierarchically ordered social and psychological structures. The analyst herself lives and practices within such structures. Even as she analyzes, she does so within a world of hierarchical beliefs, such as regulating time is better than not regulating time, charging a fee is better than not charging a fee, the treatment of psychological suffering is better than its nontreatment, self-reflection is better than thoughtlessness. Theoretically, analytically, and in the privacy of her own thoughts, the analyst believes none of these things to be essential truths; practically, and in her personal life, she is inclined to believe all of them. Her ambiguous post—midway between these irreconcilables—is both burdensome and, at the very same time, the source of her analytically complex thinking.

The analytic mistrust of hierarchical thinking cuts even deeper than this. Insofar as she is thinking analytically, the psychoanalytic theorist is unwilling to judge one mental state as better or worse than any other. This means that she is cautious about psychological formulations that embrace notions of pathology or disease. She is only willing to recognize that there are many ways to live a life and insists that, in her role as analytic theorist and practitioner, it is not her province to make any judgment about whether one way of living a life is better or worse than any other. By doing this, she strains even her own credulity but, with great resolve, she sticks to *suffering* as her area of concern, with no implication that suffering is to be equated with illness, psychopathology, primitiveness, or infantilism. What is madness to some, is genius or godliness to another. For such states to achieve thoroughgoing status as substantial illness entities, they would need to be cross-culturally recognizable. These sickness categories are, to the analytic theoretician, only conventional judgments that invite normative demands or expectations.

> Auntie Muriel is unambiguous about most things. Her few moments of hesitation have to do with the members of her own family. She isn't sure where they fit into the Great Chain of Being. She's quite certain of her own place, however. First comes God. Then comes Auntie Muriel and the Queen, with Auntie Muriel having a slight edge. Then come about five members of the Timothy Eaton Memorial Church, which Auntie Muriel attends. After this there is a large gap. Then white, non-Jewish Canadians, Englishmen, and white, non-Jewish Americans, in that order. Then there's another large gap, followed by all other human beings on a descending scale, graded according to skin color and religion. Then cockroaches, clothes moths, silverfish and germs, which are about the only forms of animal life with which Auntie Muriel has ever had any contact. Then all sex organs, except those of flowers. [Margaret Atwood, *Life Before Man*, p. 122]

It is, perhaps, harsh to compare ourselves to Auntie Muriel but, for the purpose of immunizing us against the perils of unwarranted value judgments about patients, the comparison may be worth making. Patients, after all, are mortals liable to judgment and, since we share their mortality, we are in permanent danger of lapsing into judgmental and hierarchical thinking of the same unattractive kind as that used by Auntie Muriel.

Northrop Frye (1991) tackles the same problem. The biblical idea of hierarchy conceives of man as the *soma psychikon*—what the King James Bible translates as the natural man. Frye argues that this natural man

> has, or thinks that he has, a soul, or mind, or consciousness, sitting on top of certain impulses and desires that are traditionally called "bodily." "Bodily" is a very muddled metaphor in this context: we should be more inclined

today to speak of repressed elements in the psyche. In any
case the natural man sets up a hierarchy within himself
and uses his waking consciousness to direct and control
his operations. [p. 13]

A change in this undesirable state takes place, just as it does
in psychoanalytic treatment, by way of self-reflection:

[Rebirth] cannot mean any separation from one's natural
and social context, except insofar as a greater maturity
includes some knowledge of the conditioning that was
formerly accepted uncritically. The genuine human being
thus born is the *soma pneumatikon*, the spiritual body
[into which Yahweh has breathed the breath of life.] This
phrase means that spiritual man is a body: the natural man
or *soma psychikon* merely has one. [p. 14]

The fallacy of the *soma psychikon* can all too easily lead us
into deciding that, since we are made up of separate pieces or
parts, the disturbing soma is alien to us and is located in the
"sick" other. In other words, it allows us to purify ourselves
and, by means of projection, to pathologize others.

The analytic theory builder will, as far as she is able, ensure
that her theoretical creations are free of hierarchical assumptions. She smiles when reminded that such an expectation
for a better theory is, in itself, a hierarchical expectation.
"The theory, after all, is about incommensurate realities" she
acknowledges ruefully. But, being fated to be as self-
deceiving as anyone else, one could guess that, despite her
smile, the theorist is chagrined that her critic does not yet
understand her point. She assumes, hierarchically, that his
inferior intelligence renders him too stupid to understand.
    A second characteristic of all redactors is that they are
inclined to historicism. All developmental theories are troubled by problems of a historicist nature—problems that will
be extensively discussed in a later chapter. The historicist
idea is that of *progress*. For example, the scholastic philosophers were convinced that reason can lead to a perfect
realization of truth. Ultimately, reason can lead us to a

complete coordination of all knowledge, so comprehensive that nothing would be left over—with no remainder, so to speak. Life begins with creation, and moves forward, forward, forward, until the person arrives at redemption.

Analogously, and stated in psychopathological terms, a patient might be understood to move from a position of inferior psychological status to a position of superior psychological status. I have already argued that such assertions are judgmental and hierarchical, and are akin to the idea that sin can be overcome by virtue. The resolution of such an overcoming is salvation. Psychoanalytically speaking, sin can never be overcome since, having bitten the apple of knowledge, and having thereby abrogated the power of the Father, man is eternally guilty.

Wisdom dictates that the theorist not be too absolutist about such matters. She, like all of us, needs her utopias, but it is hoped she will reflect upon her preferred Elysian Fields as conceptions that facilitate her thinking and *not in order to believe in them.* Utopias should remind the theoretician that, although she may know how such a Utopia could work, the unnerving truth about all of us is that we do not act upon what we know. George Santayana said, "Those who cannot remember the past are condemned to repeat it." But history also teaches us that, typically, we do *not* learn the lessons of history and, also typically, we all too often do *not* profit from experience. We are, indeed, Yahwehs or, perhaps, yahoos, angels, and the ordinary, all wrapped up in one. Had the Aristotelian thinking of the Scholastics the power to give us progress, we would surely have been spared our wretched twentieth century.

People, as Freud saw them, achieve none of the above forms of progress, nor do the people seen by any of us. But being human, and thereby fated to be eternally imperfect, the theorist will forever be inclined to redact her own knowledge of human frailty. At her worst, she is liable to normatively redact the insights of Freud and of "J" into invisibility.

When working on her theory, the analytic theorist is the eternal enemy of Aristotle's logic. His logical forms are good for natural scientists but hopelessly misleading to the psychological theorist. The analytic theorist will be scrupulous in her avoidance of physics-envy. In *her* theory, the gift of Grace—of transparency—was not given to the person who thinks about psychology, to Yahweh, or to real persons. The God-given ability to see some kind of real world, true and clear, is not available to her.

2

The Fundamentals of Psychoanalytic Theory

> It is certainly not the least charm of a theory that it is refutable; it is precisely thereby that it attracts subtler minds.
>
> Nietzsche, *Beyond Good and Evil*, 1885–1886, 18.

Times change and psychotherapeutic practices change—not always for the better. Enthusiasms come and go although some become institutionalized without their use having been reflected upon as rigorously as one might hope. Changes that veer away from the intent of analytic theory and analytic practice are more than inevitable in our field—indeed, they are expectable. Psychoanalytic theory is not a coherent system that students can easily master, and the human desire to synthesize and to explain is such that every idea that offers clarity or simplification is a temptation for us all. But our patients stubbornly insist on being complex, enigmatic, and will forever prevent us from reducing them to formulas and clichés despite, at times, behaving in clichéd ways.

The theory, too, is stubbornly enigmatic and complex. Every clarity come upon in a patient is eventually transformed by the analyst—on theoretical grounds—into something that is to be puzzled over and behind which she is bound to catch glimpses of an unexpected and uncanny unconscious. In some ways her groping analytic struggles are fun since she is opening up a kaleidoscopic world of wonders. To the analytic therapist's chagrin, she is also opening up a disturbing Pandora's box of horrors. As Freud (1911) said "It is the fate of psychoanalysis to disturb the peace of the world" (pp. 32–33).

Freud's disturbing discovery is not simply the disturbing psychological contents that we unearth in our patients. More disturbing is his insistence that the psychological world in which *each one* of us lives is only our own particular interpretation of a world. This is not our interpretation of *the* world since it cannot be designated who will assign final truth statements about particular worlds. In fact Freud goes further. Since every thought we have is an interpretation of a world, our own most precious beliefs are henceforth to be viewed skeptically. This skepticism is not intended to lead us to the idea that our every thought is plainly wrong. Instead it is intended to imply something more paradoxical, a paradox that says that our every truth is *also* a nontruth. Freud's interpretive science was never intended to hold to the reductionistic notion that conscious behavior is *nothing but* a manifestation of a deeper and truer unconscious truth. His theory, instead, is complexifying and diversifying. Insofar as every truth is to count only as a partial or occasional truth, it must never be treated as though it is precious.

When I began thinking about this, I realized that the theory of analytic technique has a far wider clinical applicability than just the practice of psychoanalysis proper. Full-fledged analytic treatments are, indeed, in need of continuing theoretical influence but, I thought, countless therapists who practice other forms of analytic therapy also need to be kept theoretically up to date. Indeed, in my own practice, I sometimes see patients once or twice weekly but act with those patients in an exclusively analytic way. The only substantial distinction from formal psychoanalytic treatment, apart from frequency, is that these patients do not use the couch. The question of the analytic couch will be discussed at length in a later chapter.

I also realized that, when working with students, I expect them to respond analytically to their patients, even when they are novices. Sometimes I tease them and ask when they are going to turn into psychoanalysts. By way of this, I intend to prod them to increasingly adopt the analytic attitude that is so heavily emphasized in this book. The reader might wonder how I could have such an expectation of young trainees. In response I can only say that forms of intervention that do not have an analytic intent usually seem to be part of the ordinary repertoire of compassionate commentary that could be made by any person. Since the beginning therapists of whom I speak are highly trained professionals, I have the expectation of them that, in addition to ordinary human compassion and good sense, they must offer substantially helpful interventions above and beyond what their patients typically receive from family, friends, and other associates. The "above and beyond" interventions about which I am an expert and about which I can teach, are psychoanalytic interventions. No purpose is served by interspersing interpretive work with supportive or instructional comments since these are readily available elsewhere. Their use simply subtracts from the time available for analytic work and, moreover, contaminates and reduces the effectiveness of the analytic attempts that are actually made.

It is no secret that therapists who use analytic methods do so because they believe that those methods are the best psychological interventions that can be made. Many people would be quick to disagree with that conclusion but, personally, I suspect that the supposed skepticism about psychoanalysis is weaker than is sometimes announced. If we truly believe that we have available to us a valuable treatment method, it seems to me unkind that we would withhold it from any of our patients. Since I have embarked on this book-writing exercise, I have come to an increasing awareness that the theory of analytic therapies, be they brief or long term, is obviously identical. With some reluctance I have come to realize that, whether it is to be precontracted brief therapy or whether it is a full-fledged psychoanalytic treatment, the theory—and, indeed, the method—remains the same. I say that I have come to this conclusion "with some reluctance" because I know that my conclusion is at variance with the conclusion to which many colleagues have come. For some reason it has seemed to them that the technique of brief therapies and of less intensive psychotherapies must be different from that of psychoanalysis proper.

The time constraints imposed by brief psychotherapies is undoubtedly irrelevant to psychoanalytic theory per se but, having reflected further, I can only conclude that these time constraints are also irrelevant to therapeutic practice, that is to say, to the theory and technique of brief analytic therapy. Every psychoanalytic treatment suffers intrusions and has limitations placed upon it—constraints if you will—so why should briefness deflect us from our analytic task? It is true that *less* work will be accomplished, but why, if we believe in what we do, would we do *different* work?

This book therefore has become a treatise on psychoanalytic theory, on the theory of therapeutic technique, and on how any analytic psychotherapy is to be done. I hope it can be used by practitioners of the various psychoanalytic therapies, be those therapies brief or long term.

I have already quoted the words of one of Thomas Mann's shaman/analysts. That character exemplifies certain elements in the therapist's analytic attitude, namely, the therapist's willingness to stand by as she permits the patient to envelop her in his peculiar psychological world. Another angle, more explicitly focusing on how the analyst evokes the patient's transferences, is illustrated by another of Mann's characters, this time a magician/analyst. The conjurer/protagonist of *Mario and the Magician* (1929) had made his audience wait:

> It had got to a quarter past nine, it got to almost half past.
> It was natural that we should be nervous. . . . The stalls

had filled in time . . . the guests of the Grand Hotel, the guests of Villa Eleanora, familiar faces from the beach. Everybody had come late, but nobody too late. Cipolla made us wait for him.
    He made us wait. That is probably the way to put it. . . . Then, with no darkening of the house, Cavaliere Cipolla made his entry. [p. 540]

Thomas Mann's protagonist is an oddly ambiguous figure. He presents himself as mysterious and puzzling. What is he going to do? Will he say something soon and, if so, what will he say? If we wait, will he begin the show and entertain us? The audience is in a state of heightened expectation and suspense.

The patient speaks and the analyst remains silent. "If I speak further, will she say something or do something helpful?" thinks the patient. "Perhaps I have not revealed enough yet. Let me try harder." The patient, too, is in a heightened state of expectation and suspense.

Both sorcerer and analyst have offered themselves as figures about whom the patient and audience can spin their transference fantasies. In their state of frustration they have been said to undergo "regression" (Menninger and Holzman 1973, Chapter 3). In that state (whether one approves of the word *regression* or not) every person can create his own world of wonders about the analytic theater into which he has entered. And this, of course, takes us directly to the heart of the analytic exercise. The transference–countertransference setup will be the central vehicle of the treatment, be it brief or long term.

The working assumption of this book is that analytic treatment is based on the attitude and behavior of the analyst and not upon secondary factors such as frequency of meetings, the duration of the treatment, or the various physical arrangements.

This is not to say that frequent analytic sessions over a long period of time are not desirable. Indeed, in the best of all worlds, five meetings per week, over a period of years, would be universally available for patients who need it. However, economic and manpower constraints, not to speak of research constraints, make such analytic arrangements less available than one would wish. The typical analytic expectation that the patient use the couch is not usually advocated in brief therapies, although, upon reflection, there seems no good reason why this should be the case. I say this even though I, myself, have never used the couch for brief analytic therapy and even though many may find such a possibility highly unorthodox. In formal psychoanalytic treatment the couch is used simply because most patients seem more able to lose themselves in their thoughts and associations when in the recumbent position. And even if this were not true, there is something to be said for a traditional ritual that puts all concerned in an analytic frame of mind. It may well be that the avoidance of the couch in brief therapies should be reconsidered.

The model that I use emphasizes that the patient and the analyst are together engaged in a serious and intense inter-personal setup that is best conceptualized in transference–countertransference terms. The scrutiny of this situation, along with the scrutiny of his current and past life situations, will illuminate the patient's urgently preferred interpersonal worlds. Eventually, the analytic therapist aims to understand the unconscious motives that determine why the patient so actively pursues the particular interpersonal configurations that appear in the treatment situation and in all other areas of his life.

The words *preferred* and *pursues* as used in the previous paragraph suggest that the patient *chooses* a particular personal narrative or interpersonal setup. From an analytic point of view this is seen as only one among numerous explanations for why the patient lives his life as he does. One could, for instance, also speak of the patient being *driven* to live out a particular narrative, that is to say, he is caused by blind forces to act and think as he does. Although "choosing" and "being driven" to act are contradictory notions, psycho-analysis claims that both explanatory methods have truth val·e, and that their very contradictoriness may add elements of truth to one's understanding of what is going on. Indeed, when we (or our patients) are most inclined to think that the analysand *chooses* a particular behavior, we might be wise to consider that the patient fears that he is *driven* to act or think as he does. In like manner, the person who announces that he is driven or compelled to a course of action leads us to think of choices denied, feared, or disavowed. This sort of analytic thinking is further illuminated by referring to Bowie's (1991) wry comment that "Truth is to be found in errors and misapprehensions of all sorts, in nonsense and word-play, in the wanderings of sense through the labyrinth of the dream work. It cannot inhere in individual states of mind or states of affairs, and can only be syncopated and spasmodic" (p. 114). Such intermittent truth possibilities are the occasion of all the self-deceptions that psychoanalysts focus on.

I have said that the theoretical framework adhered to in this book is the standard analytic theory. You might ask just what that would mean in an era when so many theoretical voices are to be heard. My quick answer would be that, of course I adhere to the theoretical approach used by Freud. Undoubtedly, that response, too, would be unhelpful to many readers. This means that I must now spell out exactly what I mean. In order to be clear, I must also clarify what the other major approach is that claims to be psychoanalytic.

What Freud introduced was an approach to patients different from that which had been used before. That which had been attributed to mental degeneracy, said Freud, could also be attributed to psychological reasons, motives, and intentions. This was a vitally important and novel theoretical enterprise. In effect, Freud decided that he would refrain from seeing his patients as objects that could be studied in a manner analogous to how an inanimate object could be studied and, instead, would focus on human reasons and purposes. Such a theory is a purely psychological one and has no recourse to a more fundamental biological, sociological, or historical underpinning. Some writers have tried to popularize a more scientific-sounding language for the more usual motivational terms. They suggest that Freud treated persons as intentional systems as distinct from physicalistic systems.

If one is inclined to use the language of intentionality, one must be sure that one does not confuse *intentionality* with the ordinary English use of the word as in "he intended to frighten her," that is to say, "he did so on purpose." In the theoretical and psychological sense, intentionality is the "mark of the mental." This meaning of intentionality is sometimes referred to as Brentano's thesis. Psychoanalytic theorists might be expected to have a particular interest in this approach to theory building because Freud attended Brentano's lectures on philosophy for several years and was undoubtedly influenced by him. The thesis in full is as follows: *all mental phenomena exhibit intentionality and no physical phenomena exhibit intentionality.*

The idea of intentionality as a theoretical term to be used in theory building is particularly popular among workers in artificial intelligence (Dennett 1981). Dennett points out that one of the values of intentionality theory is that it is uncluttered by notions of consciousness, an attribute that also permits psychoanalytic theoreticians to enlist the idea of the unconscious. But, as will become clear later, for the theory to capture unconscious motivations, *multi*-intentionality must be invoked.

Intentional systems are understood to behave as they do because of the ordinary human motives to which we have recourse in our daily comprehension of other people. These ordinary accounts of human behavior refer to a person's hopes, fears, wishes, desires, and thoughts. For example, if I arrange with a friend to meet her at a particular time and place, I assume that she will be there. I am confident of my assumption because I am treating her as an intentional system, that is to say, I treat her as though she has plans and "intentions" to meet with me. Note that under ordinary circumstances, treating my friend as an intentional system has great predictive power—a predictive power far greater than would be possible if I treated her as a physicalistic system.

A physical (or physicalistic) system is understood in terms of linear causes that produce particular effects. All mechanical, biological, physiological, and chemical approaches to the study of human beings are physicalistic. Developmental and ethological theories are similarly physicalistic since they presuppose innate causal forces that produce any effects that are observed. In principle, anything at all can be treated as a physical system. We can, for example, treat a ghost, or an idea, or a soul as a physical system and, indeed, the very fact that we use nouns such as ghost, idea, and soul, suggest "things" or "substances" (albeit ethereal things or substances) that can be studied. Under these particular circumstances such a physicalistic approach, as is obvious, does not pay off in any scientific way. Freud came to the same conclusion about people. The things about people that mattered to him—their characters, their symptoms, their artistries, and their dreams—are, he said, ill-served by being studied physicalistically.

In a similar vein I would say that anything can be treated and studied as an intentional system. We can perfectly well attribute intention to a plant of which we might say that it is "trying to get to the light." If we wish, we can also treat an automobile as an intentional system by saying that it "pulls to the left" or that it "tries to surge forward when I come to a stop." For purposes of repairing the automobile, however, it profits us more to treat it as a physicalistic mechanical system.

The point of this discussion is to make clear that the theories that we use are scientific options. We can apply to anything whatever theoretical framework we wish. To treat a patient as a physicalistic system has a variety of consequences, just as does treating him as an intentional system. Freud's theoretical revision was to suggest that people should be viewed as intentional systems.

The phrase *intentional system* has a rather cold-blooded ring to it and moreover is one never used by Freud. It is a term that I do not wholeheartedly recommend, largely on the grounds that, like so many of our theoretical options, it is somewhat reductionistic and therefore is at risk of forfeiting much of the complexity of human beings. For example, such a designation leaves out of the human equation, first, explicit reference to the fact that humans have *unconscious* intentions, second, that humans are guilty and self-defeating, and third, that they desire and pursue sensual pleasure. Therefore, when I dub persons as intentional systems, I am also saying that the analytic point of view treats people as sensuous, desirous, guilty, striving, and doubtful. Of course, my selection of adjectives is perfectly arbitrary since the list of human reasons, purposes, and fears is virtually endless.

If one wishes, the above definition can be put forward in other words. Persons, I could have said, are to be defined as multi-intentional systems. All have kaleidoscopic aims and purposes, including sensuous purposes and self-critical purposes, all of which are both conscious and unconscious.

All who talk of psychological deficits, of weak egos and fragmented selves, are applying to their patients a preanalytic degeneracy theory, as are developmental theorists who refer to patients as immature or undeveloped. Although such theories have often been devised by psychoanalysts, I have questioned whether such theoretical systems are of the essence in analytic theorizing. This analytic debate will be examined in greater depth on a multitude of occasions later in this book.

This discussion of how a psychoanalytic theory (and theories in general) come to be framed may seem to the reader to be arbitrary, if not capricious. In a way it suggests that one can choose as a theoretical starting point any axiomatic underpinnings that one may wish. This is, of course, a partial truth, but a truth emphasized because psychoanalytic theory is always at some pains to emphasize that worldviews are forever inconstant. Like all other truths, psychoanalytic truths are true for their own unique psychoanalytic purposes. Although mutable in the sense that any theory is arbitrary, the theory is precious to its practitioners because it suits our liberal humanitarian ends.

Despite that tractability, the theory is not, after all, merely a matter of caprice. Although analytic theorists are uneasy about objective truth, they are also, like all theorists, responding to, and theorizing about, some real presences. Theorizing does not take place in a vacuum and the theoretical constructs that I have put forward must refer to something substantial regarding persons about which the analytic theorist is concerned and which she counts as having importance.

The first "something" to which I will refer is an interaction that I recently observed to take place between a father and his 18-month-old daughter. Upon arriving home from work the father crept quickly toward his child announcing "Here I come! Here I come!" The little girl squealed with delight as he lifted her high in the air, kissed her, blew noisy bubbles on her arm, and then enveloped her in an energetic bear hug. When he sat her on his knee, she reached for his glasses, to which he responded by preventing this and, with mock anger, scolded her with the words "rascal . . . don't you dare take my glasses . . . now I'm going to bite your tummy . . . monkey . . . funny little imp. . . ."

If we wish to theorize about persons, scenes such as this must, in some way, be apprehended by the theory. To apply to it a physicalistic or biological theory would miss the mark very widely indeed. The behavior of the father and of the child can, of course, be discussed in the language of mechanics, but any discussion of muscular actions, of bony leverage, or of neurochemical changes, fails completely to illuminate the human scene that we are considering. Nor would sociological truths—just as valid as biological truths—illuminate the psychological individuality of father and child. Their individual and unique psychology is, of course, the topic of our analytic scrutiny and, interesting though biology and sociology may be, they do not address what concerns us. Uniqueness, individuality, and the personal are our real presences, that is to say, our preferred object of study.

The young father is clearly a multi-intentional creature, responding to his daughter with love and with teasing. But we must be sure to remember that the intentions that we identify are never to be understood as having exhaustive explanatory power, since such an understanding would constitute an unwelcome and impoverishing reductionism. The latter behavior—the father's playful teasing—may, for example, be noted by us as having sadomasochistic qualities, but such a comment carries the risk of being heard reductionistically, thereby missing the point. Perhaps, one might say, his teasing behavior is a spicy and enlivening intention that can only *enrich* (not explain) our understanding of the interaction with his child.

We also must not decline to note the intense sensuality of the father–daughter interaction. Freud, when speaking theoretically, might well have preferred to say this was a sexual rather than a sensual interaction, a preference consequent upon his wish to ground his theory in biology. More specifically, his wish was to ground his theory in reproductive biology (Sulloway 1979). To me this is a distraction from the essentially psychological nature of psychoanalytic theory and, to me, the scene that I have described does not warrant such a quibble. Finally, one must note the introduction by the father of a moral lesson or, more abstractly, the differential assignment of value to various behaviors. His daughter is not, he affirms, to touch his glasses.

A bit later on, the child seized a fragile camera, in response to which the father responded with a stern "No!." The child looked at her father apprehensively and, while still looking intently at him, tentatively reached again for the camera. He said again, "Mariah, noooo . . ." The child then gave up her attempt to play with the camera.

Such a human story, I would say, requires us to note multi-intentionality, sensuality, value and moral designations, and the beginnings of guilt. Psychoanalytic theory, as I have proposed to formulate it, addresses these requirements. At a more hypothetical level, the theory would comment on a number of unconscious phenomena. The child, it might be speculated, has begun to suppress—perhaps repress—a fragment of her exuberant childish curiosity. The discrimination of what is to be suppressed is based not only upon the father's announcements that the child's various behaviors are assigned different values, but also upon the child's interpretation of the situation. To neglect this interpretive element would tend to render the theory far more behavioral than psychoanalytic theory intends.

One could also speculate about unconscious motives in the father. No obvious neglectfulness, exploitativeness, or cruelty are visible, although we know only too well that such traits (such intentional phenomena) are alive and active in all of us. The assumption of psychoanalytic theory is that these inclinations are at least suppressed and, in all likelihood, are repressed.

There is always the danger in analytic theorizing that the pervasiveness of unconscious motivation will be understated, and this may well be the case in the example I have just recorded. A particularly rigorous theorist, Barnaby Barrett (1984), insists that the very *kernel* of the theory lies in the notion of the unconscious but—and this is his crucial point— that unconscious motivates us to a far greater extent than is usually recognized. Crucial for Barrett are notions such as the contradictory repressed, negative dialectics (Adorno 1973), and psychoanalytic negativity, that is to say, psycho-analysis as a reflection upon and interrogation of the ideology of false consciousness and of self-deceiving dialogue. To him, psychoanalysis is indeed *"eine entscheidende Neuorientie-rung in Welt und Wissenschaft"* (a critical new direction in the world and in science) (Freud 1916–1917, p. 22). The book in question is dense and difficult. Indeed, Barrett seems to be at some pains to use as many obscure terms as he can—as though he wants us to have difficulty discovering philosoph-ical and psychoanalytic secrets. Nevertheless, his book is a remarkably penetrating investigation of the philosophical grounding of psychoanalytic theory and, especially, an inves-tigation of how the theory is *not* to be grounded. Barrett's book repays careful reading. For a reader who, like me, is not philosophically trained, such a reading is like having another liberal education.

What now follows is an example of another explanatory method—this time an ethological formulation of another real presence. The infant's smiling response is an innate behav-ior, universal to the species, evoked by a specific sign stimulus. At a certain age, human infants smile in response to a crude face drawn on a piece of cardboard or paper. The only requirements are that a circle be drawn, that simple marks for eyes, nose, and mouth be added, and that this piece of cardboard be moved. If one reports this finding to fathers of young infants, they understand what has been described but, typically, are unimpressed by their new knowledge. They do not, for example, prepare cardboard faces in order to elicit smiling responses from their infants. Instead, just like their psychoanalyst wives, they gurgle and coo to their infants. When their infants smile, they beam and exclaim with joy.

From such a parent–infant scenario one can glean some of the issues that lead the psychoanalyst to theorize as she does. "Ethological theory is interesting," she might say, "but it seems to miss out on what is really important. Where is the juiciness and the passion and the joy that is so centrally characteristic of what goes on between parent and infant? Ethology has something interesting to say but that is not how we conceptualize—that is to say, theorize about—infants. To parents and to analysts, infants are loved and adored and, in return, love and adore their parents. They smile, we assume, because they love their fathers and mothers, and parents live by this assumption no matter what ethology describes. What this teaches us is that ethological theories, in and of themselves, fail to capture important aspects of the real presences that psychoanalytic theorists wish to explain. To reductionistically afford privileged explanatory power to ethology—as do many object relations theorists—is a misapprehension of what it takes to be a person, that is to say, what it takes to be understood psychoanalytically. Those who use mechanistic terms like *bonding* and *attachment* may well be missing the point."

When she argues this way, the analytic theorist is in agreement with Stephen Vizinczey (1986) when he referred to "the kind of barbaric incomprehension that would describe a woman's glance by saying that she had twenty-twenty vision" (p. 106). Concomitantly, the theorist is disagreeing with the ethological speculations of John Bowlby (1960, 1961) and, as well, with some of his biologically oriented critics (A. Freud 1960, Schur 1960, Spitz 1960). Human longings, desires, fears and hopes are, plain and simple, the basic stuff of psychoanalytic theorizing.

I am insisting that a truly psychological theory—in this case psychoanalytic theory—must be embedded in the steaminess, the joys, and the torments of real life. To further that project, I propose now to bring forward another splinter of life but, this time, an example of behavior that is morally repellent. During the Second World War, in Poland, it is said that rabbis were required to clean latrines with their beards. Rather than being treated as persons, these rabbis were to be treated as physicalistic objects. Polish, Jewish, rabbinical beards were to be designated as latrine brushes. Such a designation was not genuine, of course, since those enforcing such actions recognized only too clearly the personhood of those who were to be humiliated in this way. To treat a man's beard as a latrine brush is to degrade him beyond measure and that degradation is a consequence precisely because it denies personhood. The persons—and they were, indeed, persons—who imposed such abhorrent edicts, were clearly aware that their victims were made of the stuff of humanity and would suffer from self-revulsion, humiliation, rage, and terror. A theory that attempts a beginning comprehension of such grotesque behavior cannot revert to notions of psychological deficits. Those who perpetrated such acts must be understood to be of ordinary psychological competence because, otherwise, they could not have invented such devilishly cunning tortures.

The offenders may even have known that their prey would experience guilt—a paradoxical guilt that psychoanalytic theorists, too, know about. Why would there be guilt? Could these victims, like all of us, be claiming agency for the misdeeds of their persecutors, a type of claim that is perhaps most transparent in the beliefs of children who assume that they are responsible for the misfortunes and misbehaviors of their parents or their siblings?

On other occasions humans, although psychologically competent, oblate their own psychological abilities and mis-recognize persons as not possessing the qualities—or, at least, some of the qualities—of personhood. Such is the case when humans enslave one another, when we practice racism and genocide, or when people are used as gold weights or as ballast.

The point that I am trying to make is that all persons, including monstrous persons, are capable of having a thoroughgoing awareness of psychological matters, albeit an awareness that is not explicitly codified by them. Such an explicit codification is what the psychoanalytic theorist attempts. She may well wish that her theoretical formulations were more coherent and logic-tight but, in her awareness of her impoverished predictive powers regarding human behavior, she is content to build her theories without overall coordination. The analytic theorist does not even *aim* for a comprehensive theory because, being constantly immersed in the unanticipated byways of her patients' lives, she knows that such an aim is profitless. The reader will discover for herself that, in my theoretical formulations, I repeatedly attempt to illuminate an issue and then, because of my uneasy recognition of the paradoxical nature of man, I become wary, make a cautious withdrawal, and announce that "on the other hand . . ."

Some readers will be troubled by the fact that, in a chapter devoted to theoretical issues, I have neglected the traditional theoretical constructs such as ego, id, superego, drives, and energies. The reason for this neglect is that, personally, I use these constructs only as a series of reminders, and prefer to confine formal theory to issues of the unconscious, personal motives, self-deception, the ubiquity of psychological conflict, and the pervasive sensuousness of human life. I also try to remind myself that these are Latin terms that have been grafted onto Freud's ordinary German usage and that can easily mislead us about his theoretical intent. Since this is a book on psychoanalytic praxis, I have found it best to keep my theoretical formulations as close as possible to the clinical and the personal.

My theoretical commentary has, I fear, been highly discursive—if not rambling. I will therefore conclude this chapter with a summary statement of what I consider to be the two indispensable ingredients of a psychoanalytic theory. Psychoanalysis (which I understand to be a discipline *sui generis*) is, first of all, the study and illumination of the patient's representational world. Second, it is the teasing apart—the analysis—of that representational world into its motivational components. These conflicting motivational components create a representational world that is the solution to a moral dilemma.

Psychoanalysis is a *theory of representations*. Every person, the theory says, represents the world to himself in a particular way. That system of representations is unique to each individual and the existence of such a system constitutes the very grounds upon which we can decide to call anyone an individual.

Having said this in the language with which most of us are familiar, I must now, in a sense, take it back. This is so because psychoanalysis starts with an assumption that is more radical than I have implied. In fact, psychoanalysis does *not* claim as its field of study a person's representations but, instead, claims that the representations *are* the person. The person or the self are, plain and simple, the representations in question. In other words, there is no anterior subject who does something—in this instance represents things to himself—but, instead, *representing is being a person*. When we say "It is raining," we have no particular "it" in mind. The purpose of the word *it* is merely to fulfill a linguistic custom and the *self* or *person* who represents is only another linguistic custom. Peculiarly enough "Raining!" or "Representing!" are logically preferable.

The reader will, however, forgive me if all too often, I turn out to be guilty of violating these assertions in favor of the more familiar language of persons as "representing things." The issue at stake is how the theoretician can steer clear of the kind of positivistic thinking that results in the metaphysical intoxications that I aim to avoid. The reader who wishes to pursue this matter further will profit from reading Barrett (1984), Spence (1982, 1993), and Rorty (1993).

Despite what we often think, the theory does *not* lead us to study the patient's family, his lovers, abusers, and ancestors. Rather, psychoanalytic practitioners and theoreticians study how the patient *represents* to himself and to us his family, lovers, abusers, and ancestors. I cannot emphasize this point too strongly to the student. This is so because the point is, in a way, an odd one. Here it is again. Psychoanalytic theory and practice is not about finger–thumb reality, about the soup and dumplings of life, or about tables, chairs, cats, and dogs. It is, rather, about how we humans *construe* the world. Insofar as it claims reality to be a psychological stance rather than a more or less accurate reproduction of an external reality, the theory can be said to be dialectical, linguistic, and post-Kantian.

To remind the reader of the central place of representation in psychoanalytic theorizing, I will elaborate upon a number of well-known terms used by various theoreticians, all of which, if not perfect synonyms for *representational world,* are at least very close to it in meaning. My arbitrary list includes the terms *narrative, interpretation, psychic reality, self state, compromise formation,* and *signifying chain.*

Donald Spence (1982, 1993) invites us to focus on the patient's *narrative,* a term that is gaining currency as a linguistic equivalent to *representational world.* Indeed, linguistics in general has come to play an increasingly important role in psychoanalytic theorizing (Lacan 1954–1955, Schafer 1976). Every symptom, we might say, can be viewed as a narrative. The patient with a psychologically paralyzed arm, for example, speaks to us by way of his symptom. He might be saying to us (or so we might hypothesize) that he could not have acted injuriously toward his dead father as evidenced by his physical handicap. Furthermore, his handicap punishes him for whatever he may have done. An anxiety symptom, in equivalent fashion, would announce that the afflicted patient is a nervous wreck and that—since he is that weak vessel known as a "nervous wreck"—no one could attribute to him aggressive or potent qualities. In this manner every human thought, act, and symptom can, and perhaps should, be understood as an analyzable statement or narrative.

It may not have occurred to the reader that *interpretation* is another synonym for the representational world that the psychoanalyst studies. The individual's representations are his interpretations of the world. Psychoanalysis is, of course, an interpretive theory and, at least in psychology, it is *the* interpretive theory. Outside of science, in fields such as literary criticism and biblical exegesis, interpretation is also the key theoretical instrument. There are important similarities between psychoanalytic and literary interpretation—similarities that will be spelled out later in the chapters on interpretation. In those chapters, interpretation is designated as the paradigmatic therapeutic intervention of the psychoanalytic therapist.

Psychoanalytic practitioners and theoreticians should keep in mind that we attend to interpretation in two senses. First, our clinical attention is on how the patient interprets the world—that is to say, our attention is on the system of representations being discussed in this theoretical summary. Second, we must be aware that in our analytic praxis we interpret in another sense. Clinically, we the practitioners make interpretations about the representational world in which the patient so resolutely resides. In other words, we reinterpret the patient's interpretations.

The patient's *psychic reality* is the enduring focus of the analytic therapist's attention and, to put it more strongly, that psychic reality is the urgently and resolutely contrived world that she, the analyst, tries to enter. That world *is* reality for the patient, and is just as concretely real for him as the analyst's own psychic reality is for her. Such a reality is the patient's unique way of conceiving the world, that is to say, it is the patient's system of representations. Theoretically, psychoanalytically, and poetically, these realities are as legitimate a representation of the world as is any other. Naturally enough, in our preferences, tastes, and in our public lives we believe otherwise, perhaps advocating and promoting liberal or humanitarian causes. Privately, though, we hold to our odd relativistic truth posture. Other synonyms for psychic reality include expressions such as *reality, truth world,* and *universe of discourse.*

Heinz Kohut's (1984) later formulations successfully capture the sentiment intended by the postulation of the representational world. In that work Kohut argues that psychological   development   progresses   from   archaic   forms   of
narcissism to mature forms of narcissism. This means that
individuals create their own personal worlds or universes—
that is to say, their own representational systems—based on
their unique and idiosyncratic motives. For now I will leave
aside any comment on Kohut's disposition to talk of narcissistic *needs* rather than of personal motives. A final word
about Kohut's formulations: his reference to "self states" is
another rendering of how the patient represents himself, that
is to say, it refers to his resolute psychological stance, his
posture, or, in Wittgenstein's terms, his typical language
game.

The term *compromise formation*—the expression preferred by Brenner (1976, 1982)—has the same referent as do
all the other terms that I have drawn to the reader's attention.
That which is manifest (in other words, the representational
world) is, according to the theory, the result of myriad
contradictory ideas and forces. All thoughts, feelings, and
behavior, and all symptoms, dreams, fantasies, and parapraxes as well, are to be understood as compromises between
various elements in the person—elements that are, by and
large, outside of awareness.

Compromise formation has an advantage over many of
the expressions that I have drawn to your attention. The
advantage is that compromise formation suggests to us that
there is a compromise between certain unspecified psychological forces. Very roughly speaking, those unspecified elements are the various aspects of the unconscious. The unconscious or, more specifically, the unconscious motives,
constitute the second major element of psychoanalytic theory.

The free associations of our patients are representational
worlds that we are witness to in the clinical situation. Although they tell us their narratives, patients do so in an
unfettered style that may, at times, resemble the stream-
of-consciousness writing of some modern authors. Lacan

would call such associations "signifying chains"—yet another synonym for my list.

I turn now to the second fundamental tenet of the theory: Psychoanalysis is *the analysis or unraveling of the system of representations* that constitute a person. When patients come to us, they complain that they have a problem. We the psychoanalysts can, of course, only agree. And yet, even as we agree, we also pursue a line of thought about which we cannot immediately speak to our patients. That line of thought conceives of these matters in a completely different way. Rather than thinking of the patient's symptom or distressing character trait as a problem, we, on theoretical grounds, think of them as *solutions* to problems.

The reader will recall that Freud, from the very beginning of his work, conceived of symptoms as the result of a conflict between painful memories of a traumatic event and the patient's warding off of that memory. That defensive warding off was motivated by moral offense at the memory in question. In other words, the patient's symptoms were to be understood as a defensive solution to the problem of moral disquietude. Later on, of course, Freud was more inclined to conceptualize neurosis in terms of defense against disturbing fantasies rather than against disturbing memories. The key point is that symptoms in particular, and the representational world in general, can be redescribed as serving a purpose and that, when so analyzed, the redescriptions of the patient's unconscious system of representations can be achieved.

The universe of discourse of every person is thrown into existence as a consequence of the inevitable human dilemmas to which all persons are heir. Personal desire is forever in conflict with the cultural mores. Each person's uniqueness competes eternally with demands to conform with social convention. Brief hypothetical examples such as those to which I will now return must always, I fear, be crudely simplistic. Nevertheless, in order to make my point, I will return for a moment to the example of the man with the psychologically paralyzed arm. One can see that, formulated psychoanalytically, the patient's personal desire is that his father should come to harm, but, in conflict with this, is his own allegiance to his father and to the cultural mores. The same sort of psychoanalytic understanding can be applied to the patient who suffers from an anxiety symptom. What is personal and unique to him is a sense of potency and power; the conventional cultural mores (at least to the patient in question) demand restraint of such forms of effectiveness. The psychological stance of being the anxious man satisfies such a demand for restraint and, in conformity with public morality, denies any perception of himself as hurtful.

The patient himself is conscious only of his presenting system of representations (that is to say, of his narrative, his symptom, his psychic reality, his narcissistic construal of the world, his impulse–defense configuration). But of the conflictual elements themselves, he is unaware. In other words, both that which is warded off *and* the censoring forces are unconscious. The theoretical position of psychoanalysis is that the unconscious is *never* conscious. Therefore if, by way of self-reflection or with the help of the analyst's interpretations, the patient becomes aware of a warding-off element in his behavior, that behavior is then understood to be part of his *conscious* representational world. Although previously unconscious, it is now conscious and part of the patient's personal narrative (a compromise formation, his universe of discourse). If the time is right, it is now subject to analysis just as is anything else. Such an analysis once again aims to discover additional unconscious meanings. The censoring and the warded off forces are both, of course, merely *theoretical* formulations. The attribution of unconscious motives is *never* intended to announce the intrinsic nature of the narrative or of the representational system. Such attributions are intended only to shift the patient's (and the analyst's) attention to new interpretive descriptions of the patient's world and to place that world into a context.

Freud was firm in his insistence that sex is the thing that is warded off—at least much of the time. Why sex? In response to that question I might ask other questions. Why is sex so great a preoccupation with most people? Why does every culture surround sex and marriage with complex rituals of so many kinds? And why is sexual training so determined to convince children, usually successfully, that sex is a private matter? Is it because sex is the first powerful vehicle for the child's sense of uniqueness, privacy, and separateness? After all, sex is early on deemed to be a private matter that children are urgently taught neither to talk about nor to practice in public. In addition one might speculate about the cultural value of the incest taboo. These matters are perhaps best left in the hands of anthropologists except for the psychoanalytically important issue of cultural mores. These moral codes—perhaps especially codes concerning sexual behavior—are powerfully implicated in psychological conflict. The reader can judge for herself whether this answers the question "Why sex?"

The reader may well have noticed that in my statement of the fundamentals of psychoanalytic theory I have included no commentary on biology or on mental development. On many future occasions in this book I will voice my uneasiness about including these fields in a specific psychoanalytic theory. For now I will only say that, like the analytic study of a patient, every psychological novel is the study of character and how particular characters struggle with moral dilemmas. I am tempted to say that, for all intents and purposes, psychology is the study of moral conflict.

Biology, I suspect, is a false lead. Erik Erikson (1963) made a brave attempt to include the notion of conflict in a developmental theory, and, insofar as he succeeded, his work was on the right track. He ultimately concluded that each developmental conflict *ought* to be resolved in one way and, by taking a moral position ("ought"), he unfortunately lost his psychoanalytic footing.

3

The Therapeutic
Contract

The cautious seldom err.

Confucius

Before discussing in detail the complexities of the therapeutic
contract, let me give a brief outline of how the contract is to
be set up. It is assumed that a diagnostic examination has
already been carried out by the analytic therapist (or by
someone else) and that a recommendation has been made
that the patient should enter analytic therapy. In effect, these
guidelines are for the first psychotherapeutic hour.

The analytic therapist should begin with a request that
the patient give a symptom review. The aim is to obtain from
the patient a simple listing of those concerns that caused him
to seek help. Such a review should be very brief since, either
because she has done the examination herself or because the
analyst will have received the examinational findings from
the referring physician, the results of the diagnostic examination are already known to her. To repeat the examination
will give the analyst no information that she will not have

access to in the therapy itself. Freud (1913) explicitly recommends that the analyst should keep the preliminary arrangements simple. The symptom review is helpful because it allows the analyst to hear the patient voice his complaints in his own words. Naturally, if the analyst herself conducted the diagnostic evaluation, and if there has been a time interval since the completion of the examination, the analyst may ask only whether anything new has come up or been thought about since the last meeting.

After reviewing the symptoms, the practitioner must see to it that practical arrangements are made. An appointment schedule should be agreed upon at times that are possible for patient and analyst. The analyst should tell the patient that it is important to meet regularly and to indicate what is to be done if patient or analyst cannot keep an appointment. Ordinarily both parties would agree to make substitute arrangements whenever possible. Some analysts have particular policies regarding vacations and this should be made clear before proceeding.

Analysts, if they are paid by way of a service fee, should explicitly mention that (in 1994) each appointment costs $100 and that, in the event of a cancellation, one of the parties will suffer a $100 loss. It should be clear (but not obsessively clear) that the analyst reserves the right to charge the patient for missed appointments. This is particularly important in jurisdictions in which a third party pays for the service. In these circumstances, patients are liable to assume that the service is free whether or not they attend. These mechanical arrangements will typically take up only another short segment of the appointment and the remainder of the time can be used to begin the treatment proper.

If the patient is to be invited to use the couch, this should be made clear now. Following this final "mechanical" arrangement, the analyst must advise the patient how he should proceed. Most often the analyst does this by giving the traditional basic rule, a suggested version of which will be given later. However, she may well give more cryptic instructions. At times analysts simply fall silent and allow the patient to proceed. With this, the therapeutic analysis proper is under way. These brief admonishments belie the subtle complexities of the contractual arrangements, an extended discussion of which follows.

All analysts should study Freud's important technical papers in Volume 12 of the *Standard Edition* of his works. In a paper entitled "On Beginning the Treatment" Freud (1913) argues that preliminary discussions with the patient should be simple and tentative, avoiding elaborate explanations and instructions. This directive is deceptive because, although Freud counsels briefness and tentativeness, it must be recognized that these contractual arrangements structure the whole analytic enterprise upon which patient and analyst are about to embark. A cardinal goal in setting up the contract is, of course, that there should be the fewest possible restrictions upon the patient's revelation of himself. There is an odd thing about all of this. Even if the treatment arrangements were more restrictive, the patient would still reveal himself upon the psychotherapeutic stage. If one thinks about this, what else can the patient do? Whatever the patient may do, he reveals who he is. In a peculiar way, the patient can hide nothing. Although we aim to discover what the patient keeps hidden, we are peculiarly aware that any behavior of the patient is revelatory, even as it masks something else. The contractual idea is that the analyst wishes to impose upon the patient as little of *her* agenda as possible, and yet, limitations there certainly are.

First, I should mention certain tacit contractual demands that the analyst makes. Most of all this consists of the expectation that a number of social conventions be obeyed. Ordinarily the patient should not injure or touch the analyst, should not soil or damage the analyst's office, and should not violate the comfort of people who use adjacent premises. None of these tacit expectations need be discussed with the patient. All members of our culture are aware of these social rules, and most obey them. Furthermore, the analyst does not discuss these social injunctions because she is not sure just what she would do should there be violations. But more about "what one does" later.

The great problem in making a contract is that the tacit expectations that our cultural norms place upon the patient are enormous and the possibilities for unique or new behavior is thereby considerably restricted. Every expectation placed upon our patients that they behave in normative ways is a restriction. The revelation of the patient's idiosyncratic side does, of course, take place, but normative demands limit the patient's ability to show his foolishness, genius, cowardice, and selfishness. In a more subtle way, the patient feels constrained to hide from himself and from the analyst his uncomfortable insights about the world, including his detection of the analyst's flaws.

Insofar as we ought not be "too smart for our own good" and not too single-mindedly accomplished, the talents and unusual abilities of the patient may well be hidden. This could be summarized by saying that the analyst, because she is interested in the patient's evil, mediocrity, and genius, will abstain from explicitly expecting socially conformative behavior. Although she, the analyst, may decline to tolerate socially disapproved behavior, she will aim to do so only after careful thought about the ways in which she may be responding, and about the possibility that she will proscribe behavior for her own personal reasons rather than doing so for therapeutic purposes. It is hoped the analytic therapist will take such actions only with regard to behavior that will definitively disrupt the analytic work—behavior such as personal intimidation, damage to the office, or serious legal infractions committed by the patient that the analyst knows about. Typically, the analyst will be tempted to respond in precisely the same way in which the patient has previously provoked the world to respond to him. In other words, she fears that she may enact with the patient the very maladaptive pattern for which he seeks help.

Even the necessity that we share a common language with our patients causes problems. To the extent that we share a language, we limit ourselves to conceiving of the world in particular ways. I suspect that this is why we psychoanalysts are puzzled and yet intrigued by the peculiar language habits of Jacques Lacan. I suspect, too, that this is the reason why we are also intrigued by certain colleagues who speak of patients in oddly evocative ways and who are sometimes said by us to be "in touch with the unconscious."

What, then, is this simple contract to be? The analyst must bring to the contract the assurance that she is properly qualified and certified to conduct psychotherapeutic work (Menninger and Holzman 1973). Ordinarily this need not be spelled out, although some patients may wish to inquire about this explicitly. Typically, patients are agreeably silent on this score. One can assume that this silence represents early evidence of a positive transference, a development that characterizes many patients. One need not, of course, speak to the patient about this fragment of positive transference at this early time, although later in the treatment continuing positive attitudes will become the focus of analytic scrutiny. Most analysts find it less agreeable when the patient asks questions about professional qualifications. Young therapists, especially, are liable to bristle a bit when faced with such early (albeit often trivial) evidence of negative transference. Such immediate doubts about the psychotherapist are far less frequent than is an immediate faith in the analyst and his qualifications. Before illustrating how such a negative moment—trivial though it may be—might be dealt with, let us be clear that, despite what may seem obvious, a *mixture* of attitudes toward the analyst is ubiquitous.

Let us suppose that the patient voices a doubt:

"Doctor, what is your theoretical orientation?"

"I hope you aren't one of those psychoanalysts who never speaks . . .?"

"Did you finish your training very long ago?"

"Have you ever worked with a patient like me?"

"Since I am an 'x' do you think it would be better if I saw a male analyst? (A Jewish analyst? A homosexual analyst? A feminist analyst?)"

I suppose there are innumerable responses that could be made to such questions. A colleague used to say, simply, that the analyst must reply using her native wit. Most important in all of this is that the analyst must be aware that whatever her response—be it subtle and wise, silly and impulsive, or defensive and cranky—she should keep to her idea that her response is a product of the therapeutic interaction. The response and the context in which it appears, can be pondered for purposes of illuminating the therapeutic interaction. In any case, here are some possibilities:

"Hmm . . . one of your early thoughts is to doubt me . . .?"

"Might I appear less promising an analyst than you expected?"

"I wonder have you any thoughts about the question?"

"Typically I like to look beyond the surface meaning of such a question. I wonder if there is more to it than meets the eye?"

"Oh, I'm pretty straightforwardly analytic in my approach. If I have to have a label, I suppose I could be called a Freudian."

The first three of these responses aim to illuminate the manifest content, that is to say, to expand the patient's conscious awareness of what is going on. They are also moves into the analytic therapy before the contract is fully made. And probably all three are psychotherapeutic and interpretive in an expectable and acceptable way. The fourth response is partly didactic and partly interpretive. I suppose that only a pedant could complain about such a response, although I will admit that I prefer to remain analytic and interpretive. The fifth response is a straightforward realistic answer to the question. I can imagine strong opinions to the effect that, while establishing a contract, the analyst is honor bound to answer the patient's questions. I can also imagine an analytic scrupulousness that disapproves of giving such an answer. Personally, I doubt that it matters very much one way or another. I am of the opinion that the analyst's ongoing attempts to take an analytic posture will, as often as not, lead her to (mildly) ponder and speculate about why the interaction is taking the form that it does. She asks this question of herself whether she has responded to the patient's concerns interpretively, didactically, or informationally.

Consideration of the immediate reaction of the patient to the analyst leads me to digress briefly to the question of how the patient should go about finding an analyst in the first place. Much has been said about this but, in my view, most of the advice given is empty rhetoric, always well meaning, but typically made up of a variety of clichés. For example, the advice that one should find an analyst with whom one feels comfortable has a certain common sense appeal. Yet, analytically speaking, this comfort is only the manifest situation. Analysts who promote comfort may well be conspiring with the patient to remain oblivious to disturbing issues that may well be at the heart of the neurosis.

Similar considerations apply when one is advised to see analysts who have established a good reputation. I am sorry to say that I have known a number of senior colleagues with splendid reputations who were, in fact, abusive with patients and, in a way, were quite mad. Other colleagues, with low or nonexistent public profiles, I have come to suspect of being profoundly wise and analytic in the best sense of the word. Probably those patients who themselves are mental health workers have a slightly better chance of linking up with competent analysts.

A woman I know once said that having a good marriage is a matter of luck. There is much to be thought about in such a statement and, perhaps, the same can be said about finding a psychoanalyst. Perhaps fortunately, there are many circumstances in which the patient is spared the problem of choosing an analyst, for example in public clinics and in research projects.

Menninger and Holzman (1973) wisely observe that the provider of the service—the analytic therapist—can promise only that she will try to help. Both words, *try* and *help*, are important here. Tentative though they may be, they capture the spirit in which the analyst will work. She will certainly not talk of cure. I sometimes teasingly suggest to students that patients are cured when they realize that there is no cure. Had I ever said such a thing to a patient, I would certainly not reveal that fact to the reader!

My francophone colleagues sometimes tease me about the fact that we anglophone psychoanalysts are excessively medical and health oriented in our work. To them, psychoanalysis is a much more philosophical and intellectual pursuit. This attitude caused me to be surprised one day when a colleague from Montreal talked repeatedly about cure. This, I thought, was my opportunity for revenge and I proceeded to tease him in return about his sudden nonphilosophical references to cure. He, in his reply, was puzzled by my remark. His Gallic shrug indicated that, of course, a cure was in order. I persisted in my teasing and reminded him of how he had chuckled at the medical frame into which we anglophones tend to place psychoanalysis. Suddenly he understood what I was talking about. "No, no," he said. "I am not talking about a medical cure but, rather, about a different cure. You know," he said, "like a cured ham."

I also avoid talking about solving problems. If one reflects for a moment one will realize that the patient has already solved his problem. His neurosis is his solution. When we say that a patient has resolved a problem, or that there has been a resolution of the neurosis, we do not mean that it has vanished or evaporated away. We only mean that new and different solutions are developed. To resolve means to re-solve, that is, to solve again. All we can promise to our patients is that many people are helped by this form of treatment and that in this instance one can only "see how it goes."

For her services, the analyst expects to be paid. Most typically, a fee is levied for each psychotherapeutic session. Under certain circumstances this fee is paid for by an insurance scheme or by some other third party. In still other circumstances, the analyst works for a salary.

Beginning analysts only reluctantly discuss fees with their patients. Most learn the hard way. The important point here is that the analyst discusses fees with the patient just as straightforwardly as she discusses anything else. Be it coarse sexuality, personal achievement, cowardice, or money— plain (but not vulgar) talk is the order of the day. Among other things, plainspokenness about money communicates to patients that the analyst's attentions are not personal. Although she may be intimate, concerned, involved, and impassioned about her patient, ultimately this is how the analyst makes her living. Please do not misunderstand me. It is not necessary that this message be communicated to the patient explicitly. If a patient is inclined to understand the analyst's ministrations as personal, he will do so willy-nilly— no matter what the analyst communicates by way of financial plainspokenness. Contrariwise, those patients who construe the analyst as impersonal, objective, and cold will do so no matter what the analyst considers the nature of her own interventions to have been. Nevertheless, in an area as fraught with the possibility of misunderstanding as is money, an initial clarity is worthwhile.

Patients should be told that money is at stake if an appointment is missed and that cancellation does not necessarily imply cancellation of the fee. As has already been mentioned, misunderstandings are especially likely to occur if payment is made by an insurance scheme. For patients so covered, payment for a missed appointment may be the only payment they ever have to make.

The practice of billing for missed appointments, whether there is insurance coverage or not, is variable among practitioners. Freud's opinion (and many agree with him) was that the patient leases the analyst's time and is responsible for the fee whether or not he attends. That practice often includes the expectation that the patient take his vacation at the same time as the analyst, or at least, that he must pay for his appointments if he takes his vacation at another time. Another group of practitioners act differently with regard to fees. If a patient misses an appointment, they believe this to be merely one of the risks involved in operating a small business and that the analytic therapist must accept such losses. A

third group takes the position that fees for missed appointments should be determined on the merits of the case. If there
has been a family death, these practitioners would not
charge. If the patient has spent the time at the movies, he
would be charged. Most cases would fall between these
extremes and would require individual consideration, usually with the participation of the patient.

I cannot claim that any of the above options is preferable.
The first two options are, of course, simpler since one can
apply a predetermined contractual arrangement. The third
option promises to make a more analytic approach possible
but may also be well-nigh impossible in practice. The choice
between a simple and a complex solution and between a
financially attractive and a financially unattractive arrangement, is not the key point. For the analytic therapist, such
arrangements are to be understood as part of the transference–countertransference setup in which patient and analyst
find themselves.

A more analytic position is to not expect uniform billing
practices regarding missed appointments. Rather, it is expected that analysts examine their billing practices analytically. They are to consider their idiosyncratic methods as an
example of their participation in the transference–countertransference situation. For example, those who *always* bill
for missed appointments, and those who *never* do so, would
be expected to view this as reflecting important features of
their own psychological status vis-à-vis their patients. Analysts who bill according to the merits of the case will be
expected to do likewise. Analysts are expected not to believe
that there are correct or incorrect policies regarding such
matters—especially since analytic thinking is characterized
by reflective caution regarding fixed rules.

In the past, in situations where the psychoanalyst was
salaried, I have at times recommended that, at the time the
contract is made, the patient should be informed that a
canceled appointment has consequences even though there
is no direct financial loss to the analyst. Since other patients
are interested in receiving the psychotherapeutic service, and
since psychotherapeutic time is at a premium, the patient

should feel a responsibility to use the time. I now find this recommendation to be rather moralistic and superficial and advise against saying such things. If the patient misuses the services of the analytic therapist, such misuse should be subjected to the same reflective analytic consideration as is anything else.

Many have said that a fee helps the patient. This may be so but as of now this is merely an opinion. I admit that I myself am of this opinion. For me, analytic thought is skeptical of opinion—especially strong opinion. Analytic thinking is far more likely to be ironic, wistful, and doubtful. This sort of thinking is unexpected in science but its rationale should become clear in later chapters.

Ordinarily, analytic therapies have no fixed time limit. The duration of the treatment is left open-ended. But at times external constraints demand that the treatment be limited to a specific number of sessions. This can happen, for example, because of limitations imposed by insurance coverage or by the requirements of research. In such cases the required time constraints should be spelled out by the analyst herself, even though research personnel may well have explained these matters previously. Should patients demand expansion of the designated research period, this should be treated by the analytic therapist as an issue to be analyzed. It is not analytically elegant to make excuses such as, for example, to say that the research does not permit such changes. But of course, from time to time, the analyst will find herself being defensive in this way. Such defensiveness is not, in fact, an analytic *faux pas*. Actually it is a countertransference reaction that is not to be squelched or extruded but, instead, is an honorable analytic event that can only illuminate what is going on. Such analytically inelegant acts do deviate from the analytic ideal to which we hold. But it is never possible to be perfectly analytic and the record of our therapeutic acts is a testimony to the fact that this is, indeed, the "impossible profession." Don't worry about such matters. Think, rather, about why you may have done it, which is what you ought to do about your most elegant utterances as well. The splendid analyst ought to contemplate her self-imposed requirement that she be splendid just as diligently as another analyst contemplates her ungainliness.

Psychoanalysis proper is conducted four or five times weekly. Time, money, research, and bureaucracy often prevent so thoroughgoing a treatment but, when such constraints are present, I personally am reluctant to see people less than twice weekly. My argument to myself on this score is that at a lesser frequency I have difficulty keeping my finger on the pulse, that is to say, I feel less attuned to the patient and less involved with him. Despite my reluctance, many analytic psychotherapists report that patients seen less than twice weekly benefit from their treatment. Despite the accumulated wisdom of years of psychotherapeutic practice, we cannot definitively announce that any particular frequency is to be recommended or prescribed. My own rationale to myself and my patients is to say that self-knowledge, like the skill of piano playing, is best achieved by frequent exercise of the function. Probably our desire to be scientific deflects us from truths about analytic frequency that are perfectly obvious when one considers how tennis players and pianists learn their crafts.

In the clinical situation I say to patients that I practice psychoanalysis and that this requires four or five meetings per week. Were I in other circumstances I would feel quite comfortable recommending twice weekly treatments. In a research situation, I do not hesitate to conform to a research protocol since I know that patients benefit and also because I know that these patients might well not receive psychotherapy outside of a research situation. It is therefore legitimate, I am arguing, to contract with a patient to meet once, twice, or five times weekly and, if the context entails specified time limitations because of research, this, too, is legitimate.

Such arrangements about appointments are made in the first meeting. But after the contract is made, a curious yet crucial change takes place. Once the treatment has begun, the analytic therapist has quite a different attitude toward the patient's appointments. No longer does she make recommendations about attendance, nor does she make recommendations about anything else. The analyst is thereafter resolutely analytic with regard to the patient's behavior—with one proviso: the one requirement placed upon the patient is that he is responsible for the analyst's fee. Otherwise, except for severe violations of social proprieties, anything goes. Whether the patient be silly, lazy, industrious, or silent is of only analytic interest to the analyst. However, since this is how the analyst earns her living, the fee must be paid.

If, for example, a patient is participating in a research study and, after a few appointments, decides to end his cooperation with that study, the analyst will not deviate from her therapeutic task. She will analyze and interpret and elucidate and clarify. For example, if indicated, she may well talk of the patient's provocativeness in agreeing to the study and then withdrawing. The same considerations hold for a patient who initially attends five times weekly and soon thereafter decides to come only once or twice weekly. The responsible analyst will not eject the patient since this would simply mean that the analyst is unwilling to know and tolerate certain aspects of the patient's being.

If the patient does not pay his bill, the analyst will not act peremptorily. Naturally, she will discuss the matter and attempt to analyze what is going on. No specific time limit for payment is recommended but, from bitter experience, most analysts know that an unpaid bill should not be tolerated for too long.

In summary, analyst and patient contract to meet at a certain frequency but, if a patient later decides to reduce his appointment frequency, the analyst will neither object nor impose sanctions. The exception to this would be a proposal by the patient to meet at a frequency that cannot be accommodated by the analyst's schedule. For example, a frequency of less than once weekly would be difficult for most analytic psychotherapists to accommodate. An increase in frequency would be accommodated by the analyst as her schedule permits. In the case of a decrease or an increase in the number of appointments, analysis of the motives for change is, of course, pursued.

Patients in formal psychoanalytic treatment are invited to use the couch. Most experienced analysts find this arrangement facilitates analytic work (Brenner 1976, Chapter 7), although others might disagree that the use of the couch is required. Some analysts suggest the use of the couch to patients seen only once or twice weekly. Many have opinions about this—often strong and divergent opinions. I would suggest that there is little evidence supporting or contradicting such methods, and that benign indifference to the matter is best.

One or two additional "mechanical" matters must be mentioned. It goes without saying that the analytic therapist provides for her patients a situation of privacy, confidentiality, and relative quiet. Many claim that the consulting room should be modestly furnished and that personal items such as pictures should be kept to a minimum. The rationale here is that this will prevent the contamination of the transference manifestations that develop. I suspect that such opinions are based on a misapprehension of transference phenomena. It seems to me that, theoretically speaking, transferences are inevitable since all interpersonal attitudes are grounded in previous interpersonal situations. More than that, they are grounded in the fantastic imagery and belief that lies beneath the surface of all thought. It is doubtful that furnishings could prevent or impede the entry of conscious and unconscious transference imagery into any and every situation in the patient's life.

A symptom review has been carried out, a contract has been made, and all that remains is to advise the patient how he should proceed. I am old fashioned and tell patients a slightly modified version of the basic rule (Freud 1913).

> The idea is to say your thoughts as freely as you can. Say everything that comes to mind, even if it seems silly, irrelevant, or impolite. As far as possible, say everything. This is what is called the basic rule and I recommend it to you—with one proviso. I, personally, prefer not to think of it as a rule since a rule seems to violate the spirit in which we will do our work. But in any case, it gives you an idea about how we will proceed.

There is nothing precious about my way of advising the patient how to proceed. Many analysts begin in quite different ways. Some, for example, say nothing at all, and others slip imperceptibly from contract into the analytic therapy. Here are other examples of what might be said.

> "It is important that I know as much as possible about you. Can you now go ahead and speak of yourself?"

> "Why don't you start in . . .?"

> "Well, what will you now talk to me about?"

And, more flamboyantly:

> "Now you can start to tell me of your world of wonders, your house of horrors, your tales and triumphs, your trials and tribulations."

> "And now you can let yourself appear on our stage, our therapeutic stage. I wonder what play, what novel, will emerge?"

The reader can see that the analyst's counsel to the patient about how to proceed in therapy ranges from earnestness and didacticism, to playfulness and evocativeness. All are satisfactory. Typically, the analyst will be inclined to choose the sober options, partly because we analysts are usually, by nature, earnest, and partly because our patients, especially when the treatment begins, are not in a frivolous frame of mind.

I sometimes like to specifically use the word *analysis* in order to hint to the patient that our therapeutic task will be to tease apart what he says, does, and feels. But this is certainly not a necessity.

Kernberg and colleagues (1989) suggest that the basic instructions to the patient may have to be returned to a number of times, at least with borderline patients. For example, a silent patient would need to be reminded of the expectation that he should speak. My own reaction to these words is to become a bit uneasy. Such advice seems to me to be a misunderstanding of the intent of the basic rule and, although any of us might admonish a patient to speak, we certainly do not believe that we behave analytically if we do so. The silent patient is as dramatically revealing of himself as is any chatterbox. He is, moreover, concealing, hiding and wearing a mask just as is any patient who speaks openly and freely. Whatever the patient does or says is a compromise formation (see Brenner 1982, Chapter 7) or an impulse-defense configuration, and cannot be anything but perfectly acceptable material for our analytic attentions. Often we are dissatisfied or troubled if a patient is silent, but this is a perfectly ordinary and commonplace countertransference to which the analytic psychotherapist will attend—or not attend—with a mixture of chagrin, amusement, and bemused resignation. I prefer to heed the advice of Menninger and Holzman (1973, Chapter 2) and of Freud (1913) who have recommended that we keep the contract as short and sweet as possible.

Kernberg and colleagues (1989) also suggest that the analytic therapist should explain to the patient why she talks only intermittently. Here is what they recommend that she say.

> Let me remind you that my task is to speak whenever I feel I have something to contribute to your understanding of yourself. And that is what I am doing. If I am silent, it is because at that point I don't feel that I have anything to contribute. If I feel I have something to contribute, I'll say it, sometimes, as you remember, to your annoyance because you feel I am not letting you talk. [p. 26]

Keep in mind that the writers of this passage are diligent and experienced practitioners and theorists. Despite their undoubted good intentions, I find this remark to be nonanalytic and outside of the range of commentary to be recommended to dynamic analysts. It is not that we dynamic analysts do not say such things because, of course, we do. It is simply that this is not what is *recommended* since it advises the patient to suppress his reactions to the analyst. The comment to the patient seems to be an airtight argument that it would be improper of him to be frustrated or annoyed by the analyst's behavior. I could interpret the above comment as follows:

> Please do not become annoyed with me. If I am silent, then this is for your benefit. You ought to feel guilty if you are annoyed when my intentions are so good. Let me remind you that you also were annoyed when I *did* speak on another occasion. Can you see how unfair you are? You should be ashamed of yourself and please don't complain any more.

Telling the patient what we are doing, and why we are doing it, is typically done to suppress the patient's reactions—precisely what we do not wish to do. This point is so important that I am impelled to repeat it. Whenever we explain our behavior to our patients it is likely that we are frightened and wish to calm our own distress by squelching the patient. Both patient and analyst are eternally inclined to evade unpleasantness—as are all persons—and the analytic therapist, in particular, ought to be eternally on guard against such evasiveness. The inevitable expectations for social conformity by both parties to the treatment contract make for the greatest difficulties in maintaining a space in which the unattractive can appear.

I have already mentioned many things that the analyst is not to do. She will, of course, do them anyway since the analytic posture is only a guiding idea to which one can never live up. What follows are further suggestions of things the analytic therapist is not to do.

Once again I turn to Kernberg and colleagues (1989), who entitle a section of their book "Structuring the Treatment." I pick this book to comment on because the authors advocate technical behaviors that contradict what I consider to be the analytic attitude. The only argument that I can imagine that they could muster against my complaints would be that their way works. But so many people in our field claim that their way works that one can only believe that their injunctions to structure the treatment are based on their preferences rather than on evidential, theoretical, or practical grounds. By now it must be plentifully clear to the reader that my preferences are different.

Some remarks have already been made about the risks to an analytic approach that are entailed in placing injunctions—in this instance structure—upon the patient. In the case of Kernberg and colleagues (1989), I would add that their structuring attempts are clearly interventions that all of us *want* to make but, unfortunately, when we do speak this way to patients, we are usually voicing moralistic clichés. Here are some of their recommendations:

> "I insist upon your being open and honest with me if I am to help you."

> "If you feel the desire to kill yourself, you must take steps to get immediate protection."

> "If you don't stop getting pills from other doctors, I will have to terminate our work." [p. 39–40]

One can see in their text that Kernberg and his colleagues are aware of the risks involved in doing this but, nevertheless, they firmly instruct patients to act according to social norms. I expect that such instructions have been given to these patients on countless previous occasions by countless friends, family members, and professional helpers. Why would the authors believe that their interventions would carry more weight than anyone else's? Surely patients come to the analyst because she offers something different from what other helping persons have offered. And surely the analytic psychotherapist is far too expensive to intervene in a way that most other decent citizens could just as well intervene.

I suppose it could be argued that the patient may have a

particular transference to the analyst that he has not had toward previous helpers. This would be some form of submissive, masochistic, or obedient transference. But why not analyze this? And why would a transference appear *de novo* toward the analyst in contradiction of our theoretical understanding of transferences as ubiquitous? And do we not say that transferences are clearer when the analyst is a somewhat ambiguous figure who declines to take a definitive stand on most issues? I have mentioned already that the analytic therapist's bill is the most prominent exception to the analyst's abstention from applying rules. And that demand for payment seems to me an adequate structuring of the treatment—apart from the implicit expectation that the patient not act toward the analyst in a physically forward manner. The patient must pay and must not touch the analyst. Life, of course, instructs us that absolute rules are silly. Some patients delay payment and yet we know perfectly well that the bill will be attended to. Others shake hands before and after vacations. I have been kissed twice, once by each of two patients, at Christmas time. Although full of meaning, these "violations" were not violations after all. As always, I would say simply that the therapist should resolutely maintain her analytic intent.

During my career I have been physically threatened—and frightened out of my wits—by two patients, one of whom was a bodybuilder with a record of having assaulted a previous therapist. Although I imagined to myself that a threat by him would be best managed by the purchase of a pistol, I did manage to maintain an analytic stance without untoward consequences. Like all analysts, I have also been confronted by blatantly seductive patients. An attractive young woman responded, when I commented on her sensuous wriggling on the couch, by unzipping her skirt and dropping it to the floor. I am as prone to blunders as any other psychoanalyst but, on this occasion, I again held to a strict analytic attitude. Some might complain that it was seductive of me to do so and, perhaps, it was. In fact, I assume that my response was analytic and was many other things as well. At the end of the appointment the patient put on her skirt and,

as she walked out, declared "I was just mooning you."
Perhaps she was "mooning" me but, like the analyst, she was
doing many other things as well.

That the patient can disrupt the therapy or bring it to an
end is undoubted. Analytic efforts will be made to understand
such disruptive attempts but no injunctions or levies should
be imposed. The patient's record is often filled with examples
of other people's previous failed attempts to structure the
patient. The analytically oriented therapist has typically
been chosen because it has been recognized that something
else is indicated. That "something else" is the analytic
approach.

Kernberg and colleagues (1989) advocate their methods
in a book concerned with the treatment of patients carrying
the diagnosis of "borderline." They would presumably say
that the severe psychopathology of these patients requires
that the therapeutic method be modified. As I have already
suggested, it may well be that with these particular patients
it is especially important not to deviate from our analytic
stance. These patients present themselves as foolish, weak,
impulsive, and lacking in judgment. Rather than participating in the patient's behavioral self-definition of himself,
thereby agreeing that the patient is a damaged specimen, the
analytic therapist acts otherwise. She respectfully, but with
great resolution, insists on working with her patient analytically. She is convinced that to do otherwise is to participate in
and to help perpetuate the patient's disturbing variant on
psychoneurosis. David Rapaport (1959) said it better than I
can:

> Therapies and analysts end up establishing their own
> McCarran Act: sooner or later they announce that this or
> that kind of patient is not the right kind of patient for their
> kind of therapy. However, not infrequently, they will fur-
> ther announce that this or that kind of patient is "not
> treatable." [p. 115]

It takes resolute analytic thinking and courage not to fall into
this trap.

Patients are sometimes urged to talk honestly (Kernberg et al. 1989), to try and to cooperate (Menninger and Holzman 1973). Such common-sense admonitions are, in my view, less valuable than one might think. At best, such requests for cooperation suggest a failure to recognize the ubiquitous power of unconscious motives. At worst, such urgings patronize and infantilize patients who perfectly well know about honesty and cooperation. They do not cooperate for reasons that are beyond their ken, at least for the present.

Some analysts inform patients that suicidal attempts will lead to a discharge of the patient from treatment. One can understand the disquietude of those analysts, but I cannot agree with the threat of enforced termination. It is as though they say to their patient "I will only work with your madness if you stop having your madness."

My colleague, Dr. Howard Gorman, used these words when he asked me why I had devoted so much attention to this chapter:

> If transference is conceived of broadly as a person's unique, comprehensive, and pervasive worldview, including both conscious and unconscious dimensions, the notion of objective reality loses its usefulness and must be replaced by that of a collection of individual realities (transferences) interacting with varying harmony. The therapeutic contract can now be more appropriately defined as a text given meaning by the transferences of both analyst and analysand, helping them govern the analytic situation, becoming itself a subject for analytic interpretation and best understood at the end of the analysis rather than at the beginning. The analyst wishing to address this issue might say: "In our attempt to bring understanding to your situation, you and I have agreed to some conditions governing our relationship. In this, we may, however, be deceiving ourselves. Our agreement may involve thoughts, feelings, and intentions which we do not suspect. Our analytic experience together may give us a fuller understanding as we examine it like anything else in our relationship."

As Dr. Gorman has pointed out, all of our good intentions regarding the contract are merely conscious intentions. The unconscious goals and strategies of both analyst and patient will inform the analytic process just as much as do our conscious contractual intentions. The contractual arrangements are, of course, intended to facilitate the patient's unconscious elaborations. But even though the analytic situation is not designed to facilitate the analyst's unconscious elaborations, she will nevertheless have every scoptophilic, exhibitionistic, domineering, and passively neglectful attitude that one can imagine—and every other human desire as well. Her personal neurosis will influence her far more than she realizes. The analytic therapist is forever poised between the requirements of her professional situation and her personal madness.

4

Regressive and Progressive Diversification

Even a thought, even a possibility, can shatter us and transform us.

Nietzsche, *The Gay Science*

Once the contract is made and the therapist is ready to adopt the analytic attitude, the treatment begins. The analytic therapist listens and, occasionally, intervenes. Her interventions are interpretations concerning that which the patient, ardently or reluctantly, is communicating to her. But discussions of interpretation must wait. Another phenomenon must be described first—the unfolding of regressive and progressive shifts. This refers to qualitative changes that take place as the patient speaks to us, and our interpretations must be less than satisfactory if we do not see and understand the transformational changes that are taking place.

The notion of regression is tricky. It is a term widely used by analysts and probably is so used for good reason. It refers to the disposition of the therapeutic situation to induce in the patient increasingly novel and unexpected ways of thinking and speaking. One might also call this an increasing use of creative and poetic ways of speaking and, contrapuntally, an increasing use of disturbing and primitive speech. The important point here is that the changing ways in which the patient speaks can be viewed as implying changes for the better or, contrariwise, as implying changes for the worse.

I strongly urge that a double judgment should always be made about the various alterations that take place in the patient's communications. I so urge because analytic therapists so commonly assume that regressive change implies only primitiveness, pathology, and infantilism. This despite the well-known notion of regression in the service of the ego. I suppose an argument could be made that the word *regression* should be dropped from our clinical and theoretical vocabularies. The word itself means the opposite of *progress*, and the phenomenon that I intend to describe is just as much a progression as it is a regression. Also, the word has been used so often to refer to severely and chronically disabled persons—the so-called regressed patients—that the word, in this sense, cannot be rehabilitated. Brenner (1982) for example, insists that the word regression simply does not apply to what goes on in analysis. But I will use it nevertheless, mainly because it points to essential features of the time-related speech changes that we see in patients. Patients do, indeed, sink into their own minds, their own depths or, one could even say, into their own souls. And so, with the proviso that I refer only to another of the human mind's multivalent activities, and not to any negative or sickly thing, I will herein use the term *regression* freely. It refers, therefore, to what is, in fact, a matter of theme and variations.

Regression has also been used to refer to a move from secondary process thinking to primary process thinking. Freud, with whom I disagree on this score, often equated rational secondary process thinking with health and, in parallel, irrational primary process thinking with pathology. In contrast, I believe that thinking can be categorized into two distinct types, but that both have equivalent value and equivalent health status. Furthermore, I suggest that all persons constantly use a mixture of both these forms of thinking. For example, the splendidly rational man, Aristotelian that he is, may argue that by way of his secondary process thinking, he has a privileged access to truth and to the practical solution of problems. But is this not magical, that is to say, primary process thinking? Does rational thinking give him access to poetic and artistic truths? Can he, with his rationality, solve the problems of love? When he places value on his rationality how, in fact, does he derive the value that he places on secondary process thinking? Does he use for this assignment of worth primary process methods? Since value is derived by way of a thousand quirks and identifications, both conscious and unconscious, the rational person would have to concede that rational preference is irrationally grounded. In other words, it is a matter that can only be understood as having to do with taste.

A complementary argument can be made with regard to the man who prides himself on his access to primary process thinking. One might use as one's target Jacques Lacan, who is a legendary case of proud, primary process obscurity. Although he is poetic, evocative, and even inspiring, are his texts of any value if even serious thinkers give up on him? Could he not have given a tip of the hat to secondary process thinking so that a majority rather than a minority of his potential readership could have had access to his brilliance? And, one might ask, how can one enter into an enriching dialectic with a mind that one cannot comprehend? I suspect that Lacan would have contempt for minds so mundane that they could not, in proper primary process fashion, appreciate his poetic truths. In his contempt he could only be likened to the rational person who I invoked in the previous paragraph, a person equally prone to contempt, except in that person's case, contempt for the poetic.

Freud's value judgments about these forms of thinking are, in my opinion, not a true reflection of his actual theoretical position. Freud, after all, was the one who initiated us into an awareness of the role of dreams in normal psychic life and taught us how to listen for and value the primary process. I, like every analyst, appreciate the value of reason. I also insist on the equal value of the poetic and the primary process. The psychological shifts that our patients undergo during their analytic therapy are comprised of excursions into both the primary and the secondary process. Excursions into both forms of thinking may be novel (and therefore potentially enriching or self-injurious) or they may be stereotyped (and therefore potentially stabilizing or stagnating).

The analytic patient finds himself in a strange situation. He has probably heard snippets of information about couches, interpretations, the unconscious, and about the importance of sex—all of which lend an aura of mystery to the psychoanalytic process. The cryptically negotiated contract and the unfamiliar, if not peculiar, nature of the analyst's behavior, often lead the patient to react both with disquietude and fascinated engrossment. Furthermore, during the initial appointment, he will often have found the analyst to be unexpectedly quiet and noncommittal, behaviors that can only contribute to a beginning puzzlement, awe, and impatience. Even during that initial appointment the patient may well begin to show signs of psychological shifts, both progressive and regressive. Finally, the analytic therapy having begun, he finds that he himself tells much to the analyst, but that she says little in return. In fact, he notes, she says virtually nothing at all. Most of the time she is silent.

Typically, patients respond conventionally, that is to say, they defer making a judgment about the silent analyst. Surely, they expect, she will soon say something and, if only they fulfill their duty to speak, the analyst will offer help, treatment, relief, cure, a unique inspirational experience, a magical transformation. Such a sequence is commonly called a regressive sequence, that is to say, a return to more primitive or infantile modes of thought. If a patient can permit himself such a psychological shift, could one not just as well call it a progressive sequence? Such changes can take place in the patient's speech during the course of one appointment, or over a period of days, months, or years. Commonly, these hopes and expectations are, in a certain sense, frustrated. In fact, Menninger and Holzman (1973, Chapter 3) are inclined to believe that the analytic therapist's frustrating silence is the precipitating occasion of the patient's changing verbalizations, a change that they opt to call regression. These authors are clearly guided by Chapter 7 of Freud's *Interpretation of Dreams* (1900), in which Freud postulated that, during sleep, the motor apparatus is inactive and that because of this the psychic apparatus is blocked from discharging its energies—in other words, the apparatus is frustrated. In consequence, says Freud, the energic flow is reversed and travels in a regressive direction. This is the model Menninger and Holzman are using to explain what happens to the frustrated analytic patient. And as the patient talks and tries to fulfill his part of the analytic contract, he indeed receives little comfort and no advice. Here is what Menninger and Holzman say happens:

> Gradually the sense of having contributed in vain, of having failed to please or satisfy or even provoke the analyst, begins to weigh upon the patient, first as mild uneasiness, then as anxiousness, and finally as frank frustration and resentment. Phyllis McGinley probably wasn't thinking of psychoanalysis when she wrote, very aptly:
>
> > Sticks and stones are hard on bones,
> > Aimed with angry art,
> > Words can sting like anything.
> > But silence breaks the heart. [p. 54]

Keep in mind that, frustrated though he may be, the patient may not complain. In fact, a large proportion of patients, even in their state of frustration, will think well of the analyst and, to be more technical about it, will tend to idealize her. For months and years patients will continue their struggle to fulfill their part of the therapeutic contract, even though the analyst does not yet seem to have reciprocated by fulfilling her vague implication that she will help. Sometimes such positive idealizing transferences can be dramatic.

Dr. L., a 40-year-old physician, entered therapy upon the urging of a psychiatrist friend. He had been seriously depressed for nine years and had seen numerous psychiatrists, had been hospitalized six or seven times, had been treated with many drugs and, a few months before the therapy began, received electroconvulsive therapy.

The analyst—who had a special interest in the analytic therapy of major depressive disorders—saw Dr. L. three times weekly using the couch. Although the analyst had no opinion about whether or not she could be of help to this patient, she had a determination that this man, like any other patient, had the right to receive the benefits of a resolutely analytic approach to his problems. She worked with him in a singlemindedly analytic way.

The patient spoke for six days in a stereotyped way about his stupidity, his harmful effects on his family, and about the futility of the treatment that was being attempted. This style of his was in keeping with the psychiatric records—going back nine years—that the analyst had in her possession. The analyst spoke little, but on one or two occasions in each appointment made brief comments on what she was observing:

"You are at great pains to convince me of your inferior status."

"Every word you utter aims to establish that you are 'the wretched one.' "

"It has been your fate for the last nine years to be exclusively understood by yourself as stupid, burdensome, and without value."

In the seventh session Dr. L. reported that he had had wild dreams all night long. This was unusual because he had not dreamt for many years. When he awoke he was not depressed for the first time since his illness began. In fact, he said, he had been depressed for longer than the nine years in which he had been a psychiatric patient. He recalled, he said, being depressed since he was a teenager. But, he said, after being free of depression for a few hours that morning, the depression had returned.

During the following weeks his depression gradually waned and after seven weeks, was gone, never to return. Dr. L. claims that he was fortunate indeed to come under the care of a physician as skilled, concerned, and humane as his analyst. He is of this opinion still (seven year follow-up), although he understands with wry amusement that this is also part of his aggrandizement of her.

This idealization of the analyst is extreme—regressively exaggerated, if you will. Attempts were made to analyze this positive transference—with some success. As is common, this analysis left the idealization only modestly modified. As the analytic therapist in question said, her analytic attempts were typically met with further idealizing comments. Her humility in the face of his praise and her attempts to analyze the motives for his praise were clear evidence for the patient that his analyst was a woman of fine character. Here is another variant on the positive transference:

A 37-year-old engineer had suffered from repeated manic and depressive episodes over a period of 16 years. During the year immediately preceding his referral for psychotherapy, he had been hospitalized eleven times. His hospital doctor, perhaps in desperation, had insisted that Mr. R. consult the psychoanalyst.

The patient agreed to see the analytic therapist only once weekly. Throughout the first year of therapy he spoke almost exclusively about his skepticism about the psychotherapeutic enterprise, about the fact that he attended against his will, and about the unremitting vicissitudes of his depressive mood. Both patient and analyst (as the analyst said to me) almost died of boredom.

After one year of such tortured meetings the patient, with great despair, said, "Doctor, I just cannot bear this any longer. I ask you very seriously to now answer my questions: What would you do if you were in my circumstances?" The analyst's answer is not necessarily one that is advocated but, nevertheless, here is her reply. "If I were you," she said, "I would urgently ask me to see you five times weekly and to allow you to use the couch." The patient was dumbfounded. "I don't get it," he said. "Why in the world would you do that? Haven't I told you how futile I think this all is? What do you mean?" The analyst then pointed out that, although the patient had been hospitalized eleven times in the year prior to beginning therapy, during the past year of psychotherapy he had had no hospitalization whatever! The patient, for want of a better word, was flabbergasted. The following week the patient made a request to begin analysis.

The analysis began a few months later. The patient lay on the couch and began with complaints and insisted in his usual way that psychotherapy was futile. But after twenty minutes a remarkable change took place. Suddenly he announced, "This is amazing! Lying here lets me think more easily. I feel all freed up." He then began talking in detail about his life, his family, and his opinions about his illness. He spoke of the analyst, associated to this and that, and to everything. In short, in a period of twenty minutes he was transformed into an "ideal" patient. I suppose that one of the essential ingredients of this idealness was that he thought that the analyst was wonderful. She had—thank God—given him the treatment he had needed all along.

He was seen three times weekly and behaved like any typical patient in analytic psychotherapy. He was depressed and "high" at times but such periods were analyzed straightforwardly. The analyst's view of this was that the straightforwardness of the analytic process was part of the positive transference that had so suddenly developed. She attempted to subject to analysis the fact that Mr. R. was such a splendid patient and, like the splendid patient that he was, he industriously tackled this issue too. His idealization of the analyst was never subject to the wry amusement that the previous patient, Dr. L., was able to muster.

After fourteen months, this analytic therapy ended because the patient was transferred to another city. The ending was uneventful. Eighteen months later the analyst happened to meet Mr. R. at a social function. He reported that during the last year "my manic-depressive illness has been worse than it has ever been." Upon questioning he blandly reported that he was working without interruption and had had no further hospitalizations (although for over a decade prior to his treatment he had had multiple hospitalizations each year). The analyst found him to be cranky and full of complaints, just as he had been during the first year of psychotherapy.

What can one say about the nature of this man's overall transference reactions? Were the reactions positive, negative, or both? Could the transformations in his attitude toward the analyst be called regressive transformations? If they are stages in a sequences of regressive changes, which behaviors should be seen as being more deeply regressed? Or are they *pro*-gressions? Or are they just changes? Is the phrase *theme and variations* safer, after all? The essential point here is merely illustrative, that is to say, an exemplification of the vicissitudes that may be seen in the transference. The two case examples cannot even be said to demonstrate particular patterns that patients in general show. What happens in practice is that each person arrives in therapy with a particular transference reaction to the analyst that then unfolds in a unique narrative pattern typical of the patient in question. The analyst monitors this narrative and analyzes it as skillfully and creatively as she can.

As has already been said, many patients have positive attitudes toward the analytic therapist and only rarely become annoyed or negative. When they do, the most typical pattern is for negativity to be retreated from in short order. After a particular instantiation of annoyance, patients are inclined to do a number of things. First of all they may do an about-face and make an excuse for the analyst's behavior. Alternatively, they may shift to a criticism of someone else. Yet another possibility is that they may be overcome with guilt and remorse and enter into self-criticism.

The point I wish to make is that, with such patients, their anger is precious. Although the patient's complaint about the analyst may be improper, incorrect, and unfair, this is usually a good time to hold one's tongue. The patient himself is all too ready to inhibit himself. Almost anything the analytic therapist is liable to say will hasten the disappearance of what is, after all, a psychologically dangerous and novel experiment that the patient is making.

The analyst is apt to be evenhanded and fair in what she says and by her fairness in the face of criticism will prick the patient's conscience. It is best to wait in silence—even in silent chagrin—if and when the patient can bring himself to tear a few strips from the analyst's hide.

It is quite another story with the patient whose transference pattern is negative from the start or who, when he develops a negative attitude, persists in it. Under these barrages of complaint, criticism, and argument, there is little need to treat the annoyance as a precious gift from the patient, that is to say, a behavior that must be handled with kid gloves. Since it is a public and obvious pattern, attempts to analyze it are in order. Here is a tip: those who must argue, quibble, and criticize eternally are, if one takes pause, at great pains to make the therapeutic situation unpalatable, ungainly, and ungratifying. Such patients often fear tenderness—and any form of interaction that is worthy and satisfying. Quibbling and arguing spares such patients what to them is forbidden.

The wise analyst will not wildly, or suddenly interpret the above formulation. First, it is a generalization that does not apply to all patients and, second, no interpretation of unconscious contents can be made without preliminary labor—sometimes brief and easy, and sometimes prolonged and arduous. Such regressive modes of interaction must first be made ego alien, that is to say, the patient must be aware of the pattern and, at least to some extent, be offended by the pattern. The analyst's native wit and her background of therapeutic experience will allow her to know when the patient is becoming curious about such a pattern. Then, and only then, can attempts be made to unravel the unconscious elements that lie behind the pattern. In this instance, forbidden interpersonal satisfaction may well be uncovered.

There is also the patient who is afraid to regress, who urgently clings to the identical interpersonal pattern that was to be seen at the beginning of the treatment.

> Thirty-two-year-old Miss A. complained bitterly that the analyst did not tell her what to do. It was necessary that she sit up and look at the analyst to discover clues to what it might be that he thought would be the right way for her to proceed. For many months she proclaimed in a stereotyped way phrases like the following:
> "I can't do this. I just can't."
> "What do you want me to do ?"
> "This doesn't work for me."
> Eventually it became clear that the phrases she had spoken since the first day of the treatment referred to a highly charged understanding of the treatment session, namely, that she and the male analyst were involved in a stimulating and dangerous sexual scene. "Innocently," the patient had given the analyst two inexpensive penis-shaped objects. She "jokingly" an-

nounced that she had heard his secretary offer to get coffee for him and teasingly added that she could undoubtedly make a better cup of coffee than could his secretary. On the immediately following days the patient anxiously repeated in a stereotyped way that "I can't do this." When this sexualized transference scenario became clear, it quickly became associated with a period in her life when she was home alone with her stepfather for many hours a day. The phrases applied exactly to that incestuously charged story.

This patient did not regress. Her words and behavior were exactly the same at the beginning of the treatment as they were when their significance became clear. But something did change. Was her insight the opposite of regression, that is to say, *progression*? But if regression means, as I said earlier, a movement toward the inward look, then could not the word be used for this sort of mutation as well? Unfortunately, when patients behave as did this woman, the analyst is inclined to urge the patient to try, as though the patient were foolishly reluctant and ought to get on with it. In retrospect, this would have been a transparent countertransference enactment in which the analyst would have been actively urging incestuous cooperation—"Try!" The patient would have gained temporary relief, since the actively incestuous person would not be her but, rather, the father-analyst. In effect, the therapist would have been the ally of the patient's wish to project her desirous statements onto the analyst.

An important point that Menninger and Holzman (1973) make is that recovery may take place as part of a disorganization–reorganization process. There is a truth in this—to wit, King Lear's clearer perception of Cordelia after he has become mad and recovered. As has often been said, a man must lose himself to find himself. There are many such expressions in our language. Karl Menninger himself used to talk of our psychiatric patients, after treatment, being "weller than well." What he meant by this was that, in psychiatry, we may well have higher goals for our patients than do other branches of medicine. We expect that, after breaking down and being successfully treated, our patients will function at a level higher than that at which they have ever previously functioned. Ordinarily in medicine, we hope only that our patients get back to where they were.

The hesitation one might have about this is the implication that the patient must disorganize before he reorganizes. It is true that we can, at times, be witness to disorganization–reorganization sequences in our recovering patients but it is not a necessity. Certainly, some of our patients do not seem to do so. They simply move in the direction of wellness. And also certainly, no analyst should aim to have her patients regress or disorganize. Some patients may do so but it is surely not an inevitability or a requirement.

We are all cautioned, I think, when we consider the grotesque admonitions of the primal therapists, perhaps the definitive advocates of disorganization as the route to recovery. Perhaps more worrisome is the work of someone like Davanloo, whose reification of the theoretical terms of psychoanalysis leads him to conceive of analytic therapy as an attacking or breaking through process, in other words, a disorganizing and reconstituting process:

> Pressure toward the experience of feeling. Challenge to the resistance. Unlocking the dynamic unconscious. Direct access to the unconscious . . . resistance, which is now easily penetrated . . . direct view of the unconscious. [Nahmias 1990, p. 172]

More disturbing is the resemblance of such methods to the suggestive insistence of certain therapists that their patients have suffered sexual abuse in childhood. Even patients who remember no such events are exhorted to admit that such events have occurred—usually with the firm assurance that the memories will come if only an admission of abuse is made (Wright 1993). Even the alleged sexual abusers themselves, including alleged perpetrators of satanic and ritual sexual crimes, are urgently persuaded to admit to crimes of which they have no memory. They are assured that, having confessed, they will quickly remember what they have done.

Menninger and Holzman (1973) acknowledge that, to some colleagues, regression simply refers to the patient's increased awareness of himself. I myself am inclined to be sympathetic with that view.

On occasion, I like to speak of the analyst's reverie. By this I mean her way of suspending linear sequential thought and listening to her patient with, as Freud said, "evenly hovering attention." This is, I would say, a type of regression that the analyst voluntarily undergoes. This will be discussed further a bit later on but I mention it now in order to introduce a particular angle on the patient's regression.

The patient, too, can enter a reverie. Or it might be a dreamy state in which daydreams, sleep dreams, and the therapeutic situation blur together. Occasionally, patients are frightened by this but, on many other occasions, they experience this as a state of peacefulness. Indeed, they may fall completely silent. They may even fall asleep. There was a time when this caused me considerable disquietude and in my state of uneasiness I typically said things to the patient such as "Are you asleep?" or, "Are you having a dream?" After all, that is what my analyst said to me once or twice. I no longer say anything. Why should I? If the patient is quiet or sleeping he may well be communicating to me a powerful statement of relaxation, comfort with his own vulnerability, or something of that order. Why in the world would I want to suppress this? My job is, I assume, to analyze it. This means I must be unobtrusive, take note of what is happening, but certainly avoid any interruption of what is, usually, novel behavior.

Analysts typically feel guilty when they allow patients to sleep. This suggests to me that they are possessed by a moralistic industriousness that demands that the therapy be a conscientious piece of tangible work. I recommend only that, when circumstances so dictate, the analyst will interrupt the patient's sleep by saying "The time is up." I might, however, add that if the patient wakes up spontaneously—as they usually do—I typically say "Did you have a dream?" I can't say why I ask this. It just seems to be what a psycho-analyst ought to say!

There are other kinds of silence as well. We all know of silences of terror, stubbornness, grief, and rage. Often one can recognize what type of silence one is encountering, but not always. A brief inquiry is sometimes called for.

When I was a student psychotherapist, one of my first patients did not speak for three months. In my state of anxiety and frustration I wanted badly to kill the supervisor who had assigned the case to me. The patient was a deeply disturbed adolescent youth who had one of the most spectac-ular recoveries I have seen. He had been institutionalized for many years and, as I found out later, his forty hours of silence were spent daydreaming about Martians. He continued in therapy once or twice weekly for three years. Ten years later he appeared on my door step in another city a thousand miles away. He was rather withdrawn and quiet but was em-barking on a trip to Europe. He was, he told me, the tri-state chess champion. There are, as I have said, many kinds of regressive silences.

I have already emphasized that the analyst, when observing a patient (or any other person!), sees only the manifest content. Be it a dream, a narrative, a character style, or a fragment of body language, analytic theory begins with the assumption that we see only the manifest. Behind this is the latent content, which is, of course, what our analytic efforts aim to uncover. The manifest is a compromise formation made up of many conflicting intentions, hopes, fears, and desires. The latent is also made up of hopes, fears, and desires, but, in this instance, of hopes, fears, and desires that are unconscious.

Analytic theory makes a strong claim about human psychology, which may not be immediately apparent from the above comments about manifest and latent content. The claim is that the subject is fundamentally divided and that the subject, divided as he is, never knows himself compre-

hensively. Every conscious experience or thought forbids and
oblates all other possible universes of discourse, thereby
rendering the subject self-deceived. Particular conscious–unconscious configurations are understood as dynamically motivated.

The phrase *personal desire versus social conformity*
apprehends another way of conceptualizing the divided self
that characterizes each of us. It refers to the unresolvable
tension between personal wishes and the claims, demands
and obligations of the social realm. On the grounds of prudence, guilt, fear, or love, we may relinquish our personal
desires, especially when they conflict with the social mores.
In other words, we restrain ourselves. But the most important
prudence is barely prudence at all, since it is an unconscious
inhibition against the violation of superego strictures, that is
to say, the internalized repository of social mores. This
self-restraint is very powerfully built in. One might say that it
is built in with a vengeance. Superego restraints and constraints are typically harsh, arbitrary, and unforgiving. Consider the storm of self-defeating behaviors that we can see all
around us and, in particular, in our patients. Such self-
attacks are punitive restraints that persons mount upon
themselves because of real or imagined crimes, that is to say,
because of improper personal desires. The reader will know
already that such crimes range from incestuous and patricidal ideas, to the most trivial of social infractions. And do not
forget the crime of knowledge—the crime of original sin. This
is the crime of seeing the truth about parents, and seeing
beyond the hypocrisy of the moral slogans that most of us
proclaim. The crime of knowledge is also the biblical knowing
as in "He knew her." The knowledge of sex is the original sin
and is a sin still.

Personal desire versus social conformity: how is the
breach of social conformity punished? Think of addictions,
reckless driving, smoking, and other urgent bad habits.
Think of the whole range of neurotic suffering. Think of the
paradoxical guilt—painful guilt—of those who have been
abused. Criminal behavior and the socially inept behavior of
so-called borderline patients are transparent and skillfully

calculated strategies to evoke negative and punitive behavior from others. One need only think of the blatantly self-abusive thoughts and attitude of depressives. They sometimes kill themselves, as well. Here is a story of how drug dealers, in effect, commit suicide.

> The crowd fell silent. Other soldiers in green riot helmets marched 28 convicted drug dealers across the field. The prisoners knew they would be dead by noon. Right after the rally, they were taken to a secluded execution ground and shot in the back of the head.
>   This is China's new Opium War . . . "Every drug dealer knows there is a death penalty, but they still sell it. Every addict knows he'll be sent to labor re-education, but they don't stop." [*Toronto Globe and Mail,* July 17, 1992]

Our patients are self-defeating in many more subtle ways. Low self-esteem, for example, is simply a manifestation of a series of negative thoughts about oneself. "I am stupid and no good," is what such patients are saying to themselves. In response we, the analysts, think, "For what psychological crime do they inflict upon themselves such hurtful and self-punitive accusations?"

A variant on the low self-esteem tactic is the eternal determination and resolution-making of many patients to do better and to behave more sensibly, more industriously, or more sociably. A common form taken by this is that the patient is eternally "trying." The psychological maneuver that such patients use is a downward definition of themselves. They are, in effect, "no good," since only a person who is no good needs to try to improve.

One can immediately see the ineptness of the analyst who asks the patient to try. She, too, has decided that the patient is no good. What she might do, instead, is to discuss with the patient the details of his convoluted psychological efforts. This whole business of low self-esteem, of needing to improve, and the patient's self-definition as sick, infantile, or primitive, is fraught with difficulty for the analyst. Despite her best intentions, she will endlessly fall into the patient's traps. Early in her career she will fall into these traps blatantly; once highly experienced, her entrapment will be subtle and hard for her to detect. Does this mean that the experienced analyst has greater difficulties than do her junior colleagues?

Regressively self-defeating behaviors are gross and obvious in patients who carry diagnoses of borderline or of schizophrenia. The analyst can easily see the regressive nature of the behaviors in question, but there is a danger that the word *regressive* will deflect the analyst from her mission to discover further and additional meanings to what is seen. Words have a peculiar ability to lead us into closure. When we hear the word regressive, we are liable to think that we have come upon the explanation for something.

We may well say to ourselves, "Aha, that's why he is doing this (saying this, feeling this, believing this), it's because he is in a state of regression." Analysts should keep in mind that *regression* is a merely theoretical word and, at that, is a word that is at a very high level of abstraction. It is, in fact, so general a term that its usefulness is less than we might wish. It really doesn't do the work that we expect of a theoretical term. The analyst should, perhaps, keep in mind that many terms in psychoanalytic theory suffer from the same problem. And rightly so. It must be remembered that they refer to psychological phenomena of enormous complexity and the most that we can expect of them is that they should be rough guides.

The bulk of the literature on the analytic psychotherapy of such difficult patients urges upon the analyst modifications in her usual analytic behavior. I would give the opposite counsel. I believe it unwise and nonanalytic to deviate from our standard practice. You have already heard some of my arguments against authors who urge analysts to set conditions, give warnings, and emphasize structure. It is true that patients such as those under consideration will place the treatment in jeopardy. Since conditions, warnings, and structure have not in their past histories had any effect upon their behavior, there is little hope that they will have an effect in the psychoanalytic situation. The only hope that I see with such patients is to aim for analytic changes—by way of diligent interpretive work.

I am personally inclined to say that it is particularly important to maintain an analytic stance with these patients. Any participation in their neurosis such as advice-giving, encouragement, or explanation of reality (whose reality would one explain to them?) is really a participation in a particular transference–countertransference setup. In this setup, both parties agree that the analyst is a person of superior merit to the patient and that the patient, since he has lesser abilities, should go along with the analyst. In fact, I would say both patient and analyst conspire together to maintain this particular interpersonal configuration; by doing so they neglect to search for the motives that lead them to posture themselves in this way vis-à-vis one another. This agreed-upon interpersonal posture is also the place in which the patient has previously and repetitively contrived to situate himself.

The argument favoring the introduction of atypical—that is to say, noninterpretive—behaviors by the analyst has, of course, been rationalized by its adherents. They claim that there is a fundamental difference in the psychological organization of borderline and schizophrenic patients—a difference that I deny. The argument that I make is that psychoanalytic theory affirms a priori that all behavior—including schizophrenic, manic-depressive, and borderline behavior—is to be apprehended as a compromise formation and hence, in principal, is analyzable. My theoretical ally on this score is Charles Brenner (1982), whose formulations on psychoanalytic theory are unswerving in their intellectual rigor. Some might complain that he is dogmatic, but he has made a convincing argument that, psychoanalytically speaking, all behavior is to be viewed as a compromise formation. As such, all behaviors, including disorganized and asocial behaviors, are, in principle, analyzable.

An odd thing about all of this is that no claim is made for better therapeutic results using a strictly analytic approach since that which is better is so elusive. I personally have a heavy bias in favor of the changes consequent upon a purely analytic approach but, ultimately, that preference is based on theoretical, esthetic, and moral grounds rather than on mere clinical betterness. But one can nevertheless hope for a better clinical result since, for most of these patients, nonanalytic approaches have been used by many helpers before us. Why should we repeat what has already been tried?

5

Changes in Language

In France a man who has ruined himself for women is
generally regarded with sympathy and admiration; there is
a feeling that it was worth while, and the man who has
done it feels a certain pride in the fact. In England he will be
thought and will think himself a damned fool. The English
are not an amorous race and are only sufficiently sexual for
purposes of reproducing the species. That love should
absorb a man has seemed to them unworthy.

Somerset Maugham

In writing of the patient's reaction to the therapeutic situation—his so-called regression—Menninger and Holzman
(1973) emphasize and give examples of linguistic mutations.
The patient initially wants one thing which, as time goes on,
becomes transformed into wishes for something else. Here
are some transformations they make note of—transformations that can take place in a few hours or, on other occasions,
take place only after months or years:

I want:

audience
help
relief
cure
sympathy
forgiveness
acceptance
approval
praise
scolding
punishment
rejection

I also want:

soft reassurances
comfort
caresses
fondling
embracing
oral and/or genital contact

One need not invoke, as Menninger and Holzman do, an explanation of this in which frustration is deemed to be a causal agent. Safer to simply note that this is a reaction to the therapeutic situation and the analytic therapist's behavior. Safer because, first, it is not clear that so specific a word as frustration adequately characterizes what is going on and, second, one would certainly not want therapists to believe that they ought to consciously impose frustration upon their patients.

I mention that Menninger and Holzman specifically refer to transformations in language usage when patients regress. This is much in keeping with a linguistic emphasis that has crept into analytic thinking in recent years. I have already mentioned Schafer (1976) and Lacan (Bowie 1991). It is important to note that the linguistic turn in analytic thinking corresponds to a linguistic turn in philosophy early in this century.

> It is now popular to mark shifts in philosophical method and preoccupation as "turns." In the modern period, for example, philosophy turned from its previous preoccupation with metaphysical questions to a primary concern with the possibility and nature of knowledge. This "epistemological turn" was to dominate philosophy for two centuries, only to be replaced in the early part of this century, at least for Anglo-American philosophy, by a "linguistic turn." Recently . . . the basis for the epistemological turn [has] been called into question [which has led] to a new direction in philosophy characterized by an interest in interpretive activities. [Hiley et al. 1991, p. 1]

Such philosophers are now preoccupied by their interpretive turn and, from their point of view, psychoanalytic theorists have done things back to front. Analysis began with an interpretive turn away from causal explanations of dissociated psychical contents. That which had been explained via defects such as brain or mental degeneracy was now to be interpreted as a symbolic statement of one kind or another. In analytic theory, scrutiny of linguistics and interpretations have always gone hand in hand. But in recent years there has been an explicitly linguistic turn nevertheless.

Faust struggled with the question of how he should translate the word *logos*. He was acutely aware that the translation of that biblical word would create a world of difference or—more accurately—every possible word that he might use would lead to the creation of a whole universe of meaning.

> In the beginning was the "Logos"
> In the beginning was the Word
> In the beginning was the Sense
> In the beginning was the Force
> In the beginning was the Deed
>   Goethe, *Faust* (my translation)

I recall an occasion on which I was at a large dinner gathering in a foreign country. To my disquietude, someone at a nearby table passed out and fell to the ground. Since I was a physician, I got up and walked toward the man but I did so with some reluctance because I did not speak the language. To my relief, another person, obviously a physician, stepped into the situation ahead of me, and took over. Quickly he examined the stricken man. A crowd surrounded him and anxiously awaited his verdict. Finally he rose to his feet and announced "Kollaps!" Everyone heaved a sigh of relief. How peculiar and yet how obvious. The word had the power to explain, to reassure and to bring the disturbing event to some sort of closure.

The language of illness and the language of analytic theory are just as powerful and one way of approaching the psychotherapeutic process is to see it as the conversion of the patient to a new linguistic universe. Even the words that I now write upon this page could be understood as my attempt to convert the reader to a different linguistic universe. If this is so, my attempt could be understood in different ways—depending upon the language used:

> I am inviting you to join me in an expansion of the theoretical imagination.

> I am subtly and repetitively suggesting my ideas to you—in short, brainwashing you.

> I am manipulating you and charming you with cute, tricky arguments.

> I am putting forward a point of view for the interested audience to observe.

All of us have sets of words with which we justify our actions and our beliefs (Rorty 1989, Chapter 4). By way of this final vocabulary we praise our friends, denigrate our enemies, explain our own shortcomings, and justify the wickedness we participate in. We also have a final language with which to discuss illness and, especially, mental illness. Such final vocabularies are precious to us and are preciously hard to change. Philosophers like Rorty have noted how reluctant we are to change our final vocabularies, but analytic theorists have some additional things to say on this score. Final vocabularies are hard to change because each person has personal motives—to a great extent unconscious motives— for thinking and speaking as he does. These motives are idiosyncratic to each person. In addition, allegiances to pre- vailing final languages are conditioned by prevailing social practice. Powerful superego injunctions, say the analytic thinkers, impel us to think according to social conventions and make alternative language patterns hard to introduce.

I have already suggested that the analytic therapist is uneasy about using the vocabulary of illness and sickness with regard to her patients. She may well explicitly raise doubts about that language although not, as you might expect, because she feels that she has a better language. What she has in mind is simply a *different* language, and her great interest is in why a particular patient might so reso- lutely commit himself to a language of sickness with regard to himself. She wonders, too, why society by and large has analogous linguistic preferences. This point—made as starkly as this—has caused some of my critics great concern. In essence, their complaint is that, for me, illness has an almost mystical nature. Although I deny this, that complaint has led me to the assertion that such a view of illness (or, better, of madness) addresses the fact that the most essential thing about human life is that it is not mystical but, rather, a mystery.

Other patients, fewer in number, are deeply committed to a final vocabulary about themselves that strongly avoids any implication of sickness, victimhood, or affliction. They prefer to speak of how they must stand on their own two feet, how they have made their own bed and must therefore lie in it, and that they must be mindful of past errors and henceforth choose more wisely. The analytic therapist will once again wonder whether other languages are possible and, concomi- tantly, will wonder why the language of self-determination and free will are so moralistically preferred by them. What motives drive them to be so self-reliant, she asks? And if they are driven are they really as self-reliant as they believe? Could they, perchance, be so self-determining that they could stop so single-mindedly seeing themselves as self-reliant?

As the psychotherapy progresses, patients will, in their regressive or transformative way, elaborate such vocabularies with greater vigor. The sick and afflicted may pronounce upon their sick and afflicted state more vehemently. The self-reliant may become more indignantly self-reliant. Since their psychological economy depends on these precious views of themselves, patients will oppose and be offended by the gentle liberties that the analytic therapist takes with regard to all final vocabularies—indeed, to all final positions, opinions, and beliefs.

The dialogue with a depressive patient may go something like this. The therapist has voiced mild skepticism about the patient's repetitive assertions that he suffers from a disease and that he has a chemical imbalance. "It's just common sense that it's a disease," is a common countermove by the patient. Recourse to common sense is, of course, how all of us defend our final vocabularies. "It's only common sense," we say, "that socialism is wrecking the country." Or one hears the complementary "It's only common sense that capitalist exploiters are wrecking the country."

The analytic therapist, too, can understand such disorders in the same biological common-sense terms—especially since she is likely to reside in an occupational world in which that particular brand of common sense is popular, influential, and taken for granted. And yet, being adventuresome, curious, and concerned that seriously depressed persons be understood in the most therapeutic terms possible, she insists on exploring vocabularies that might lead to better help than is currently available. After all, she is liable to say, the rhetoric of biochemical imbalance is supported by little of the usual evidence required of a biological hypothesis.

Statements such as these are easy to make about depressive patients since they are often willing to participate in psychoanalytic treatment and, in my experience, often do well. I only wish that the same could be said for manic patients who, unfortunately, usually won't come to analysis regularly enough to make such treatment feasible. On infrequent occasions I have done satisfactory analytic work with manic patients (one of these has been mentioned in an earlier chapter) but most are elusive candidates for what analytic therapists have to offer. Patients must, after all, be able to follow *Pogo's First Rule of Cooking:* "Don't let the meat get away!"

The analytic therapist, when at her best, does not participate in these final positions. She knows what the patient means about his common-sense positions, but she has doubts nevertheless. She worries a lot about whether she is participating in the wrong language game. As Rorty says, she worries that she may have been born or educated into the wrong language tribe. She wants badly to hear about vocabularies other than "manic-depressive illness" and "major affective disorder." Perhaps, she wonders, she is not observing a manic-depressive disorder but rather is witness to a manic-depressive life. Perhaps her patient lives an alternately elated and depressive life. And most of all she wants to experiment with a motivational language. The analytic therapist thinks:

> He must have reasons for living his life as he does. I wonder what his motives are for debasing himself? When depressed, he himself is an agent of his own self-abuse and self-denigration. When elated he convinces his anxious family (and all of the anxious persons in the world who deal with him) that they must intervene and regulate his life, that is to say, he convinces them that they should think of him as inadequate and as lacking judgment. They therefore judge him to be an inferior and sickly individual. If I agree that he is sick, I will be a full participant in the final vocabulary to which he so desperately clings. This vocabulary is the guarantor that he will remain unwell.

She ultimately wants to have a detailed knowledge of her patient's motives for his deeply held final vocabulary. All too often, this is exactly what the patient does *not* want to know.

The therapist is, as tactfully and patiently as she can, pursuing the unconscious.

"Maybe," thinks the therapist, "what I am observing is not a matter of scientific facts but, rather, a poetic achievement." She wants to try out new languages, such as the language of poetry, because she suspects it may be a readier route to the unconscious motives that she seeks to elucidate. She is participating in a dialogue that undoes, or unglues, the final vocabulary of the patient.

> Mrs. H., when she was a child, moved into a new home. The previous tenants had left behind an old piano and, in the piano bench she found sheet music. Since she was taking piano lessons at the time, she played the music she had found. Her family disliked the classical music that she now began to play, since they had more popular tastes. Mrs. H. was extremely troubled by this turn of events since, to her, this meant that her family failed to recognize fine art, a recognition that had come to her instantly. Later, she had a similar experience when a neighbor took her to the theater. Once again her parents reacted in a way that indicated to her that their tastes were "low brow." Later still she realized that her mother flirted in a vulgar way with the teenage boys who visited the home. She herself, Mrs. H. realized, was much more appropriately modest than her own mother.
>
> Mrs. H. resolutely and repetitively described herself as an inferior and despicable "low brow" for the first two years of her analytic psychotherapy. Only then did the above modification in her narrative begin to appear.

So go the narratives of most depressed patients—narratives that are a posture of unfulfilled potential by way of an identification with the imagined inferiority of others. The other is thereby relatively elevated.

A new vocabulary for depression would no longer talk about depressive disease but, instead, would talk about depressive character style or about a person's "inferiority propaganda." Such persons resolutely define themselves as inferior and, just as resolutely, elevate others and see them as powerful or better. Furthermore, they throw up as a comparison a different life that they claim would be better than the one they have. There is a great discrepancy between that imagined better life and their actual life. And in that discrepancy lies their depressive character style. To them, life is elsewhere.

If this is a character trait rather than a disease, then we must have a different and more ambitious attitude toward depressive and elated ways of life. There are, the analytic therapist says, many ways to skin a cat and many ways to live a life. She has no expectation that the patient's life should change, although she is puzzled, worried, and concerned that someone should live his life in such a painful way. She advocates no health measures or symptom relief but, rather, is ready to enter into an analytic dialogue with the patient should he desire it. Besides, she is cheered by reading that the rates of manic-depressive illness are ten to thirty times greater in geniuses such as Lord Byron, Shelley, Melville, Schumann, Virginia Woolf, Coleridge, Aldous Huxley, Alexander Graham Bell, Einstein, and Matisse (Jamison 1993, Ludwig 1994). Such information allows her to be more thoughtful and less nervous about her depressed patients. What is more, she begins to have a greater interest in Ivan Illich's idea that our typical medical urgency to relieve suffering may well be misplaced. What he proposes is that "medicalization of health beyond a certain intensity increases suffering by reducing the capacity to suffer and destroying the community setting in which suffering can become a dignified performance" (Cayley 1992).

In her analytic work, two ideas eternally intrude into what she is doing. First, she assumes, with great resolution, that the patient is competent. Second, she attempts to position herself in between.

> In between—it is the dwelling place of Thomas Mann's chief characters, the residence too of anxiety and disquiet, of irony and humor, of tragedy and comedy; that is to say, the accustomed place of man. [Heller 1958, p. 13]

The analytic psychotherapist is content to allow herself the disquiet that follows upon such an uncertain locale. There-

fore, if the patient speaks of wellness, she is led more deeply
into her disquietude; if of disease, she thinks of another style
of life; if despairingly, she thinks of hope. Her interventions
with the patient may clarify and simplify matters but not
necessarily, since they may, instead, lead to confusion, to
increased complexity, to greater density, and to subtlety.
Despite Freud's remark to the contrary, for the Freudian, a
cigar is *never* just a cigar. Typically, the patient's reports and
narratives become more compelling and show less of the
banality so usual in stereotypical neurotic behavior.

> It still strikes me as strange that the case histories I write
> should read like short stories and that, as one might say,
> they lack the serious stamp of science. [Freud 1893–1895,
> p. 160]

World I is a term that I use to refer to the conventional
everyday psychological world in which most of us reside.
That world is filled with rules, customs, and rituals that most
of us are happy to be in accord with. Without ceremony and
order, I could ask, how can beauty and truth be born? But
World I can also be spoken of in derogatory terms. It is the
official world, the bourgeois world, or the world machine.

I sometimes think of the patient's regression as an entry
into a different world. Commonly I think of this other world—
World II—as a fascinating place. With depressed patients,
however, this place is gloomy, heartbreaking, and frightening—at least for a while.

World II is the way of thinking that is less conventional
and that frequently calls in question the values of *World I*. It
is the world of paradox, poetry, and creativity. The analytic
psychotherapist values *World II*. She believes life is enriched
by regression, that is to say, by familiarity with *World II*.
"Except," she hastens to add, "for those patients who characteristically reside in *World II* and decline to pay serious
attention to logic and the concrete. They eternally privilege
the poetic over the prosaic. One wonders whether they can
risk dabbling in *World I*, that is to say, risk regressing into
World I."

The analytic therapist is as troubled by suicidal threats or suicidal behavior as is any other person. Yet, troubled though she may be, she is inclined to respond differently to such crises from the way in which most helpers respond. To understand this difference, and before saying just how she does respond, it is necessary to make a few theoretical remarks. To this end, the following is a rather long-winded theoretical digression that uses as its vehicle the depressive style of life.

What goes on between therapist and patient can be conceptualized in many ways. The most common way is to say that the patient is sick and the therapist takes care of the sick patient. The greater the degree of disturbance, the greater the degree to which the helping therapist intervenes, helps, takes over. In extreme cases the helper—in this instance someone medical—takes over the patient's bodily functioning including his eating and breathing functions. This is the *in loco parentis* model. The helper, like a parent, takes over the patient's functioning for him. The patient is clearly understood to be disordered and the parentlike helper protects, corrects, and functions for him.

This model has been utilized by psychoanalysts and analytic psychotherapists more in the past than it is now. In effect, therapists were considered to be healthy objective observers of the patient—and especially of the patient's illness. Somewhat troubling was the idea that the therapist understands what is real, whereas the patient is liable to distort reality. Such assumptions were partly based on the idea that psychotherapists have often had some treatment themselves, and, having been thereby cured, have a purer vision of reality than they had before their own treatment.

This is, of course, at considerable variance with reality as it is nowadays philosophically understood. Instead of a singular reality it is more common to speak of a plurality of realities. Each of us, one might say, lives in our own personal array of preferred realities—not to speak of another array of warded-off realities. Therapists are not viewed as having any privilege with regard to particular realities. The only concession to the above would be the acknowledgment that there are rough social conventions regarding what is to count as real. Psychoanalytic therapists, uneasy as they are about leading patients into conventionality, are inclined to remain as neutral as possible about these socially designated realities.

The objective real illness model is nowadays less popular with psychotherapists. It is, after all, only one of many models available for comprehending the therapist–patient dialogue or dialectic.

The intersubjectivity model is much bandied about nowadays but I do not like to distinguish it too sharply from an analytic model that I will, for want of a better term, call *dialectical negativity*. Perhaps it is possible to get by with simpler terms but very clearly our models must adequately emphasize the interpretation of all interpersonal stances or, within the analytic situation per se, the interpretation of the transference–countertransference setup.

Now here is what happens when one uses the first model, that is to say, the model of the objective therapist who observes and treats/manages an objective illness/problem. The patient states that he intends to kill himself. The therapist attempts to prevent this by way of explanation and persuasion and by invoking consequences. If this does not work, the therapist may enlist family members or other guardians and, eventually, may hospitalize the patient. In extreme cases constant observation and monitoring of the patient is introduced. This is the *in loco parentis* model.

Unfortunately there is little evidence that such modes of intervention reduce the incidence of suicide (Liberman and Eckman 1981, Linehan et al. 1991). There is even evidence that the use of a rescue model may *increase* the incidence of suicide (Hendin 1982, Meissner 1986, Searles 1967, Zee 1972). If it is indeed the case that suicide is not reduced by using the *in loco parentis* model, explanations ought to be offered as to why this is so. Those who focus on the transference–countertransference setup do, indeed, have an argument to make concerning this point. Although they are convinced that they have a worthwhile explanatory position, they are also uneasy about what they themselves have to say because, first, a person's life may be at stake and, second, because they fear professional or legal repercussions if they use a model that is less well known and a suicide takes place. But here is their argument nevertheless:

Suicidal threats and suicidal behaviors are part of an interpersonal configuration that certain patients prefer to locate themselves in, that is to say, they compellingly enact a linguistic and behavioral game in which they threaten suicide and the analytic therapist intervenes in ways designed to prevent suicide. The analytic or dialectical negativity model, however, helps the analyst to level certain complaints about such a turn of events. The analytic therapist (who very much wants to use a strictly analytic model) points out that, since the patient is attempting to coerce a psychologically vital scenario, attempts to prevent suicide are liable to lead the patient to redouble his efforts to kill himself. Then, contrapuntally, the therapist is liable to redouble *her* protective actions, and so on. In this vicious cycle, says the analytic therapist, the possibility of suicide is *increased* rather than decreased. Suicide, she says, is not a disorder in the usual sense of being a tangible or objective problem but, rather, is dialectical.

The therapist must be extremely cautious about committing herself to rescue attempts for fear that she will do more harm than good. She is, of course, mindful of the fact that no one has certain knowledge about whether patients are less likely to commit suicide when she deals with them analytically, or contrariwise, whether they are less likely to do so when they are dissuaded or prevented from killing themselves. She wishes there were airtight research data available concerning this issue, and is worried about how ethics committees will respond to proposals for studying this matter. Being as egocentric as any other person, she is inclined to think her model better but, when at her best, smiles ruefully about her own egocentrism.

So what does she do when she applies her analytic method with her suicidal patient? What she does is to operate, as much as her courage will permit, according to a few analytic principles:

1. She will insist that this suicidal inclination is part of an interpersonal strategy that she and her patient

have embarked upon. She will include herself as part of this dangerous dialectic, and will point out that as a mere mortal, and a humane one, she will obviously be inclined to give protection. But, she will tell the patient, her primary goal will be to keep analyzing.

2. She will refrain from guaranteeing that she will not actively intervene to prevent suicide. She will tell the patient that she wishes not to get into the game of no-you-won't-kill-yourself versus yes-I-will-kill-myself but that she may well become frightened and shift to a protective role.

3. She will resolutely (but not urgently!) point out that suicide is, among other things, a regressive or flamboyant example of the patient's ordinary characterological style. She will, like any analytic therapist, connect everything to everything. In other words, she will liken the suicidal behavior to all other self-injurious, self-demeaning, and self-insulting behaviors and speech. She will do this with regard to the patient's current life, the transference–countertransference situation, and the past.

4. She will interpret as well as she can the identificatory aspects of suicidal behavior. The patient, for example, is enacting upon himself a punishment deserved by someone else, or is volunteering to suffer a deadly fate in place of a loved one. All too often the suicidal act is seen by the patient as a strange form of justice for imagined crimes. The analytic therapist will, despite her anxiety, work at the best level of analytic wisdom that she can manage.

5. Whenever the analytic therapist finds herself knowing better than the patient or protecting the patient, she will point this out so that he will see that the aggrandizement of therapist and diminution of himself is maddeningly persistent and pervasive. She, the therapist, may even chuckle self-deprecatingly about her own vanity.

Despite the above counsel—all of which is known to most of us—therapists tend to avoid taking on as patients persons with serious depressive disorders. This is due to many factors. First of all, some analytic therapists react with depression of their own in the face of the eternal pessimism and gloom of such patients.

The distracting problems of hospitalization, drugs, and suicide only add to the disinclination of therapists to take on depressed patients. But I suspect and submit that there is yet another important reason why fewer of these patients are treated psychotherapeutically. There is a current rhetoric that all depressions are biological—especially serious depressions—and a concurrent rhetoric that claims that drugs are therefore the intervention of choice. Therapists should keep in mind the words of Rapaport (1959) that I quoted earlier and remember, too, that the evidence from biology is meager. Finally, evidence from outcome studies is unconvincing with regard to which forms of treatment are preferable. More and better research, especially in areas as critical as suicide, is necessary.

The problems of research are manifold. Because of the elusive nature of the data and because psychotherapists use uncommon logical formats, endless problems arise. Here are some of them:

1. Instead of objectivistic and empirical methods, analytic psychotherapists view data with ironic skepticism.
2. Instead of anticipating generalizable and expectable results, they emphasize the ambiguity and uniqueness of all human phenomena.
3. Typically science thinks in terms such as "A causes B, that is to say, B is a direct consequence of A." Another common logical paradigm in science is "If A = B, and B = C, then A = C." Analytic theorists are much more likely to say things like, "A resembles B but also resembles D, E, and F, and, in addition, resembles a babbling brook." In other words, analytic psychology affirms that A and B are related in a multitude of metaphoric ways.
4. Research questions come to have quite a different form. Analytic theorists want to know whether the

major depressive disorders in general, and individual
cases in particular, are scientific problems at all? Are
they, perhaps, social problems? Is every case best
considered to be a complex human drama? What kind
of theories, asks the analytic researcher, give courage
to psychotherapists? Or, contrariwise, do courageous
therapists pick theories that validate their natural
abilities? And what is courage? Can research be done
on this? Does courage cure patients? What is cure
anyway? Do courageous therapists deny that patients
have diseases? What is psychiatric disease? Can one
do research on cruelty, genius, and mediocrity using
empirical methods? What about greed, vanity, and
pride? Can we do empirical research on why we prefer
the disease vocabulary to the style-of-life or interpersonal dialectic vocabulary—especially since empiri-
cism is part of the final vocabulary that is being called
into question?

Here are some other questions that may be more optimis-
tic. Why, very roughly speaking, do so many psychotherapeutic and psychiatric treatments have a 70 percent positive
success rate? Could research also include more of a focus on
the old idea of the university, that is to say, encouraging
people, by way of funding, to think? Could they ponder the
philosophy of mind, the history of human thought, literature,
art, and music, and see how these may pertain to psychotherapy?

Biological discoveries have led to a flurry of hope about
the plight of mental sufferers. Could fresh analytic thinking
about psychological matters also lead to new hope, perhaps
hope for more lasting improvement, lower suicide rates, and
fewer hospitalizations?

Finally, is the invitation to try new vocabularies an
invitation to enter into a creative regression?

Such a changed vocabulary, such a creative regression, is
precisely the seminal discovery with which Freud was concerned. In a certain sense one could say that these were not

really discoveries. Perhaps one could say, instead, that the accepted final vocabulary used by late nineteenth century psychiatrists was called into question by Freud, and a new language introduced. This new language turned out to be of interest to those who became his adherents.

Psychiatrists in the nineteenth century were well aware of what they termed *dissociated psychical groupings*. They had become aware of this through the study of conversion hysteria, dissociative states, hypnosis, and the compensation neuroses. The explanation for these states was given in the currently prevalent final vocabulary used for such matters. The most typical explanation was that these mental contents were dissociated because of mental degeneracy.

Freud reconceptualized how such phenomena could be explained. An hysterical paralysis, instead of being explained by the postulation of mental contents dissociated from consciousness because of mental degeneracy, was now to be reconceived. The language of lesions, of mental degeneracy, and pathological causes was abandoned and replaced by a language of motives. An hysterically paralyzed arm might now be spoken of as a kind of communication or announcement made by the patient. I would remind the reader of the example I gave in Chapter 2: "I am not to be understood" says the patient by way of his symptom, "as someone who could injure or kill my father. Note that I am paralyzed and weak. And if there is any possibility that I have an ungenerous attitude toward him, I am adequately penalized by my affliction."

Freud went even further. His idea of multidetermination avers that all behavior has a host of influencing motives and ideas behind it. Implicit in this is the further idea that no one can easily, if ever, fully know all the determinants of his own behavior. Analytic therapy, therefore, has no ultimate end point and analysis or self-analysis, in principle, can go on forever. One could even go so far as to say that patient and therapist struggle to get glimpses of motives here and there and that it is futile to hope for exhaustive analytic enlightenment.

One might want to take note of another interesting fact.

Neither mental degeneracy nor unconscious motives are based on objective evidence. So which theory should one adopt? Although I could argue for the analytic theory that I favor, at this point I would say only that in the human sciences, the choice between theories is largely based on rhetoric, tradition, and taste. If this sounds unscientific I can offer only this reassurance. Science is based on the eternal questioning, doubting, and disposing of hypotheses—including doubt of well-established hypotheses. Since it represents doubt and challenge, experimental modification of preferred final vocabularies is clearly in the best scientific tradition. This arbitrary definition of science—arbitrary in the sense that it sounds as though anything goes—is far less true of traditional sciences than it is of psychology. This is so because traditional science usually has practical goals and consequences as, for example, in mechanics or optics. But in fields such as quantum mechanics or particle physics, many theories actively compete for explanatory priority. This is also the case in psychology. In our field, many theories compete for priority.

Freudian theory pushes such thinking even further since, fortunately or unfortunately, all theories can be proven *and* disproven. Since scientific theories come and go, one must ask why particular theories, especially in the mental sciences, happen to prevail at any given time. I have already suggested that rhetoric, tradition, and taste have an important influence on which theories hold sway at a particular time. But analytic theory holds that personal motives influence the choice of theories as well. In effect, the analytic theorist asks, "Why do I prefer the theories with which I work, and why am I so much in their sway? Why, as well, do my patients (theoretically) explain their lives as they do?" In other words, analytic theory twists back upon itself and theorizes about why it theorizes as it does. If this sounds peculiar and paradoxical, it is so because all of us are just that—peculiar and paradoxical.

The patient has regressed. He has, at times, become saner, and at other times, greater madness has prevailed. In our moments of common sense we have hopes and expecta-

tions of what will have transpired in our patient. Will regression have become transformed into a progression that will
serve him in good stead? Naturally, we hope that he will be
more realistic, more grown-up, and more integrated. We
assume too, that he will have worked things through. Ironically—and ours is the ironic science, of course—we also
suspect that regressive capacities are quite all right, that
multiple realities may be more refreshing than any unitary or
fixed reality, that grown-up common sense can be boring,
and that integration may well mean blandness.

What we do know is that, after their analytic therapy, be
it brief or long-term, most patients will be better, at least
according to our conventional ways of measuring these
things. What I personally count as better will be clarified in
my final chapter. For now it is enough to say that, after
analysis, patients will at least be different.

6

The Analyst's Regressive and Progressive Participation in the Treatment

In physics we don't seem to be finding out about the nature of the world, we seem to be finding out about the nature of the equipment we're using.

Nicholas Mosley, *Hopeful Monsters*

As is true of every person, the analytic therapist is prone to regressive and progressive psychological shifts. This change is neither a good thing nor a bad thing. It is just what happens. The treatment situation is, of course, designed to maximize the possibility of regression in the patient and, although it also is designed to permit regression in the analyst, other factors keep the analyst's regression at a modest level. In other words, relative to the patient, the analytic psychotherapist is an enduring figure of stability.

This relative stability is extremely important since it is the guarantor that the treatment situation can endure. The therapy is not, as some might think, an exercise in regression, that is to say, an exercise in which a patient plunges into the chaotic and the brilliant, the prosaic and the profane.

These things can happen, of course, but they happen in the context of the treatment contract and the therapeutic situation as a whole. The responsibility for the treatment situation belongs to the analyst. Her stability relative to the patient permits her to take on this responsibility.

When I refer to the analytic therapist's stability, I do not mean that the analyst is psychologically more stable than the patient or at a higher level of psychological health. In this situation stability refers only to the analyst's ability to exercise her professional responsibilities during the treatment. Why should this be so? Why can the analyst more firmly maintain the professional context than can the patient? Why will her regression be more modulated and less flamboyant?

A number of reasons come to mind although there may well be factors at play of which I have not thought. First, the psychoanalytic therapist is a highly trained professional, a training that prepares her to deal with the regressive forces that impinge on her. Second, she is focused on a specific task, namely, the therapeutic analysis. Such a focus is not demanded of the patient who, instead, is invited to be *without* focus. The patient, after all, can drift in whatever direction he will. A final point—very important—is that the analyst has many other patients. Her life does not revolve around her patient with nearly as great an intensity as does the patient's life revolve around his analyst. Intensity there is, even for the analyst, but woe betide the therapist who comes to center her life satisfactions too exclusively on her patient. It is hoped that the immunizing factors listed above prevent this from happening.

The analytic therapist, as I have already said, regresses nevertheless. And so she should. Should she remain too sensible, rational, and realistic, she will miss out on the imaginative possibilities of unconventional thinking and, to that extent, will be less able to imaginatively understand her patient. In this regressively more fluid state of mind the analytic therapist finds herself making remarkable and unexpected connections. To the patient's surprise (and sometimes to her own surprise) the analyst discovers links between what she is listening to and what she has heard from the patient on other occasions—sometimes occasions many months ago. Trivial things that were mentioned in passing by the patient, sometimes long ago, suddenly come to her mind and can prove to be uncanny paradigms for what is currently being heard about. The analyst, when in this imaginative state, often realizes that the patient is enacting and describing the roles, stories, and activities of archetypal figures and events from mythology, literature, and history. Suddenly she may become aware that the patient has become an uncanny incarnation of one of his family members.

When speaking to her patient, the analytic therapist typically speaks briefly, clearly, and logically, but on other occasions, will speak allusively and poetically. For example, she may intervene using odd transpositions of persons as in the following example. The reader is reminded that incubi and succubi are male and female devils that copulate with humans while they sleep. In this example the analyst is male, and the patient is a female. The central issue with this patient was her terror that she was a sexual bombshell and her typical way of dealing with this was to discover sexual bombshell behavior in others.

> The patient spoke of a movie she had seen in which pod-like creatures enter and take possession of human bodies. She was afraid to fall asleep because, she said, "that is when humans are vulnerable to these 'body-snatchers.' "
> The analyst spoke of incubi who might come and copulate with her. "And when I do so," he went on, "I will come to have possession of your body. And furthermore, there are no succubi in your fearful thoughts. You are clearly not a sexual 'bombshell' [the patient's word] . . . unless, of course, I am unaware that you come to me in my sleep."

The analyst blurs together and interchanges the pod creatures, incubi and succubi, himself, and the patient herself. Everything connects and alternates with everything else. The analyst caricatures and loosens the obligatory projections of sexuality onto others. In effect he says to his patient that there is a sexual bombshell in her narrative, but that its location is urgently indeterminate.

The same patient had described a series of remarkably plain women, including her mother, who were in one way or another linked to her father. When the patient referred to her own attractiveness, the analyst commented that father, being surrounded by hunchbacks and dwarfs, must have been dazzled by the patient's appearance.

In this instance the analyst has caricatured the patient's universe of discourse and, by doing so, helps her to see with great clarity and starkness the imagery with which her psychological world is populated. The analyst has been listening with the "third ear" and the patient, by now attuned to the analyst's periodic lapses into unusual but evocative logic, joins him in linking everything to everything else. Together, patient and analyst weave a web of interconnectedness into the patient's psychological world. That world includes the patient's past, present, and future, her joys, hopes, and despairs, her language, tastes, and passions.

No analyst need feel bound to participate in the treatment in the odd artistic ways described above. Not all of us are James Joyce pretenders, nor should we be. The analyst who can participate in the patient's enlightenment in this particular way does so because when she and the patient in question are in the therapeutic crucible together, they find this brand of dialogue to be fruitful. It is worth doing only if both parties to the dialogue understand and prosper from it. Do not forget that the analytic attitude and analytic theory demand that we expect such intellectually playful interactions to hide certain things from both parties, even as it enlightens them.

Other analysts, whose style is sober and industrious, may well be just as creative as their flashier colleagues. Rigorous and rational unearthing of psychological subtleties is merely another possible dialectical patient–analyst incarnation. One must not fail to remember that sober industriousness, too, hides even as it illuminates.

Any number of styles can be identified. Some analysts have a concern for their patient's well-being that is always somewhat apparent; others constantly reveal in their voices a ring of confidence in themselves and in their patients; still others find a touch of wittiness to be irresistible. Every analyst is very much herself and the way she and her patient interact is subject to analytic scrutiny as is anything else.

I am inclined to caution the reader that, despite the liberalism of the above remarks, it is not true that anything goes. Analysts, even when witty or playful, are conscientious and industrious. They never play around. Or at least I *think* that they should never play around. But is there not a problem with people who are always conscientious? Always so bloody conscientious? Are they not guilt-inducing and self-righteous? And then, of course, can anyone pretend to know the answers to such questions?

So far, the discussion of the analyst's regressive participation in the treatment has focused on benign and imaginative transformations that she undergoes. But as we all know, the analyst may regress in nontherapeutic and unwholesome ways as well. The blatant examples of this require little discussion. A nontherapeutic regression has obviously taken place when analysts bully and scold, when they dismiss or fire patients, or when they befriend them or betray confidences.

Nor is it necessary to discuss our thousand little avoidances, our self-deceiving tricks, and our distracting therapeutic enthusiasms, enthusiasms that betray our preferred appreciation of the complexity of therapeutic change. These issues are the very stuff of therapeutic work and I have tried to point these out to the reader on many previous occasions. The principles of analytic work, proper training, and experience, will keep analysts alerted to such endless dilemmas.

To me, our great concern should be the unhelpful regressive changes in the analyst that are condoned or sanctioned by public opinion. By public opinions I do not mean the public at large but, rather, the public opinion that springs from certain segments of our own professions. The reader can, by now, probably anticipate what my concern is—it is that certain patients induce us to think of them as unfit to participate in analytic work, and that we regressively agree to believe and participate in what they have induced. They are, it is sometimes said, too sick. They suffer from ego defects, ego weakness, or ego distortions. They have a fragmented self. Parameters must be introduced. They are in danger of undergoing a dangerous regression. And so on.

To introduce this argument, I will quote from Menninger and Holzman (1973):

> It is as if the patient by mere repetition of the experience was enabled to regress back through the years so that instead of saying, "Doctor, I want relief from my headache, from my fears," the patient says, "Mother, I want to be taken into your arms." [p. 71]

The following footnote is appended to the above passage:

> Dr. Earl Bond, in a lecture to the Fellows of the Menninger School of Psychiatry, March 1957, described a patient afflicted with severe mental illness of lengthy duration in the course of which she expressed overtly many sexual wishes. One day her physician in an experimental mood picked her up and held her in his arms, thrusting the nipple of a nursing bottle between her lips. She drank the milk avidly, expressing great satisfaction. "This", she said, "is what I have always wanted, this non-sexual love." This episode marked the beginning of a rapid return to recovery. *Cf.* also the work of Marguerite A. Sechehaye. [p. 71]

The authors do not propose that this is how therapy should be done. However, by using such a quotation, they hint that they might approve of such therapeutic measures. In effect they seem to condone the enactment of a transference–countertransference moment with no recognition that such enactments are errors or, more accurately, that these are dialectic moments that must be puzzled over, that we must be surprised by and fascinated by, and that must be analyzed. I use this particular example because these authors typically are not inclined to forget the proper analytic attitudes and so, what I call their lapse, is all the more instructive.

The argument that I am making is that such lapses are evidence of regressive thinking in analysts, in this case, unhelpful regressive transformations. The example itself is probably a trivial one. However, such thinking is a serious problem when analysts do a number of things. First, based on such deprivation models (rather than analytic models), certain unattractive behaviors can be used as exclusion criteria for psychoanalytic therapy and the concomitant recommendation of some form of replacement therapy. Common examples are the behaviors seen in borderline and depressive cases. These patients are all too often not referred for analytic psychotherapy on the grounds that they need something else. There is little data supporting the exclusion of these patients and yet a tradition exists whereby they are often systematically barred from receiving psychoanalytic treatment.

The second consequence of such professionally sanctioned thinking is the institutionalization of other countertransference practices, which are technically referred to as parameters. Patients with serious disorders are more likely, it seems, to earn nonanalytic interventions than are healthier patients even though it can be argued that they are precisely the patients most in need of analytic treatment. The rationale for this has been most explicitly spelled out by Kurt Eissler (1953). His term *parameters* refers to interventions by the analytic therapist such as instructions, prohibitions, and the setting of nonanalytic conditions. The patient can come only on condition that he conform to certain predetermined injunctions. These parameters are necessary, it is argued, because certain psychological functions (ego-functions, Eissler would say) are weakened, distorted, or absent. Such a function would be judged as absent or weakened if, as Eissler says, "the basic model technique does not suffice" (p. 111).

At that point in the argument, one can no longer follow the logic. First, how does one know that the basic model technique does not suffice? In the practice of analytic psychotherapy, one never knows just when a symptom or a character style will yield to interpretation. Second, and perhaps even more important, the analytic therapist, at least in her guiding tactical imagination, does not actually want anything substantial to happen. She does not want behavior to change, symptoms to disappear, or anything else. She is, as we say, neutral. To explicitly want change means to her that she is making a judgment that she, the analytic therapist, knows a way of living that is better for her patient than does the patient, and that she wants for her patient that which *she* has decided is the better way. In fact, the analyst knows that all ways of living a life are problematic and suspects that if she prompts, insists, or instructs regarding any behavior of the patient, she is joining the patient in an habitual and paralytic transference–countertransference dilemma. On the other hand, despite the opinion to which she has just given voice, the analyst anticipates some sort of change in the patient, some new awareness, or some other difference. Paradoxically, she is reluctant to maintain the status quo even as she is reluctant to advocate goals for the patient. The analyst knows perfectly well that patients unconsciously act against their own interests and wish they could have better lives, but she has grave doubts about the notion that a better way of life or a better behavior can be specified. And so, to her, the idea that the basic model technique does not suffice makes no sense.

A third argument against Eissler's point is that, in practice, one finds that parameters have been used with every difficult patient on countless previous occasions. What Eissler calls a parameter is simply what family, friends, and colleagues offer to all patients before they ask for analytic help. Analytic therapists have no wish to give more of the same, especially since it did not benefit the patient before. It is often for that very reason—that actions analogous to parameters did not work—that patients consult us.

Abstaining from the use of Eissler's parameters does not mean that the analytic therapist remains silent in the face of dangerous or immoral behavior. In addition to her interpretive work (or, rather, as part of her interpretive work) the analytic therapist may say, for example, "You've got me worrying about you just like everyone else in your life. What purpose does it serve for you to worry me?" Or she may say, "What an unpalatable plan that is—if not a wicked plan. You are determined that I should make moral judgments upon you." The analyst is a concerned and sympathetic participant in the analysis and her neutrality is not neglect of the patient or indifference.

Eissler is not the only analytic colleague who has advocated modifications in technique. Others, including many writers who have made enduring contributions to analytic technique, also feel compelled to recommend nonanalytic interventions in certain circumstances. The writings about brief therapies and supportive therapies abound with such suggestions. Here is a comment by Merton Gill (1954):

> [In supportive psychotherapy one] does not foster a regressive transference neurosis . . . but on the contrary actively discourages the development of such a transference by conducting the interview more like a social interchange of equals, by avoiding free association, by emphasizing reality rather than fantasy, by creating an atmosphere of temporariness and similar measures. [p. 771]

I hope that Gill would nowadays take back these words. Why would one discourage the transference, and how would one do so in any case? All human relationships are transference drenched, and discouraging this only distorts the transference elements that will appear. Is not every therapy—analytic, supportive, or otherwise—a "social interchange of equals"? And how could one avoid free associations? Every act and every statement made by a patient is, a priori, understood to be an associative self-revelation. Whose reality, I might ask, is to be emphasized? If it is the analyst's, this hardly sounds like an exchange between equals. To me, Gill's counsel sounds troublingly like a recommendation to avoid psychotherapy of any kind and to remain superficial and chatty.

The analytic therapist, in her regressive/creative dialogue with her patient, emphasizes the elusive goal of self-knowledge and, by way of her words, indicates her belief in the contingency of every psychological position. The self-knowledge aimed for is the knowledge that all is relative, and that every psychological event is multivalently linked to every other psychological event in the patient's world. By way of her perpetual analytic posture, the analyst implies that there is no bedrock human nature, that there are no basic human needs, and no correct or better ways to do it. The yield of analytic work is the revelation that everything can be broken down into parts such as various drives, wishes, needs, prohibitions, and similar inclinations. Those inclinations are then also analyzed yielding more parts that are, in turn, analyzed. Freud was magnificently unwilling to commit himself to any final positions. He said of the drives, for example, that they were "our mythology" even as he pursued his parallel goal of demonstrating that we are not as free as we think.

Although she may personally value liberal or humanitarian goals, and publicly pursue these goals, the analyst remains privately ironic and, perhaps regressively, finds this twin agenda to be a proper way of life for herself. The analyst, being human (and therefore self-centered), hopes for the same kind of life for her patients. Nevertheless, she recoils from any explicit advocacy of this personal philosophy. She therefore also enjoys imagining herself to inhabit only a world of wistfulness, amusement, resignation, and fascination.

Solace for this uneasy stance is to be found in philosophic positions such as those of Kant. Pure reason, he said, demonstrates to us that we can never know the real world; practical reason leads us to choose lives of one kind or another nevertheless. Analytic reason demonstrates to us that we can never know a proper way to live a life; in our practical day-to-day life we will choose a way of life nevertheless. The analyst hopes only that self-injurious ways of life can be relinquished or, at least, deprived of their power to so heavily influence our patients' lives.

7

Transference and Countertransference

Hamlet. Denmark's a prison.

Rosencrantz. We think not so, my lord.

Hamlet. Why, then 'tis none for you, for there is nothing either good or bad but thinking makes it so. To me it is a prison.

Hamlet (II.ii.243–251)

I fear that after many chapters in a book intended to be both theoretical and practical, you have so far heard little from me about how to do it. But I hope that by now the reader will realize that this apparent lack, at least partly, is understandable in view of the ambiguous nature of the analyst's task—a task that is ill served and narrowly defined by using so industrious and practical a phrase. What she does is, at least in part, without a goal and how then could this be a task? She is earnest but is also playful; definite and pensively ironic; and often speaks poetically, allusively, and magically about apparently concrete matters. On the other hand, with a resolutely lyrical patient, she may take the poetic and render it literal and concrete. In effect the analyst plays a powerful imaginary role in the patient's life and when she speaks from time to time, her utterances may well lead the patient into an increasingly imaginary vision of the analyst. This imaginary image is what we call the transference. Let me begin with Menninger and Holzman's (1973) definition of transference, which I like:

> the unrealistic roles or identities unconsciously ascribed to an analyst by a patient in the regression of the psychoanalytic treatment and the patient's reactions to those representations, usually derived from earlier experiences. [p. 83]

Having said that I like it, I now will try to demonstrate what I find to be its weaknesses. If it seems that all of it dissatisfies me, this does not mean that their definition is without value; it means only that the analytic view of all human psychological phenomena is enormously complex and that there is no end to new angles on understanding.

Every experienced psychoanalyst and, surely, psychoanalysts of all persuasions, can understand why the word *unrealistic* is used in this definition. To our amazement, amusement, anxiety, and annoyance, our patients regularly will have attributed to us every human characteristic imaginable. Although sometimes the analyst agrees with the patient's perceptions, on many other occasions the attributes with which she is labeled are quite unrecognizable to her. When the analytic therapist is described as humane, sensitive, and perceptive, she will be tempted to agree, and when she is described as cold, without understanding, and critical, she will, contrariwise, be tempted to disagree. Such attributions, since they are fairly obvious, ought to be recognizable but, human frailty and vanity being what it is, analysts will always have difficulties with both idealization and denigration; both are, of course, unrealistic.

Are such attributions really unrealistic? Perhaps they are like delusional thinking, of which it has been said that it always contains a grain of truth. Surely analysts, like all persons, are a mixture of good and bad, do their best, and are from time to time judgmental and neglectful.

And then there is the idealization of analysts who control their patients, sexually exploit them, or use them for their public aggrandizement. Surely idealization under such circumstances is unrealistic? The problem here, I am sorry to say, is a philosophical one. It has to do with the nature of reality. In practical affairs and, for that matter, in ordinary social situations, we assume a standard reality against which practical and social events are measured. In psychology things are different—unless our aim is to standardize our patient's behaviors to some social norm. In psychology we would say that every person lives in his own reality—his own universe of discourse, his own resolute paradigmatic structuring of the world. This means that the way in which the patient sees the analyst is in keeping with his own reality but may well be in sharp contrast with the analyst's reality.

Certainly it is incumbent upon the analyst not to attempt to make the patient become more realistic since this could only mean converting the patient to her, the analyst's, universe of discourse. Naturally, she will, to some extent, try to do this—often with the patient's eager cooperation. However, it is not her aim. Her goal is only to analyze the meanings, motives, and origins of why the patient construes reality as he does. If that reality becomes different, this is well and good. The changes will not, after all, necessarily lead the patient to occupy a reality that corresponds more closely to the analyst's reality.

And so, immediately, a definition of transference that on the one hand, I find to be a good one, on the other hand is found to be off the mark. Is my objection to be considered trivial or profound? To the practical person my argument will be seen as a quibble. To the philosophically inclined, I will have hit the nail on the head. We all live in different realities, after all.

Shortly after their reference to unrealistic roles, Menninger and Holzman (1973) refer to roles or identities unconsciously ascribed to the analyst. There is something to be said for limiting transference attributions to those that take place unconsciously. It places in the foreground that which is the primary focus of the analyst, that is, the reappropriation of unconscious contents. Nevertheless, I fear that this limitation can lead to confusion in the student and even in the experienced practitioner. This is the same confusion that is all too common when transference is used only to refer to the patient's *conscious* attributions to the analyst. It is preferable, I would say, to keep absolutely clear that the patient's transference reactions are always to be given a double registration by the analyst. We must remember to meticulously distinguish manifest and latent phenomena—manifest and latent being synonyms for conscious and unconscious.

Thus, if the patient consciously idealizes the analyst we typically call this the positive transference. This is in contrast, you can see, with the limitation of transference to that which is unconscious. But, my critics might respond, the unconscious part is the fact that the idealization is an unwitting repetition of a positive relationship in the past. They are quite right, of course, but I persist in claiming that clarity of clinical thinking is better served by always explicating conscious and unconscious. In the above example there are, of course, other unconscious transference elements. Might one not also expect latent disappointments, envy, indifference, or sadism, that is to say, contradictory attitudes that cast doubt on the worth of terms like *positive transference.*

The definition of transference that I am unpacking goes on to say that transference is an ascription of something to the analyst "by a patient in the regression of the . . . treatment." This statement is, I believe, too narrow and therefore misses the mark. Transference is ubiquitous in all people at all times. It does not occur only in patients, nor does it occur only in treatment or in the regressive moments of the treatment. All persons consolidate typical and paradigmatic interpersonal worlds during the course of their earliest interpersonal experiences. These they repeat ubiquitously. Such paradigmatic styles are products of a dialectic. They are not caused by the real behavior of parents, nor are they imaginative inventions of the patient in question. We cannot, in fact, say how a paranoid person or an utterly trusting person develops that particular style. As analytic therapists we know only that there are unconscious motives for eternal suspiciousness or eternal credulity. It would be safer to not use the word *know* at all; better, for example, to say that the analyst has a paradigm for understanding human behavior and that, according to this paradigm, all manifest behavior is understood to be unconsciously motivated. In saying it this way, the analytic theorist/practitioner acknowledges the relativity—or even arbitrariness—of all thought. She thereby also acknowledges that her point of view and behavior is as resolutely motivated as is that of the patient.

I acknowledge that in the regression of the treatment, transference manifestations become more obvious, more flamboyant, and more surprising. I acknowledge, too, that our special interest is in the transferences that appear in patients (as distinct from other persons) but, I submit, this should not be part of a definition of transference. That would suggest that transference has to do with sickness or that it is to be found only in treatment situations. This would incline us to think of it as something that is to be eliminated. Indeed, when colleagues talk of "resolving the transference" they sometimes seem to be implying that something pathological has gone away and that this is a desirable end. Resolving only means solving again, that is to say, looking, thinking, analyzing, and experimenting with ideas. The therapeutic situation is not designed to make transference imagery go away but, rather, is designed to make the imaginary increasingly visible. The analytic therapist's observations and truths do not make the patient more realistic. The effect of her sometimes odd interventions is to make the imaginary more imaginary, more attractive, more interesting, and more disturbing.

Before specifying my own definition of transference, let me add a bit more flesh to what I have said before. There is a risk that students will think of transference as a subtle thing—a sort of tendency or inclination on the patient's part to see things a certain way. Although this may, at times, seem true, it must be borne in mind that transferences are not additive experiences tacked to a sensible central perception of the world. Transference is the fundamental world order by way of which a person's universe is comprehended. This is most obvious when transferences are grand and detailed incarnations of fathers, mothers, siblings—and of anyone else. It can also be an incarnation of the patient himself projected onto the analyst.

To say that something is transference is actually incorrect unless we make clear that everything is transference. And to say that something is nothing but transference is even worse. Freud (1915) was quite clear in stating that transference love is simply love or, better, is simply the patient's typical way of being in love. The question is not whether something is transference or not. Instead the question is always about the nature of the transference manifestations at any given time. The question is qualitative and not existential.

In consequence of such reflections, I therefore now propose to define transference as

> the model interpersonal configurations by way of which people structure and understand the social world, in fact, the concrete and vivid social realities characteristic of a particular individual. These transference realities are defined by psychoanalysts as having both substantial conscious elements and unconscious motivational elements. Transference is ubiquitous and eternal and, rather than being static, is narrative and progressive in nature. There is, for every person, an array of typical narratives, each of which is drenched with, or constituted of, previous life narratives, and each of which is vividly populated by psychological reincarnations of important persons from the past. The vividness of these reincarnations is facilitated by the regression of the analytic treatment situation, and the presence of the unobtrusive and neutral analyst.

The first reference that Freud makes to the transference is in *Studies in Hysteria* (1893–1895). He refers to it there as the patient having made a "false connection." Most readers will know that Freud's mentor and colleague, Josef Breuer, gave up the treatment of his famous patient, Anna O. He ended the treatment, it is said, because of the patient's intense erotic attachment to him. Freud, even though his patients, too, developed erotic attachments to him, persisted in working analytically with them. One can only speculate about why one man retreated and another man persisted. We do know that Freud introduced a theoretical term that may well have helped him. "These erotic attachments," he may have said "are products of a false connection that I will call transference. I need not take such attachments to me personally since they are capable of being understood in theoretical terms."

To this day, most analysts, when faced with intense erotic or hostile transferences, find comfort in saying to themselves, "This is just another piece of this patient's urgently pursued transference narrative." In addition, analysts must periodically remind themselves that when they say something is just transference they are stating only a partial truth, since transference informs the eroticism or hostility of every person, whether he is a patient or not. It would be a deadening miscomprehension if every human love was designated as just transference. To say that the love (or the hatred) of patients for their analyst is nothing but transference is at best insulting, and at worst a failure to understand love, hostility, or transference itself. Transference is not a thing but, rather, a theoretical term that illuminates our understanding of any love or any hatred. The transference implications of events should enrich and add complexity to our understanding of them. To use the term reductionistically only impoverishes and makes banal our understanding.

Freud placed great emphasis on the fact that transference enactments take the place of remembering. In other words, in the specific instance of the treatment situation, the patient's reactions to the analyst are ways of remembering without *explicitly* remembering. One of the analyst's tasks, then, is to help the patient to apprehend as exhaustively as possible the sources of his manifold reactions to the analyst, sources that are, at least in principle, discernible in previous relationships. Eventually the patient might say, "I have been in love on numerous occasions but, strangely, it has always been with the same woman."

Such enactments, since they block remembering, can be thought of as resistances. Indeed, it has been said that transference is the quintessential form of resistance. One cannot deny that this is so but, in a certain sense, to say so has little value. This is because, theoretically speaking, everything is a resistance. Whatever position the patient takes is understood by analytic theory to obscure another position. Every thought, every affect, every action, by virtue of being performed, prevents, denies, and forbids all other psychological positions. Analytic theory insists that such forbiddens are dynamic, powerful, and that the patient has unconscious motives for incarnating his psychological world as he does. Thus, strictly speaking, every psychological action, including every transference action, is a resistance.

There is, of course, overtly resistive behavior to be discovered in patients. This, it must be clear, is to be distinguished from the theoretical term *resistance.* An example that immediately clarifies this distinction is a patient's cooperative behavior. Theoretically this is a resistance (probably a transference resistance, at that) and, as such, is to be analyzed. The distinction is between a theoretical term and the same word used to describe manifest behavior. Failure to keep this distinction clear leads to the false notion that the word *resistance* refers to something improper that a patient does and that therefore must be dealt with. A colleague once said that when a student says that her patient is resisting, she has missed the point.

The patient's resistance is, of course, constituted of the same dynamisms as are the forces of repression. The patient wards off elements in himself that he considers to be unacceptable and, when the analyst does her work—that is to say, attempts to reappropriate unconscious contents—she becomes the representative of those unconscious elements with which she has allied herself. Just as those elements have heretofore been warded off so, now, the analyst finds herself to be warded off. Voilà!—the resistance.

Often there is a fundamental distinction postulated between what are called oedipal and preoedipal transferences. Freud's theory did not make such a fundamental distinction and I fear that those who do so unwittingly lead us away from crucial insights into the human mind. I suspect that the postulation by analytic therapists of a preoedipal structuring of the human mind, leads us back to pre-Freudian theories.

The idea behind the hypothesis of a basic or preoedipal transference is that the child's first relationship, at least in the child's mind, is a one-to-one bond with the nurturing maternal figure. If things go well, it is argued, the child can, in the matrix of this relationship, build up a basic core of confidence in the world that will be a grounding for its psychological functioning throughout life. This basic relationship, preoedipal in nature, appears in later relationships as a secure underpinning for the complexities of those later relationships including the complexities of entering into the oedipal world. It also becomes a secure underpinning for being capable of doing analytic work should such a therapy ever be necessary. In the therapy this basic trust might be referred to as the basic transference, a transference configuration that guarantees that analytic therapy can take place

In that early infantile relationship, then, a core identity is established. Many terms are used for this nuclear configuration. It may, for example, be called the mature ego, the cohesive self, ego identity, or a state of individuation. The early infantile relationship, properly negotiated, leads to the establishment of stable internal objects.

These ideas and terms are commonsensical and refer to desirable human events. Every analytic therapist appreciates what is being driven at by proponents of such ideas. If I may be so unkind, I would suggest that the analytic therapist also worries about such notions because they seem to be motherhood statements. She thinks about such ideas just as she thinks about her patient's ideas and, for that matter, about her own ideas. Her thought is "Yes, but . . ." That imaginary figure—the ideal analyst—does not think this with ill humor. On the contrary, she is skeptical because she finds everything to be curious and problematic. Unlike ordinary mortals, this hypothetical analyst is forever able to maintain a scientific and philosophical equanimity that permits her to ponder such theoretical disagreements with perfect dispassion. What is it, then, that she finds curious and problematic about the basic transference? "The problem is," she says, "that the ideas are pre-Freudian." In place of Freud's idea of motivated behavior these theorists have substituted causal thinking. "Mental degeneracy", she proclaims, "is no different from a weak ego, a fragmented self, or identity diffusion. These things are understood to be direct causes of symptoms, of attitudes, and of behaviors, an understanding that is fundamentally contradicted by analytic theory."

The analyst whom I have ironically invoked always knows with perfect clarity that analytic theory is a thoroughgoing undermining of the common sense ideas by which all of us usually live. The subjective experience of every patient and of every person is postulated by the theory to be fundamentally faulted or flawed. My conscious knowledge of myself may well be laudable and rich in truth but, at the very same time, is a self-deceiving error. In other words, he who claims to be strong leads the analyst to wonder whether he is weak, whether the patient speaks of someone else's strengths by way of his claim, or whether he praises the analyst's work by his proclamation. The analyst considers many cues and many clues as she attempts to unearth possible meanings and motives that might lie behind the claim of strength. She does the very same with claims of weakness, stupidity, sexual prowess, or artistic talent. Ideally, the analyst does not change her strategy when the patient says he is falling apart or when the patient claims social ineptitude.

The analyst, when she is tempted to think of patients as having a psychic defect, looks to her own countertransference. However, in contradiction of her own ideal, the analytic therapist is, at times, liable to make unfavorable judgments about colleagues who affirm that their patients suffer from psychological deficits due to failures in early development— failures, that is to say, in the basic preoedipal relationship with the mother. Sometimes she is actually angered by them and impatiently insists that they are not analysts at all. They should, she says, call themselves ethologists and behaviorists—perfectly worthy theorists—but should not claim to be Freudians or psychoanalysts or analytic psychotherapists.

In contrast to this, that is to say, when she is truly thinking like a psychoanalyst, she will not be angered, nor will she judge her preoedipally misguided colleagues. Instead she will ruefully recognize that her own strictly analytic position is just as unconsciously urgent as is the basic transference position of her colleagues.

There is, I think, a serious misunderstanding here that ought to be clarified. The idea of the Oedipus complex seems to me to be apprehended far too concretely. That concreteness robs the notion of much of its informative power. Here is the way in which I put together the series of ideas that make up the oedipal theory. It is much influenced by how Freud (1930) spoke of these matters in *Civilization and its Discontents*.

The child is born into a family and into a culture. That family, the representative for the child of the culture's rules, implicitly and explicitly instructs the child about what is good and what is bad, about what has value and what has no value, and about fairness, justice, honor, decency, and pride. In other words, they instruct the child in the cultural law. This law, for analytic purposes, is also the oedipal law. The fundamental tenets of the oedipal and cultural law are the prohibition of incest and patricide.

The child is born into a world heavily populated by models of how one lives. Be it parents, schools, books, films, television, theater, ballet, opera or the visual arts—all inform and instruct about what is to count as valuable, as good, and as bad. The abused or neglected child is as imbued with these messages as is any other child. Even if one leaves aside the informational world apart from the parents, one suspects that even abusive parents faithfully deliver to their children the oedipal or cultural law. Are we not all too often surprised and perplexed by the arbitrary conventional morality of abusive parents? When one reflects for only a moment about such parents, it is immediately brought to mind that surprisingly

often they are strict about obedience or about mildly suggestive sexual behavior. Incestuous fathers, for example, regularly beat their daughters for sitting in cars with boys.
Another group of "sinners"—prison inmates—all too often
moralistically take it upon themselves to murder—to "exe-
cute"—pedophilic sexual offenders who are their prison
mates.

The cultural/oedipal law is symbolically structured as the
law of the father. Lacan's evocative phrase was *le non-du-père*
or its near-homonym, *le nom-du-père*. In other words, the
name of the father and the *no* of the father are the same thing.
The naysaying law is symbolically structured by the name of
the father. This is (at least for now) inevitably so because we
live in a patriarchal society. Our heritage of great literature
and fine art overwhelmingly indoctrinates us with patriarchal
thinking. Those of us who think seriously about the complaints of feminists can only speculate about the degree to
which the patriarchal culture can change. Can the mother
become the bearer of the oedipal/cultural law? Can the structuring of a family or a culture be established through a purely
abstract set of rules without embodiment in a person? One
doubts and one wishes not to doubt, both at once.

The infant is born into this structured, and necessarily
rule-bound world even though at first it may be unaware of
that world's existence. But at the instant that the infant
enters into a conscious awareness of the social world, it is
immediately in a culture infused with laws and values.
Mothers smile and coo to their babies, but they also withdraw
from what offends them, at times frown and murmur "no-
no" and "yes-yes." Entering the social order and the linguistic world means entering a world of values. No mother
loves unconditionally. She loves, values, and treasures the
love bond between herself and her infant and, if it is absent or
hard to see, she is disappointed and worried. The good basic
relationship between mother and child is one of our powerful
cultural values, sought after by all, and the failure of which is
dreaded. It is not a value distinct or different from other
values, but is just one element in the web of cultural expectations. Those who do not value or respect the love between

mother and infant are judged to be callous and cold. They are violators of an important clause in the oedipal-cultural code of behavior.

There need be no father for the child to be in a structured world that strives for a particular orderliness and a particular set of values and behaviors. The father—the oedipal father, the bearer of the oedipal law—is a figure who exists in every child's symbolic world. The language and the culture guarantee that he exists. He is incarnate in every God, every man, every hero, every leader. He exists, too, in his flawed form, in every disappointing God, every weak man, and in every tainted hero and leader. He exists, of course, as the idealized and disappointing analyst. The loving and depriving mother is equally present in every woman, or should I say, every Woman. These images, archetypes, and stereotypes eternally populate and structure our world. They orient us to our world. They are the templates against which we judge, measure, and guide ourselves and others. The triangular relationship is ubiquitous. Even if we act against the law of Oedipus, we know that the father/law/culture will structure us, guide us, oblige us to obey, and punish us.

This is my version of the Oedipus complex, a complex of conflicting thoughts that is the fundamental structuring force of every human psyche. The divided subject, unconscious of so much, is divided precisely because he must repress that which he judges to be in violation of the oedipal law. The basic relationship and the basic transference are endopsychic perceptions that are as self-deceiving as is anything else.

The popular notion of the Oedipus complex is that the child wants to sexually possess the parent of the opposite sex and to displace or kill the parent of the same sex. What this really means is that any given child has, to a greater or lesser extent, desires of every sort. He experiences and longs for sensual touches, warm cuddles, and is annoyed at parents who intrude or prevent such gratifications. Boys—in accordance with cultural expectations, that is to say, in accordance with the oedipal law—know early on that their primary love is supposed to follow a heterosexual model, as do girls. Such touches, cuddles, annoyances and—yes—thoughts of

sex and murder, are violations of the value code in which
they live. To the extent that they imagine themselves to be
violators of that code, they are fearful and guilty. Children see
to it that they banish from awareness incestuous and mur-
derous ideas, not to speak of a multitude of symbolic equiv-
alents or derivatives of those ideas.

With difficult patients the analyst should keep in mind that
transference manifestations are often more obvious than they
are in patients whose behavioral status is closer to the norm.
With the latter group of patients, the more usual social cour-
tesies and conventions make transference manifestations
harder to see at least at first, particularly since straightforwardly neurotic patients commonly begin in a cooperative
frame of mind. Borderline patients, in contrast, may be insulting or accusatory from the first day on and, with equivalent immediacy, the severely depressed may denigrate themselves and insistently expect rescuing interventions from the
powerful analyst. At times, being accustomed to acting quietly and to not speaking too soon, the analytic therapist may
wait longer than is necessary before she addresses transference manifestations that are, if one takes pause, so transpar-
ently obvious. The behavior of both these groups of patients
is disturbing, if not frightening, and I have often had students
describe how they have waited, hoping to collect further information and, one suspects, hoping that more information
will help them to intervene with less discomfort.

Generally, angry and accusatory patients can be confronted with what they are doing. I would caution the reader
that the word *confront,* although accurate, is an unfortunate
one. In fact, when confronting a patient, the analytic therapist
is merely interpreting and may be quite mild and leisurely in
her manner. Often she will talk abstractedly or whimsically.

"Here in this office you have quickly found a tormentor."

"Fortune has parachuted you into a therapy where you
find as a proposed helper . . . your mother."

> "These accusations that you are making are a discovery of this analysis as ungainly and unappetizing."

> "So . . . very quickly you are on familiar turf. You are discernibly 'the worthless one' who now makes me worry and, perhaps, scold."

These imagined interventions attempt not to judge the behavior as pathological, as inappropriate, or as something that most people don't do. We are not at all aiming to get the patient to behave normatively. We wish only to illuminate the world in which he resides—especially those elements of his world that are hangovers from the past and that lead the patient to act in self-punitive ways. In other words, we try to make his imaginary *more* imaginary.

There is no point in patiently listening and waiting to say these things to the patient because, usually, waiting merely leads to more of the same. Those who characterologically worry us, frustrate us, and offend us (borderline patients) and the characterologically depressed patient, persist and insist on doing what they do. We must enter into their characterological worlds differently from the way in which others do. Those others, of course, try to persuade them to behave normatively.

If, in our interventions, we imply deviance or psychopathology, we are doing with our patients what the world always does with them. This, one might say, is the typical countertransference reaction to such patients. Thus, when we point out to them how they act, we must be at great pains not to imply that they are "doing it here again." To simply say to them that this is their pattern, even if they deny it, is to point out something that they already know perfectly well. Better, then, to try to catch hold of the broader transference–countertransference setup that they seek and that, indeed, they always partially succeed in creating.

> "Very quickly this world of therapy is a place in which I judge you as unfair and cranky."

> "I see that I am already located in a hierarchy in which I am high and you are low. I am increasingly the potent care-

giving doctor and you, in a complementary fashion, are
increasingly the sick, helpless patient." With gentle irony
in her voice the analyst will say, "Soon I must think of
drugs and hospitals, since your insistent state of wretch-
edness will induce me to rear up and rescue you."

The analyst should not be deceived into thinking that such
remarks will alter the characterological style. She should not
even *hope* that they will alter things. Her job is to quietly, at
timely moments (who can judge what is timely?), introduce
more and more imaginative interventions such as those
quoted above. In the instance of borderline cases, the patient
will stand back from his behavior and find it ego alien only
slowly; depressives usually stand back from their behaviors
sooner—at least from its grossest manifestations. However,
there is no predicting. The analytic therapist must, to the
best of her ability, keep at her analytic task.

It has already been made clear that the patient is not alone in
being in the toils of his own personal transferences. The
analytic therapist, naturally enough, has reactions to her
patient as well. Such countertransferences are, on the one
hand, enactments of the analyst's own personal past and, on
the other hand, are evoked by the roles the patient casts her
in. Like all transferences, the analyst's countertransferences
are best understood as products of the therapeutic dialogue.
This is not to deny that the analyst's personal past plays a
role in her behavior. It is just that it is strategic to focus first
on what analyst and patient are together conspiring to do.
When one has a sense of the therapeutic dialectic, one can
then also reflect upon other aspects of both participants'
worlds, present and past. In principle, it might be argued that
just as much attention ought to be paid to the sources of the
analyst's participation in the dialectic as is paid to the
patient's participation. In practice we must do otherwise.
The patient, after all, is the patient!
    When the analyst is at her best she listens to her patient's
statements and reflectively wonders about other places,
other times, and other stages that might be fitting locales for
what is being said. In fact, she asks herself, is there a locale

wherein this narrative is a *better* fit? Does it fit in his past, with his spouse, or with his friend? At such a reflective moment, when she is truly in a state of evenly hovering attention, our imaginary analyst is, so to speak, without countertransference. Or is she? Could we not wonder, too, about her remarkable and magical neutrality? Is it not also a transference repetition of her past?

Is her listening an enactment of those days when she sat at the top of the stairs listening through the banister as the adults talked downstairs? Does she listen patiently and for-givingly to her patient's foibles with the same ears with which she heard her father make weak jokes with his business as-sociates—jokes by way of which he hoped to ingratiate himself with them? Might not fascination with her patient be a defense against rage—rage at him for being a reincarnation of a weak father? What more can one say when one talks of the task attempted by the analyst—she who attempts to practice the "impossible profession"? Even at her best moment, she is self-deceived, defensive, and resisting, just as is her patient.

The analyst must know that her participation in the therapeutic encounter bears and will always bear her own unique and fateful signature. If she is tough and self-reliant, she will be calm and self-assured in her work; if she is by nature tender and anxious, the analyst will, in her work, often be a nervous wreck. These are her analytic destinies. For many of us the patient's passionate love for us—his erotic transference—will lead us into suffering. Our desire, longing, revulsion, and guilt are inevitable. The temptation to subtly or overtly exploit the transference are ceaseless as is the temptation to dismiss, reject, and ignore it. All of us prefer patients who are, psychologically, our theoretical, political, and philosophical allies. Most of us will be offended by patients who accuse us, who whine and quibble, who reveal to us their borderline legal infractions (such as minor tax avoidances), or who endlessly intellectualize into dry dust our every heartfelt comment.

Theodore Jacobs (1993) has written a brilliant descrip-tion of the myriad inner reactions of the analyst as she sits in her analytic place and contemplates the world of her patient, a description that every student is urged to read.

Here is a list from Menninger and Holzman (1973) that may help some analysts as they struggle with their difficult analytic tasks and attempt to discover their own counter-transferences. It is a partial list of clues that lead one to realize that something ungainly is going on.

Inability to understand certain kinds of material that touch on the analyst's own personal problems.

Depressed or uneasy feelings during or after analytic hours with certain patients.

Carelessness in regard to arrangements—forgetting the patient's appointment, being late for it, letting the patient's hours run overtime for no special reason.

Repeatedly experiencing erotic or affectionate feeling toward a patient.

Permitting and even encouraging resistance in the form of acting out.

Security-seeking, narcissistic devices such as trying to impress the patient in various ways, or to impress colleagues with the importance of one's patient.

Cultivating the patient's continued dependence in various ways, especially by unnecessary reassurances.

An urge to engage in professional gossip concerning a patient.

Sadistic, unnecessary sharpness in formulation of comments and interpretations, and the reverse.

Feeling that the patient must get well for the sake of the doctor's reputation and prestige.

"Hugging the case to one's bosom," that is, being too afraid of losing the patient.

Getting conscious satisfaction from the patient's praise, appreciation, evidences of affection, and so forth.

Becoming disturbed by the patient's persistent reproaches and accusations.

Arguing with the patient.

Premature reassurances against the development of anxiety in the patient or, more accurately, finding oneself unable to gauge the point of optimum frustration tension.

A compulsive tendency to "hammer away" at certain points.

Recurrent impulses to ask favors of the patient.

Sudden increase or decrease of interest in a certain case.

Since patients are not fools, they gradually come to know much of the analyst's character. They especially know what she believes in, that is to say, they have a sense of her moral character. Although the analyst knows that patients suffer from an excess of self-imposed morality, being mortal she cannot help revealing her own moral self. Fortunately, patients know as well, that the analyst, despite her subtle moralizing moments is an ironic and relativistic observer. This, patients appreciate.

8

Interpretation

The modern era has been dominated by the culminating
belief that the world is a wholly knowable system governed
by a finite number of universal laws that man can grasp
and rationally direct for his own benefit. Communism was
the perverse extreme of this trend. It is my profound conviction that we have to release from the sphere of private
whim such forces as a natural, unique and unrepeatable
experience of the world, an elementary sense of justice, the
ability to see things as others do, a sense of transcendental
responsibility, archetypal wisdom, good taste, courage,
compassion, and faith in the importance of particular
measures that do not aspire to be a universal key to
salvation. We must see the pluralism of the world and not
blind it by seeking common denominators. We must try
harder to understand than explain.

Vaclav Havel,
Speech to World Economics Forum, 1992

These comments of Vaclav Havel are worth reading more
than once. He is referring to what is, for psychoanalytic

thinkers, a difficult but profound truth. This truth goes like this: psychoanalytic interpretation has to do with the capture of truths that are unexpected, are never unitary, and have to do with the uniqueness of psychological events. That persons have a sex drive is, of course, of interest to us—both as theoreticians and as practitioners. But *it is not our specific psychoanalytic interest.* We are, instead, concerned about what a person *does* with his sex drive and what purpose and meaning it has for him. That a person is sexual (aggressive, premenstrual, mortal) is, for us, an empirical fact and is an *existential* rather than an *interpretive* matter. We are interested and impressed by this world of empirical facts, but psychoanalysts qua analysts consider such facts to be topics for students of biology. Our concern is the devilishly complicated interpretation of what these things mean to our patients.

That Freud was often preoccupied by such empirical truths (to wit, his metapsychological speculations) does not change the fact that his interpretive psychoanalytic discoveries have nothing to do with mere facts. That persons have sex drives, noses, brains, and gallbladders is true but is not of specific psychoanalytic relevance. Men have bigger muscles than do women, but this does not irrevocably fate them to be the boss. These biological attributes are interpreted in an infinite number of ways—ways that lead to the infinite psychological variety that we discover in the lives of those we study analytically.

Freud's magnum opus, *The Interpretation of Dreams,* is, in German, entitled *Die Traumdeutung.* The word *Deutung* means interpretation but in a sense somewhat narrower than our English usage of the word interpretation. *Deutung,* in this context, more specifically means the interpretation of omens and dreams. It is the interpretation done by palm readers and by dream interpreters like the biblical Joseph. We should never forget that we, the analytic therapists, have for our patients that same slightly uncanny meaning. We are today's priests or shamans—roles thrown up by every culture and that we occupy in the Western world. These are potent roles and our anticipated power to interpret lends great authority to what we say. That power may also be one of the potent factors in the recovery of patients. One need only think of the apparent satisfaction of the clients of primal therapists, television evangelists, and other pretenders of every stripe.

This ought to make us cautious about what we claim is the curative factor in our therapeutic activities. Analytic psychotherapy is characterized by the analyst's interpretive activities. In principle, and to a considerable extent in practice, the analyst confines herself to interpretations and, if she makes other interventions, they are in the service of positioning herself to make interpretive statements. The rationale for her unceasing interpretive activity cannot rely on practical grounds. After all, I have already pointed out that good therapeutic results—at least as we currently know how to measure them—are common.

From an analytic point of view one must suspect that each of us has his or her own preferred way of viewing the world (preferred universe of discourse) and that we practice as we do for a variety of unconscious reasons and motives. Those who practice directive instructional therapies, too, have their reasons for doing so.

Despite this, all persons are inclined to explain what they do in more rational and conscious terms. Very briefly, I would say that analytic psychotherapy is highly commendable in its determination to adopt no dogmatic positions. The analytic therapist promotes no particular way of living a life and, instead, focuses exclusively on the interpretive understanding of why her patients live as they do. She is skeptical of all beliefs—especially of strongly or arbitrarily held beliefs—but, contrariwise, wants not to discard beliefs too lightly. To this end, the analyst is modestly credulous about everything. Although she has doubts about goblins, gods, popular movements, and enthusiasms (Nietzsche called them "intoxications"), she also acknowledges that all have a powerful psychological reality that she honors as much as she does any prosaic objective reality. Because the analytic therapist holds to her democratic position so faithfully, she must, of course, reflect her theory back upon herself and cast doubt upon her own doubtfulness. She worries, therefore, that her campaign against ardent belief systems—systems that she is liable to call forms of fascism—is, because of its ardency, also a fascism. The analyst must, therefore, be acutely sensitive and responsive to a great variety of narratives that will be told to her by all kinds of people on all kinds of occasions.

This argument in support of interpretation as the psychotherapeutic intervention of choice is, of course, a personal one. But these principles are implicit in many discussions that one has with colleagues and I suspect that my argument has widespread support.

Brenner's book *Psychoanalytic Technique and Psychic Conflict* (1976) contains a chapter on interpretation that can help with this difficult interpretive job. His approach is very different from mine insofar as he proposes a strictly scientific and objectivistic approach to the understanding of interpretation. But my sympathies are with him because his goal, the revelation of the unconscious, is identical to mine. Despite my sympathies, I am not convinced that the distinction between objective and subjective is as sharp as he claims.

To Brenner the issue is the discovery of objectifiable facts about unconscious motives that can then be brought to the patient's attention. This is done by collecting evidence from the patient's associations, dreams, slips of the tongue, and characteristic symptoms. These data are sifted, compared, contrasted, and reworked until the analyst, either logically or by means of a bright idea, can infer what the unconscious motives are that lead the patient into his unhappy state. The inference, says Brenner, is at first merely a conjecture but, as the evidence accumulates, the analyst's convictions about that influence hardens. Eventually the conviction about the unconscious contents can, by way of an interpretation, be delivered to the patient.

I suspect that the unconscious motives that Brenner discovers are akin to those that I discover and, furthermore, I suspect that the self knowledge achieved by his patients is similar to that achieved by mine. Our difference is in our *theoretical* understanding of how this is achieved and what that achievement means. Brenner, using an objective approach, aims to discover true facts about the unconscious; I on the other hand, aim to illuminate particular worldviews, most particularly warded off worldviews. To me these are not observable facts but, rather, dialectical achievements that are to be granted no final truth value.

In keeping with his point of view, Brenner is concerned that the analytic therapist be as accurate and pristine an observer as possible. If the analyst has had an adequate treatment experience herself, then, he argues, she will be less biased and more accurate in her analytic observations. Having attained analytic truths, that is to say, bedrock true facts about herself, her worldview will have been corrected and she will be a better observer, sifter of evidence, and hypothesis builder. I, on the other hand, think of analytic therapies as interminable and consider that at the end of treatment, no correction of worldviews has taken place. The analyst, after her own treatment is completed, may well have shifted her worldview and have come to entertain new worldviews. But these new views are not better or more correct. They are simply different. She is not more accurate in her observations nor is her psyche more pristine. She is forever a prisoner of her own universes of discourse and this means that her work is more difficult than it would be had her own treatment been a corrective one. But her own treatment will hopefully have rendered her sensitive to her own biases (or what to others would be seen as distortions) and less likely to be misled into believing that she knows what is going on.

Brenner explicitly advocates empirical observation as the prime source of analytic hypotheses. This is his preferred emphasis. Attention to one's own fantasies and affective states is part of this program of observation. Others, although not wishing to deny the importance of listening and observing, emphasize other factors. Wilhelm Reich (1949), for example, outlined a logical, rational program for interpreting. Theodor Reik (1948) took the extreme opposite position and advocated an intuitive "listening with the third ear." Obviously, observation, intuition, and logic are all used by all analytic therapists, albeit with individual emphases.

Where, you might ask, does empathy fit in? I suppose that I am much out of fashion if I state that empathy is not something that analysts do, or that anyone else does. In fact, it is a theoretical explanatory term. In trying to explain how one person can understand another, the philosopher Wilhelm Dilthey (1894) argued that psychology could generate descriptive statements about people because of a psychological ability that he called *Einfühlung,* translated into English as "empathy." In the language of ego psychology, empathy would, I suggest, be categorized as an ego function. Another philosopher, Edmund Husserl (1929), also used the term *empathy* to explain the mysterious leap from one's own mind to the understanding of another person. Heinz Hartmann (1927) disagreed with this notion because, to him, nothing mysterious was taking place. Psychoanalysis, he insisted, had found a way of objectively studying psychological data and thereby making accurate observations of such phenomena. In recent years certain psychoanalysts have retreated from Hartmann's insistence on objectivistic scientific methods and have attempted to revive and refresh the idea of empathy. Heinz Kohut (1977) has been the forerunner of an enormous wave of interest in the concept—not simply as an explanatory term for our ability to understand, but also as referring to an activity of the analyst that has healing or curative powers.

The debate between objectivism and empathy is an old one, and has been framed in many languages. It raged hotly in the distinction drawn between the *Geisteswissenschaften* and the *Naturwissenschaften,* that is to say, between the spiritual or social sciences and the natural sciences. It has also been conceptualized as the distinction between *erklären* and *verstehen* (explaining and understanding). The former, it is said, is characteristic of objectivism and the natural sciences, whereas the latter is characteristic of the more subjectivistic and empathy-based social sciences. As I have already indicated, this debate has been entered into by psychoanalytic theorists who, typically, are divided into the objectivist camp (Hartmann and Brenner, for example) on the one hand, and by those interested in empathy (largely Kohut and his followers) on the other. In my view, both camps are barking up the wrong tree, so to speak. Both the objectivists and the empathicists aim, by way of their methods, to have access to the true nature of the minds of others. Such a pursuit of truth may be laudable to some but, to me, misses the crucial point of psychoanalysis, namely, that it is an *interpretive* activity. If, indeed, interpretation is our forte, we can never establish what is actually in the mind of another but can only arrive at interpretations—and an infinite number of interpretations, at that—of what another thinks.

Nor do objectivism and empathy lead us to any substantive truths. Empirical scientists and empathic observers alike can only interpret from their objectivistic and empathic standpoints. Insofar as these analytic contributors think that their methods lead them to discover true facts about their patient's minds, they are not, in my view, thinking psychoanalytically.

The psychoanalytic method does not lead the psychoanalytic therapist to wallow in the infinitude of interpretive possibilities any more than do objectivistic or empathic observers. The analytic theorist, too, has her interpretive field delimited by a number of axiomatic positions with which she begins her interpretive task. These axiomatic starting points are just as clear cut as are the methodological constraints upon objectivist and empathic theorists. First, she aims to help another person who is in a state of psychological suffering. As she does her interpretive work she makes little explicit reference to her helping role but, in countless subtle ways, that responsibility must color everything she does. This "helping" coloration is determined by the fact that patients, naturally enough, tend to talk about what is bothering them. Thus, analytic work is tilted toward that which is painful.

Second, the psychoanalyst has a definition in mind of what her patient is like; more explicitly, she makes the a priori assumption that the patient has the attributes of personhood. All persons, she axiomatically claims, are sensuous, desirous, guilty, conflicted, and make use of a natural language. She does not search for, say, conflict. Instead she assumes that conflict exists. What she searches for is the nature of the conflict, and how the patient uses his personal qualities against himself. This holds true even if the patient bears designations such as psychosis, schizophrenia, or of major character pathology.

I would add to this that the analytic therapist, as she listens and formulates her interpretive attempts, has a third axiomatic skew in her thinking. This time, her working assumption is that all patients suffer guilt because of imagined transgressions of the oedipal law. The neurosis is a compromise formation by way of which the patient is both punished for, and at the same time subtly achieves secret gratification of, the unconscious forbidden wish. The imagined crimes are as various as the number of patients we see. The common denominator is that it is a violation of familial and cultural expectations, more or less loosely related to incest and patricide. The self-punishment is just as varied and typically is tailored to the imagined crime according to the *lex talionis.* Imaginativeness, logic, and observation all come together and structure the interpretation into a format in which the oedipal crime and its punishment are illuminated. In a barbarously reductionistic way, it could be said that every interpretation is identical: "By accomplishing this and that suffering, you resolutely punish yourself for your such and so version of the oedipal crime."

Conjectures and interpretations are not easy to validate. Many patients are eager to agree with us and seemingly confirm everything we say. Perhaps a smaller number typically disconfirm what the analyst says. Brenner believes that, at times, he can predict behavioral responses to interpretations, responses in the direction of improvement or the disappearance of symptoms. I feel hesitant about agreeing with this, partly because I am reluctant wholeheartedly to endorse improvement as being the goal of analytic therapy, and partly because I am not convinced that it happens in as straightforward a way as the word implies. My version of the desired state of improvement will be made explicit in the final chapter.

But Brenner does mention other confirmatory events that have the ring of correctness. For example, the patient may react to an interpretation with surprised recognition or with a sense that what has been said is familiar. Forgotten memories may immediately come to mind or there may be confirmatory associations or dreams. The patient may experience affective reactions such as laughter, tears, rage, or guilt.

Finally, Brenner points out that the explanatory power of an interpretation can be considered to be confirmatory. I would add that this is an exceedingly important point. Interpretations, like any other explanation—including scientific theories—are never concretely or literally true. Actually they are simply ways of ordering and making comprehensible our world. There is no such thing as free will or as linear causes. These are simply ways of explaining. I may well feel that I have free will and choose to do what I do but this is merely my preferred experience of myself and my preferred explanation of my behavior. The next person may feel that he is *driven* to action and that impersonal forces impel him to act as he does. This, too, is merely that person's preferred and experienced explanation of his actions. No explanation is comprehensive but, in general, we place more value on explanations that have great explanatory power.

I strongly agree with Brenner that interpretation is the therapeutic instrument *sine qua non* in the armamentarium of the psychoanalytic therapist. Brenner (1976) puts it straightforwardly:

> To assert (or imagine) that there is a "process" of analysis that is essentially independent of interpretation in this sense of the word is a contradiction in terms. "To analyze" can only mean to help a patient know himself better. Any other form of psychotherapy is not analysis. It may be equally successful therapeutically in a particular case. It may be even more successful than analysis in some cases, but it is not psychoanalysis. [p. 49]

From early on in his career Freud was interpretative and linguistic in his approach to patients. In his theorizing Freud's allegiance to the interpretive approach was sometimes weaker than one would have hoped. This is especially true of his metapsychological speculations wherein he was inclined to adopt physicalistic and physiological formulations. Like most of us, he never got over his physics envy. But it must also be kept in mind that, despite Freud's nostalgia for positivism, he regularly disavowed his metapsychological formulations. He said, for example, that "drives are mythical creatures, splendid in their indefiniteness" (1933, p. 95) and, in reference to metapsychology, that "such ideas as these are part of a speculative superstructure of psychoanalysis, any portion of which can be abandoned or changed without loss or regret the moment its inadequacy has been proved" (1925, p. 32). Regarding his metapsychological ideas Freud also says, "They are not the bottom but the top of the whole structure, and they can be replaced and discarded without damaging it" (1914b, p. 77).

One can see in Freud's clinical case studies that his theoretical concerns were, as I have said, linguistic and interpretive. That interest is very much in keeping with the philosophical movements of this century. One could perhaps say that Freud anticipated the movement of philosophy in this century away from matters of ontology, to the world as subject to interpretation. Insofar as Freud has done this, he has moved away from the sure footing of objective truth to the uncertain excitement of interpretive truth.

But Freudianism differs from the theoretical formulations of his philosophical colleagues in one major respect. He is not content with confining himself to the interpretive worlds that any particular person brings into being publicly. The existential worlds that Proust so magically creates for us are fine, says Freud, as far as they go. But Freud wants to know, in addition, why *that* world or *those* worlds? What is the motive for creating the worlds that Proust in fact creates? There is, says Freud, another world (or worlds) that is logically forbidden by creating the world as we do. In other words, psychoanalysis acknowledges the interpretive nature of every truth world but, in addition, postulates the truth world of the contradictory repressed. Analytic theory interprets to the patient the reasons for which he interprets the world as he does. This, philosophy neglects.

Dr. R., a colleague, had for many years carried the diagnosis of manic-depressive illness. She had come to analysis because she was dissatisfied with the results of the biological treatments she was getting and, at the time of these events, had been in analysis for one year. She was reporting to her analyst, Dr. L., that she had recently attended a clinical talk that she had originally referred to as "nice." Suddenly the patient, who was characteristically sweet and gentle, began to speak differently.

What a stupid thing to say. What I should have said was that the talk was ridiculous. This guy was talking about the attitude one should have toward patients. What it boiled down to was that one should treat patients like idiots. "You should," he said, "repeat back—echo—what patients say. Don't give advice. Always look patients in the eye. Never ask questions that have a yes or no answer." I couldn't believe it when I saw a psychiatric resident taking notes.

On other occasions she would begin in a similarly banal vein. "I heard a lecture on major affective disorders today. Are you sure of my diagnosis, Dr. L.?" Or on another occasion she spoke of how superficially and naively supportive she had been in talking to a depressed patient. In fact, she never, after the first few months, doubted Dr. L.'s diagnosis—or, rather, his non-diagnosis. Nor had she spoken stupidly to her depressed patient. These statements were, one can speculate, anxious presentations of herself as stupid, lest she be strong.

Am I really so seductive? Do I really have such an effect on men? You are right not to have an affair with me because I think women really do have a terrible power over men. I saw *Madama Butterfly* last week and it was very clear in the opera. She seduced Lieutenant Pinkerton and then later she was passionately kissing her young son.

Plato and Kant and the Idealists were right. We see the world according to our preformed ideas about it and, as Freud realized, all thought leads away from other truths. Dr. R.'s truth was that Madama Butterfly was a seductress. In contrast to Dr. R.'s vision of the opera, convention would have it that Lieutenant Pinkerton was a ruthless seducer—an exploitative, psychopathic, son-of-a-bitch.

> Dr. L., the patient's analyst, had also seen the opera a few nights before. Curtain calls. Madama Butterfly emerged from the curtains and the crowd roared although he, semi-stunned by sentiment, sat silent and glum, managing only limited applause. Next on the stage was Lieutenant Pinkerton, full of bows and smiles. Dr. L. looked at the singer and thought, "I can't applaud—I hate that son-of-a-bitch." As the thought possessed him he suddenly heard the audience booing which (amidst nervous laughter, of course) was quickly transformed into polite applause. *That* is how the conventional ones understood the opera.

And yet . . . and yet if one makes demands on oneself, can one not understand Dr. R.'s position? Did not Madama Butterfly, in her purified, innocent, Japanese way, seduce Lieutenant Pinkerton? Did she not relinquish her religion, her family, and her friends in order to increase her power over Pinkerton as evidenced by his eventual guilt? And did she not have a child and could not that too have been part of an armamentarium of power? Did Puccini invite us to partake in a ritual of prejudice in which men are to be seen as rapists and women as victims? Does not Dr. R.—who finds the feminist movement ridiculous— have knowledge of a truth that is neglected in favor of a contradictory truth that is, paradoxically, just as true and just as false? The analyst spoke to his patient-colleague of these wistful, sobering thoughts.

> "How can you know things like that about the opera?" asked Dr. R. "The opera only belongs to me and once belonged to me and my father. You steal my heart from me if you know about the opera. Oh! I suddenly feel weak. I love you because I am so weak and . . . but . . . no . . . if you love me . . . goodness, this is just silly . . .

then I am powerful. I really have to know more things
about you than I do. Just knowing that you go to the
opera is not enough."

A few years after these events, the play *M. Butterfly* appeared
on Broadway. A British diplomat loves and, for many years,
lives with a Chinese woman in Hong Kong. After these many
years the diplomat discovers that his beloved is a spy and more
surprising, discovers that *she is a man!* The story is a true one
and the playwright, upon hearing the story, made the analogy with the opera *Madama Butterfly*. But the analogy is not
made with the conventional interpretation of the opera but,
rather, with the interpretation made by Dr. R.

By virtue of being an interpretive theory, psychoanalytic
theory can never claim to be exhaustively explanatory. In its
every version it is fated, a priori, to be only one interpretation
among many. All theorists share this fate, even those who
devise strict scientific theories like physics and chemistry.
Most, however, do not explicitly draw attention to their own
interpretive nature. Nor do these theorists claim that an
appreciation of their own psychological status is of the essence in determining just what their theory is. The reader can
see that, by seizing upon the interpretive nature of the theory
itself, I suddenly distance myself from the formulations of a
theorist like Brenner. Yet by distancing myself from his
theories I have no wish to distract students from the study of
Brenner's work, which repays well any effort invested in it.
But, as is obvious, I prefer to ground the theory differently.

Since it is interpretive, psychoanalytic theory cannot
pretend to be predictive and it in fact is not a single theory at
all. Rather, it is a group of loosely related theories that
sometimes contradict one another and that, at best, serve as
a series of reminders to the practitioner. Freud's structural
theory of the ego and the id is dualistic (and not tripartite as
is often suggested) and its dualistic nature is a constant
reminder that one must think of every human act twice,
registering both its conscious and unconscious aspects. The
theory of the superego reminds us that conscience and guilt
are elements in all human behavior and that this guilt is due

to violations of the oedipal code (the superego code, the cultural code). The topographic theory reminds us that everything appears in many locales, that is to say, on many stages. A transference narrative, for example, also finds a home in the past, as well as in a thousand artistic and cultural archetypal scenarios.

The interpretive bent of the theory also makes the analytic therapist skeptical of all theories that claim thoroughgoing explanatory power. The thoroughgoing explanatory emphasis placed by psychoanalysis upon oedipal crimes and oedipal punishments is only valid because it is a defining characteristic of psychoanalytic theory; independent of analytic thinking it is as dispensable as any other formulation.

This defining characteristic is responsible for the complementary theories of consciousness and unconsciousness. If one keeps in mind analytic theory's dualistic emphasis on consciousness and unconsciousness, one is struck by the degree to which this emphasis is already present in Freud's *The Interpretation of Dreams* (1900). Not that this should be a surprise; the point here is the great lengths to which Freud went in his great book to repeatedly remind the reader of the manifest and that which is warded off, the latent. The motive for that warding off is guilt over some version of the oedipal crime.

Interpretation is not practiced only by shamans, dream interpreters, and analytic psychotherapists. Indeed, some might want to make the deadening generalization that everything humans do or say is an interpretation. I suggest that, although we all understand what is meant when it is said that all is interpretation, we also understand that there are a number of fields that are explicitly interpretive and, as well, have been granted the privilege of being central in our cultural definition of who we are. This definition of what constitutes an acknowledged interpretive enterprise would therefore exclude phrenology but accept literary criticism; it would exclude astrology, but accept biblical scholarship; and finally, it would exclude orgone therapy but accept Freudian analysis.

I will use as an illustrative occasion the case of literary criticism. This example is particularly convenient since, in some literary circles, Freudian methods of interpretation inform the thrust of the literary critique in question. Earlier in this chapter the reader was already exposed to two literary—and psychoanalytic—criticisms of *Madama Butterfly*. Analytic theorists do not generally use words such as *critique* or *criticism*. Indeed, should one use them in analytic circles, one would be liable to complaints of insensitivity or of harshness. Yet, despite such objections, it is true that analytic therapy is a thoroughgoing critique—albeit a respectful critique—of a life. To understand why this is so one must understand exactly what is meant when one uses the word *critique*.

Literary criticism is the same kind of commentary that is made by the analyst. In a general way one could say that every statement made by a person is a critique since it adds to whatever has been said before. It certainly does not mean criticism in the sense of moral or moralistic judgment made upon the text or, in analytic treatment, upon what the patient has said. Critical comment is first, a mirroring of what has been observed and, second, a rethinking of what has been observed. Hence, the poverty of those injunctions to analytic therapists that they should simply mirror what the patient has said. It is, in principle, impossible to simply mirror what is said and, in addition, to try to limit oneself to such a mirroring drastically limits any possibility of rethinking things. In a sense, Dr. L. (who discussed *Butterfly* with his patient, Dr. R.) simply mirrored convention in his personal response to the opera. Dr. R., on the other hand, rethought (brilliantly? provocatively? insensitively?) the opera and opened up the possibility that all kinds of new and different images could be entertained and pursued. Dr. R. was acting in the best tradition of literary criticism. It is also in the best tradition of analytic interpretation. I stand with those who see criticism and interpretation as being the same thing.

Some will cry out that calling criticism "interpretation" empties the critical act of its raison d'être, and makes it a self-indulgent and intellectualizing end in itself. In fact, they might say, reducing critique to interpretation definitively removes it from the arena of criticism proper. The position of these commentators is that true criticism must have moral significance. It must assail false values in order to preserve those true values for which they, the critics, must stand. The answer from within the field of literature is that such complaints are from persons who fail to understand the task of critique. The task, the latter critic would say, is to be searchingly sensitive to any text at all, with the aim of illuminating as many interpretations of the text as possible, and with the further aim of teaching the love of literature to her reader. She has no fear of pursuing avenues of thought that might be immoral because, like the analytic therapist, she performs her critical task from within a contractual situation.

She is, of course, bound by the laws of her society, by her university if she belongs to one, by editors and publishers who decide her fate in print, and by her audience of readers. Should she too harshly offend the public mores or promote what the culture has normatively determined to be immoral, she will be constrained by them. Her contractual situation is a safe harbor in which her literary critique can flourish in whatever direction it will, as long as she has the talent to sell herself to an audience. She, like the analyst, has no goals of morality, maturity, or truth that she explicitly proposes in her work, except to teach her readers what it is to love books. Analogously, the analyst teaches his patients what it is to be fascinated by one's own foibles, madness, and genius. Both critic and analyst reside in remarkably similar vocational worlds because criticism and interpretation are the same thing. Both wish to open as widely as possible the Pandora's box of life and their manifest work focuses exclusively on that task. Quietly and implicitly, both stand firmly within their culture's moral tradition—a moral tradition that they themselves repeatedly call into question.

Critic and analyst alike, as they reside within the moral world of the culture, are eternally reminded of the stenches and perfumes of life by their texts and by their patients. Neither are airy-fairy dreamers and both stick their noses into the rawness of life. Literary critics, you might say, don't really do this and, in fact, fiddle and masturbate ("masturbate" because I am, after all, an analytic theorist!) in their ivory towers. Some of them probably do and some analytic theorists, in their own way, may do the same. I defend the literary critic against this charge because of the seriousness of art. Every culture has its art forms and these arts are always objects of the most earnest devotion. There is nothing airy-fairy about any serious analysis of a literary text.

Neither analyst nor critic will ever, all going well, succumb to the temptation to find grand universal themes in their subjects, nor will they find trivial that which is simple or common. The simple and the common will, in principle, be of just as much interest as the complex and the esoteric.

The analyst certainly knows that he is liable to self-aggrandizement, particularly since so many of his patients will praise him. I suppose that I know perfectly well of myself that I have intellectual pretensions and, in complement, suppose that literary critics, too, are at risk of viewing their calling as placing them on a rung higher than ordinary mortals. Such human foibles do not, of course matter, unless we, the potentially deluded ones, are deluded into believing our own delusions.

Can music be interpreted? It is said that Schumann was once asked to explain a piece of music that he had just performed. His response was to return to the piano and to play the piece again. This was Schumann's interpretation of what he had just played. It may be instructive to imagine a similar scenario with regard to visual art. Rereading, chanting, reciting, and praying are therefore always reinterpretations and not just repetitions. Biblical exegesis can also be examined in order to further illustrate the nature of interpretation. In fact, biblical interpretation is a particularly fortuitous example because it can mirror and promote prevailing interpretations or, in contrast, biblical interpretation can be transformational and mutative of prevailing interpretations. Nietzsche's announcement that "God is dead" is just such a transformational interpretation. This brief examination of the variety and prevalence of interpretive sites is, in itself, a final example of critique or of interpretation.

9

The Analyst's Paradigmatic Intervention

> Pharaoh said to Joseph, I have a dream which no one can interpret. But I have heard it said of you that when you hear a dream you can interpret it. Joseph answered Pharaoh, I do not count. It is God who will give Pharaoh a favorable answer.
>
> Genesis 41:15–16

I must now go on to describe the process by way of which interpretation takes place. To describe analytic behavior to a beginner is a formidable task and teachers often think to themselves that the quickest and surest way for students to learn the analytic art would be for them to undertake personal psychoanalytic treatment. In formal psychoanalytic training this is, of course, a requirement and, in many other student situations, is strongly recommended. I would agree that there is no substitute for the experience of being a patient oneself.

But treatment is no guarantee that the student will catch hold of the analytic idea. Some students who have themselves had analytic treatment seem nevertheless not to understand just what the analytic effort is about. These students continue to guide and urge, sometimes subtly and sometimes obviously, their patients to behave in certain ways or to take on certain modes of thought. There is no easy explanation for why this is so. Other students, sometimes students who have had no experience of personal therapy, quickly and intuitively catch on to the analytic idea. I suspect that to be an analytic therapist requires that one have a certain aptitude for it, an aptitude by way of which one can listen to patients with a kind of multimodal ear. Such a therapist can glide from concern for the patients real-life situation, to an awareness of the ironies inherent in every human situation, and, further, to drift into a respectful, magical, and poetic apprehension of everything as dramatic theater of one kind or another.

I sometimes think that, although most of us have difficulty in saying exactly what are the characteristics of analytic psychotherapy, if we could be a fly on the wall of any psychotherapist's consulting room, we could almost immediately say, "Yes this is analytic therapy that is going on" or, "No this is not analytic therapy that is going on." I suspect that one defining characteristic would be that the truly analytic psychotherapist would be endlessly looking for extra and hidden meanings.

Another problem in defining just what goes on is that it is hard to specify just what would count as a technical error. What we know is that the patient and the analyst are in the psychotherapeutic crucible together and that something happens. That something that happens is very specific to the particular persons who have been so thrust together. Although we may hope that this is infrequent, let us suppose that the psychoanalyst speaks in a harsh tone of voice or scolds her patient. Is this an error? I suppose that it is. Perhaps one should say that it is obviously an error. And yet, when these two persons are placed in the therapeutic crucible together, harshness or scolding may happen from time to time. Do we want not to happen that which . . . happens? Would we not then be asking of the analyst that she not know something that emerges when she and the patient are together? I could, I suppose, go on and further spell out the paradox here revealed. Obviously the analyst should not scold the patient. And obviously we hope that the fumes of life will not be squelched. The lesson to be learned here is that it is exceedingly difficult to convey to the student just how she should do it. One must take care not to be misled by the word *technique,* which implies a clearly reproducible analytic method.

This discussion should not be misunderstood as meaning that anything goes. Generally the analyst must be restrained and thoughtful. She is probably more subject to proscriptions regarding her activities than to prescriptive admonitions.

Proper interpretations are consequent upon proper listening. The analyst, as far as she can, listens most of the time. Most patients catch on to this quickly and recognize that the analyst is listening to their every word with an unusual seriousness. She never, he notes, chats. Some patients ask the analyst questions. I have noticed comment in recent years that we, the analytic therapists, ought to relax about things like questions and be more human. I have a strong suspicion that I am quite human and that my humanity includes compassion, kindness, and tact. But still, I don't usually answer questions. I suggest that the analytic therapist should, in fact, create an atmosphere that suggests that she never answers questions. This allows her the freedom to occasionally admit that, yes, she has seen the film that is being discussed by the patient. But, I suggest, she should not always and regularly answer such questions.

With certain patients the analyst should be more diligent about not answering questions. The instances I have mentioned above refer to those cases where the patient who asks the question does not use the question to deflect the analytic efforts. But a few patients do use questions in this way and with those it is best that questions never be answered.

If, for example, such a patient asks about changing an appointment, the analyst ought to maintain her analytic freely hovering attention. Then, when the time is done, she should say what she always says, for example, "The time is up for today." At that point the analyst can consult her diary and see whether an alternative appointment time is available.

Ralph Greenson (1967) suggests that when, in the treatment situation, the patient first asks a question, the analyst should explain that her policy is to not answer questions and, instead, to treat questions just like any other communication. She should indicate that to her, a question is like a slip, a dream or any concrete narrative told by the patient. On the next occasion when the patient asks a question, Greenson suggests that the analytic therapist should remain silent.

There is a danger that, when we keep silent in the face of a question, we aim to block or obstruct the patient from his questioning. This, of course, is a countertransference attitude that the analytic therapist will take into account as she ruminates about the question and about everything else that is going on. The patient is not misbehaving or acting improperly. He is simply being himself, and his questions, even if annoying or impertinent, are, as is said, grist for the analytic mill.

The analyst listens on. The patient's tale about his difficult wife, for example, is not taken literally. Instead the analyst understands that the patient is at great pains to live in the particular world that he does and, equally, is at great pains to report on this to her, his analyst. He could, of course, have talked about anything under the sun. In that mundane example the analyst might vaguely speculate to herself, "Is he unconsciously and metaphorically complaining about what a difficult 'wife' I am? And, contrariwise, is he almost consciously saying that, compared to his wife, I am wonderful?" She keeps listening and wondering.

Most of all she is attempting to capture as nearly as possible the exact experience that the patient is having. Although she can never fully achieve this—she and the patient live, after all, in different interpretive realities—the analytic dialogue has as one of its products, an increasing understanding of the patient by the analyst. That procedure for attaining understanding has, at times, been referred to as *vicarious introspection,* a term that continues to be helpful. The term *empathy,* on the other hand, seems nowadays to have lost its meaning and may best be avoided. Its current connotation suggests that it is the healing factor in analytic therapy, a proposition that is at some variance from what I have defined as our analytic intent. I have already been at some pains to suggest that analysts in general tend to have good results and that typically, they attribute their good results to something that they themselves do. Rather than quickly claiming to know what the healing factors are, it is best, I think, to remain cautious and modest about such speculations.

But there is no doubt that listening and the consequent understanding of the patient, are the first order of business. The practitioners of many forms of psychotherapy are prepared to believe that this is, in fact, the essential ingredient in psychotherapy. Their understanding of the patient and the communication of their understanding to the patient constitute their theoretical and therapeutic agenda. This activity can be called that of expanding consciousness. It is not, I would emphasize, a retrieval of the unconscious in the analytic sense of the term but is, rather, a focus on preconscious ideas that the patient had not previously attended to. By "preconscious" I mean knowledge that—if not immediately in consciousness—is available to the patient, that is to say, knowledge that he can remember if he puts his mind to it. This is in contrast to the unconscious, which is unavailable to the person no matter how hard he tries.

To the extent that the patient's worldview is clarified, it is, of course changed. At the moment that he sees something about himself that he has never seen before, the patient is a different person. Thus, the detailed display of the patient's psychological world, in itself, leads to therapeutic change. It is not yet, however, analytic change. Such clarifications, confrontations, and questions lead to preliminary changes that position the analytic therapist to make interpretations of the unconscious. Part of this clarifying and elaborating of the patient's universe of discourse may concern the question of agency. Some patients go to great lengths never to view themselves as the agents of their own life events. To them, they are the victims of events or merely spectators upon them. This is, in fact, characteristic of a large proportion of our patients since, to be a patient, it is necessary to acknowledge that one is afflicted with something. The task of clarification and expansion of consciousness is, with such patients, not easy since they are at great pains to not know themselves as agents of any actions. Such patients, since they view the world as casting injuries down upon them, are quite likely to hear any commentary on this matter as simply another injury cast down upon them by the world, this time incarnated in the person of the analyst.

The latter difficulty (which is often a very great difficulty) is sometimes dealt with by the analyst remaining exclusively at the level of understanding the patient's experiential world. Others suggest that it be dealt with by way of careful and tactful confrontation. I advocate both methods. The analytic therapist should, I claim, attempt to enter into the patient's immediate experience as skillfully as possible but should also, reflectively and evenhandedly, take note of the patient's radical delegation of agency to the other.

Fewer patients are agency claimers. Their lesser numbers may well be because they are reluctant to know themselves as being afflicted by something and therefore appear in our consulting rooms less frequently. At times such patients begin by announcing, "Actually I'm O.K. There are just a few things I need a bit of advice about." They approach the analyst in a self-assured way, with heartiness, and press to define the therapeutic situation as good-natured and collegial. No special counsel is necessary regarding these patients. Courteous and resolute analytic work is, as always, the order of the day. Their fears of vulnerability, of passivity, and of victimhood will slowly penetrate into the therapeutic dialogue. The "ballsy-broad" and the "hail-fellow-well-met" have more to them than meets the eye.

Analytic therapists attempt to apprehend the preconscious world of the patient in as much detail as possible but, in contrast to most other therapists, they do so for tactical purposes rather than viewing that apprehension as an end in itself. The analyst is, in fact, positioning herself to go beyond the conscious and the preconscious manifest world. Eventually, in cooperation with the patient, she will raise the question of why he lives in that particular manifest world. It is as though she, the analytic therapist, eventually says to the patient,

> We can now see exactly what world you live in—and live in with tremendous determination and diligence. The intensity with which you live this out has the quality of a pronouncement or of propaganda. You are at great pains to affirm again and again, and very dramatically, that this is the world in which you live (. . . to state that this is the world in which you live . . . to portray yourself as living in this world). Why is it that it is so urgent that you live in *that* world?

This is the question that nonanalytic therapists do *not* ask: "Why do you require yourself to live in *that* world?" By asking this question, the analytic therapist is herself making an announcement. Her announcement is that she suspects— indeed, she is convinced—that the patient has powerful motives for living in the world in which he does.

But, often enough, the analyst does not have to ask this question explicitly at all. The patient himself may come to see his rigidly patterned world and may anticipate the analytic therapist's question himself. "Why the hell do I always do this?" he might say. The analyst need say nothing or, if she does, say only that which heightens her patient's curiosity. "Yes, obviously you have powerful reasons for doing so, otherwise you would not be so resolute in establishing your world in this ungainly form."

Another important point here concerns the speed at which this stage of curiosity is reached. Some patients already have such curiosities about their psychological world during the diagnostic interview. And sometimes the skillful interviewer can, even with these patients, illuminate still other aspects of the patient's psychological world and stim-

ulate further curiosity—also in the diagnostic interview.
Other patients are the opposite. They accept their psychological world completely and, even after years of analytic work,
have no inclination to stand back and to reflect psychologically upon themselves. The former group of patients is
commonly lauded with the title "good patient" or "psychologically minded." The latter group is sometimes given less
complimentary titles such as, "not suitable," or "not psychologically minded," or "not motivated." Probably it is best to
say that such patients are simply different. And their treatments, too, will be different. Interpretive work will be easy to
embark upon with some and more difficult with others. And
furthermore, reflective patients may quickly change and
become nonreflective and resistant. In a complementary
way, the less attractive patient may unexpectedly become a
"good" patient.

I have now made a dogmatic point. Interpretation of the
patient's manifest world, I said, is a preliminary interpretive
task. Interpretation proper has do with something else: it
aims at discovering unconscious warded-off motives that,
under the best of circumstances, the patient can reappropriate into consciousness. I made this point as strongly as I
could because it underlines what is all too easy to forget, and
what is left out of consideration by many therapists, even
therapists who consider themselves to be analytically oriented. Now, hypocritically, I am going to take back my point
or, at least, to soften the starkness of the distinction I tried to
make. The distinction, indeed, was stark. For interpretations
that illuminate and display the conscious and manifest
world, I used the words *preparatory* or *preliminary.* For
interpretations that attempted to retrieve unconscious contents, I used the term *interpretation proper.* I could have
added further emphasis by using, for the latter, terms like
psychoanalytic interpretation or *Freudian interpretation.*
When Dr. L. pointed out to Dr. R. (mentioned in the previous
chapter) that she urgently adopted a posture of sweetness
and innocence, he was making a so-called preparatory interpretation. Later, when he speculated that, like Madama

Butterfly, she was resolutely sweet to deny fantasies of power and exploitation, he was using interpretation proper.

However, as I have already announced, I propose now to soften the distinction that, until now, I have been at such pains to make. To interpret the manifest is not as mundane as we might think. Every performance of *Madama Butterfly* that I have attended was an interpretation of its traditional and manifest message: Every time I saw it performed, I felt somehow enriched, even if the production was one that attempted to be absolutely faithful to the original score. Indeed, it may have attempted to be faithful to the company's own performance of the opera the night before. The reason we are nevertheless enriched by such a faithful production of the opera is because every performance of *Madama Butterfly* can only be an interpretation of it. The little nuances, angles, and styles add meaning to what we have seen and heard before. That is why we see the opera repeatedly and why we watch and think about *Hamlet,* again and again. We also reread great books, often with greater or less pleasure than on a previous reading. This is because each reading of the book is a new interpretation of it. The letters and words on the page stay the same; we reinterpret the text.

The same is true of music and art. It is true of intense love. Even though the passions and sighs of a particular love seem just like those of a previous love, it is always a reinterpretation of love. Under fortunate circumstances it is a love of greater richness; under unfortunate circumstances, it is a love of greater pain or greater vulgarity. Like art and love, conversation, even upon the same topic, is a reinterpretation of the topic. The conversation with the analytic therapist, like all of the examples I have cited, is always a new interpretation of things, even if ostensibly a repetition.

To have such an analytic dialogue without any specific commentary upon that dialogue is still interpretive. For the eager and the enthusiastic, additional commentary may seem necessary and, indeed, analytic custom is that we aim to make further comment the hallmark of our work. I mention this in order to clarify that interpretation is pervasive and that, even if we have nothing specific to say to a patient, interpretation is going on. As I have said, analysts do comment upon what goes on. Therefore, with regard to Dr. R.— who thought her analyst was a fool for seeing Madama Butterfly as a victim—additional comment about Ophelia, Anna Karenina, and Madama Butterfly (all characters who, in the usual interpretation, are viewed as victims of oppressive men), is common. Also common would be a commentary—an interpretation—of how her feminine vulnerability is also an enactment of the lives of vulnerable women who she has known in her personal life, past and present. A transference commentary might also point at her appropriation of weakness lest it make an appearance in the analyst.

In the case of Dr. R., the interpretations went further. Not only was there a commentary on her as the vulnerable one, and also on Madama Butterfly as the vulnerable one, there was also an explicit focus on the patient as the diabolical one, as a reincarnation of her greedy acquisitive sister, as the financially demanding analyst, and as the predatory Lorelei of German mythology and as the sirens of *The Odyssey*. These interpretations were dramatically revealing of something that Dr. R. had not previously known about herself. Nevertheless, such interpretations, in principle, are no different from interpretations that focus on her as sweet and victimized. Commentary upon her sweetness and upon her as ruthlessly exploitative, are both, pure and simple, interpretations. Interpretations of the manifest and interpretations of the latent are new "performances" of the patient's life and hence, are mutative.

It may seem to the reader that interpretations of the depths, that is to say, interpretation of the unconscious, can be made only after the therapy is well established. Although this is sometimes the case, it is not necessarily so and, often, unconscious contents can be addressed early on.

The following case vignette illustrates that preliminary interpretations of unconscious content can sometimes be made more quickly than is usually assumed. In this example two unconscious identifications become conscious during the course of an initial diagnostic interview.

A 30-year-old woman complained of chronic unhappiness and, in particular, of a dissatisfying relationship with her boyfriend. Mostly, she said, she herself sabotaged things by her crankiness and persistent criticism of him. During the interview she listed a series of boyfriends with all of whom she managed to find fault. When asked whether she had loved these men she insistently answered that she did not know. Inquiry about many areas of her life revealed similar anhedonic configurations wherever she turned.

A brother, two years older, had died when he was 14 years old. "He was," said the interviewer (adding an interpretive gloss to what he had been told), "on the verge of entering into the joys of heterosexual life. Soon he would have held hands tenderly with a girl, and done all those wonderful things." The patient looked stunned at this remark. Momentarily she was silent and then briefly mumbled vaguely about her brother never having known love and about how she herself could never have love. Then, just as suddenly, she said that what the analyst had said was "stupid."

"Is that the kind of crankiness that goes on with your boyfriend?" said the interviewer. At this the patient began to weep. The interviewer then spoke again. "If your brother was denied the joys of heterosexual life, would it be just if your heterosexual life was wonderful? Clearly you have determined that what he lost out on, you too should lose out on."

During the last twenty minutes of the appointment the patient realized that not only was she enacting the loveless fate of her brother but that she was also identified with a critical grandmother who had made life miserable for her father, "Just like I make life miserable for my boyfriend," she said.

Two unconscious identifications made brief but stark appearances in a fifty-minute appointment. The early months of the patient's therapy have been characterized by negativity and rather silly complaints about the (male) therapist.

Here follows a clinical example that illustrates unconscious identifications that become interpretable only after many months of treatment.

The patient in question was a young and talented pianist, much devoted to her work, who repeatedly fell in love with married, and therefore unavailable, men. The analyst, experienced and well trained, felt troubled by his patient's strong body odor. He felt that it would be hurtful and impolite to mention this and yet he knew that this must be important. Eventually he spoke with a colleague about this matter but, as soon as he began to do so, realized that this consultation was unnecessary and that speaking to the patient about her smell was obviously indicated.

Later that day the patient came to her appointment and complained that, on the previous day, the analyst had been completely silent and, in her view, had been greatly preoccupied. The analyst took this opportunity to agree that he had been preoccupied and that the reason for this was because he was ruminating about speaking to her about her body odor. "I suppose," he said, "I was worrying that you would be offended if I mentioned it." The patient was nonplussed. She saw no reason for offense.

"When I was a girl," she said, "Rubinstein used to come to our house and play and *he* had a smell. Artists have no time to worry about things like that. My father worried about that stuff. He used to wake me every morning and I remember his perfectly pressed suit and his shining shoes walking toward my bed. If you go to Vienna you can visit Beethoven's apartment. There are still shit stains on the carpet from where he let his chamber pot overflow."

Although the patient loved the analyst and, as a child, had loved her father, she affirmed by her odor that she was innocent with regard to any heterosexual intent. She had no time for personal hygiene and personal attractiveness. When the analyst said that she was Rubinstein and also was Beethoven—both times a man—the patient reaffirmed her nonheterosexual stance. "Of course. Women are ridiculous. Men think properly and can be artists. I am a man." This despite the fact that the patient was both feminine and attractive.

A few days later the patient said, half seriously and half teasingly, "Really the smell is my genital. I am sexual and that is the scent which you have noticed." These words were followed by the surprised realization that she had never told the analyst about her grandmother who had been a pianist, who had studied in Europe, and who had been elegant and refined—in short, a lady. The patient blushed and said, "I guess I'm more of a woman than I thought."

Her smell and her identification with men had been a preconscious defense against her "improper" unconscious heterosexual desires toward both her father and the analyst. But secretly, that preconscious defense had also been an identification with her very feminine and admired grandmother.

Later it became an identification with someone both feminine and offensive—her mother. In mother's bathroom there had been disturbing smells and blood-stained tissues. That identification allowed the patient to imagine herself as the rescuer of her mother by taking upon the patient's own shoulders the injured status of the mother. This she felt compelled to do because she was (unconsciously) convinced that, as a child, she had so improperly "out-sparkled" her mother. She, the patient, although feminine, was thereafter fated to be an unattractive heterosexual loser.

> Her current boyfriend's wife was very feminine and perfumed. She, the patient, was not. But secretly she was. Her sexual smell was the genuine article and no false perfume. And besides, "all the perfumes of Arabia will ne'er . . . how does that go? Who was that? Lady Macbeth? 'Unsex me now' . . . isn't that her, and me, again. Venus rising out of the sea. Wasn't it a shell that she came out of? Don't shells smell . . . smell like a cunt. They look like a cunt too . . . now filth comes out of my mouth."

Not all cases are as dramatic as this but partly it may be that we, the analytic therapists, are inclined to not take seriously enough the reality and intensity of the identifications by way of which all of us enact our lives. If I act like a man, do I not enact an identification? Might it be that every action of every person is the embodiment of an identification? Of course we are typically unaware of this unless someone points out to us that "you walk just like your father." The analyst is curious to trace the various identifications by way of which her patients have built up their personalities. She expects them to be unconscious, ubiquitous, and unexpectedly powerful. "What model do you follow and whose life are you living, if you act like a scholar?" asks the analyst. Or, she asks, "Whose life is acting you? What identification lives you? In your dreams, who dreams you?" This unconventional mode of thought is the interpretive mode of thought, that is to say, the mode of thought in which many, often contradictory, interpretations of the world are tolerated and encouraged.

This way of thinking is fun. But we must take care not to indulge in it simply because it is enjoyable. The young pianist described above illustrates that danger. Her dramatic associations were enlightening but, at the very same time, were a resistance. In what sense? The problem is that her associative wit was also a character style that deflected her from the concrete realities of her life. By way of her wit she dramatized the heterosexual bond between herself and her analyst—secretly, of course—and denied the fruitless agenda she was playing out. Her analyst, too, was unavailable, by virtue of both his professional and his marital status. The invitation that we tender to patients that they should dip with us into the marvels of primary process thinking—into *World II*—is only one of our invitations. We also invite them to take hard looks at concrete realities, and extend that invitation most heartily and with the greatest resolution to those who characterologically defend against the prosaic.

When the meaning of a behavioral pattern, a symptom, or a narrative is interpreted, the analyst should not expect that it will disappear. Such personality features are deeply stamped into the patient's very being and do not yield easily to interpretive efforts. Patterns always return and it may be that patterns endure forever. The obsequious man will, in all likelihood, show at least a variant on the theme of obsequiousness even when his analytic treatment is ending. But perhaps his obsequiousness will no longer be so blatant and so self-denigrating. Perhaps it will simply be politeness. And perhaps he will smile as he notes the lockstep way in which he tends to defer and allow the first move to the other. And perhaps it will no longer be something that can clearly be called obsequiousness.

This raises an interesting technical point. Since patterns are persistent and insistent, perhaps forever, the analytic therapist, once she knows her patient, knows what is coming next in her work with the patient. After making an interpretation, she knows that the patient, true to his pattern, will, in his next pronouncements, be saying the same thing. The analyst's intelligence will be taxed nevertheless because, even though she knows the content of what is coming in advance, she does not know the form that it will take. Her masochistic patient will speak but she, the analyst, will not necessarily easily see the way in which the patient's masochism penetrates into what he is currently saying. But this is her task because she must discover the pattern—the same pattern—in every nook and cranny of the patient's life and thought. Then she must repeatedly interpret it, always with freshness, novelty, and with ever-widening and unexpected connectedness. And, when the patient reports a dream, she will sense and know some of the deeply patterned aspects of the dream before she has analyzed its particulars. Each time that the pattern reasserts itself is an instance of resistance, that is to say, an instance in which the patient repeats instead of remembering and understanding.

Some authors have suggested that priority should be given to pointing out the defensive aspects of the resistance; others, in contrast, suggest that the unconscious content should be pointed out; still others prefer that priority be given to the resistance as it appears in the transference. Their varying opinions suggest to me that none of these instances of resistance warrants preferential treatment. I suspect that in practice most analysts do as I do, that is to say, interpret a mixture of content and defense, of past, present, and transference. And I suspect too that most go for "where the action is." By this I mean focusing on what seems to contain intensity for the patient. Some have called this attending to "that which is economically most important."

I would, at this point, only remind the reader again that every interpretation is oedipal and clarifies aspects of that eternal human dilemma. The dilemma is that self-interest (including incestuous, matricidal, and patricidal desire) is always countered by social responsibility (including the harshest imaginable superego sanctions). The patient's behavior is broken down—analyzed—into its multifaceted and conflictual components.

Menninger and Holzman (1973) are of the opinion that the patient's material emerges in a particular order. Typically, they say, the patient begins his appointment talking about his present life, then shifts to talking about his analyst, and then shifts to material about his past life. There is also a tendency for this directional bias to take place over the course of the treatment. Early in treatment the topic is everyday events, later there is more emphasis on the analyst and, later still, there is increased attention to past events. This pattern is cyclical:

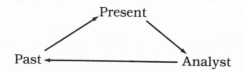

I have a sense that there is a certain truth in this although I also sense that the direction of flow is sometimes in the opposite direction. Menninger and Holzman are of the opinion that if such a reversal takes place, something is going awry. I cannot say that such reversals cause me any particular disquietude.

There is another directional matter, however, that does have great importance, particularly since it is so often misunderstood. The matter in question is that the directional flow of the material must be analyzed *within* each of the three "way stations." Topographically speaking, one would say that analytic issues must be unraveled in the topographical locale in which they appear before linking them to their appearance in other locales. The failure to do so leads the analyst into analytic error.

For example, a patient may complain that the analyst is constantly criticizing him. The direction of the talk shifts to the past and now the patient bitterly recalls that, as a child, his mother criticized him repeatedly. The analyst, at that moment, is at risk of making a serious error. She can, unfortunately, conclude that criticism by the mother *caused* the patient to misperceive the analyst as being critical, as was his mother. This conclusion is a nonanalytic one and is referred to as the genetic fallacy. The proper interpretive or analytic approach would be to search out the hidden motives that lie behind the patient's perception of the analyst as critical. Perhaps he dreads that his analyst might unduly favor him, or that she might make unwarranted special allowances for his scheduling difficulties. To such a patient, to find himself favored is forbidden, and any idea that he might be favored is blocked from access to consciousness by a resolute perception of the analyst as critical. In other words, in this hypothetical example, the patient uses a form of reversal to ward off what is unconsciously feared.

Only then, after the transference configurations have been analyzed, can the analyst obtain a clear analytic view of the patient's past. In a patient whose brother suffered from cerebral palsy, the analyst chose to reconstruct the past as follows:

> Since you so much fear that I favor you, it must be that you saw criticism in your mother for the same reason. Because you feared that she favored you, you seized on every possible evidence that she might *not* favor you, in fact, that she criticized you. Perhaps the bad luck of your brother made you feel at a grossly unfair advantage.

This interpretation uses the transference perception as an analytic opportunity for uncovering hidden motives both in the transference and in the past. Such interpretations can be then extended to the patient's present life and be woven into a myriad of pertinent narratives and symptoms with which the analyst is familiar.

The analysis and interpretation of dreams tends to be afforded a special place in many books on therapeutic technique. Menninger and Holzman (1973) seem to agree that dreams serve a special function in treatment, and that they are the *via regia* to the unconscious. My own inclination is to agree with Brenner that we have no warrant to give special status to any particular psychic process. Dreams, character style, symptoms, slips, body language—all are analyzable mental products to be dealt with as they come up. Dreams, as Freud made insistently clear, are manifest elements of the patient's psyche and the dream takes its particular content and form from the patient's character structure—just as does every other manifest psychological element. The analysis of the dream fascinates some beginners and intimidates others. This has importance only insofar as it reflects the personal countertransferences of particular analysts.

It has often been said that dreams are easier to analyze than are other mental products, ostensibly because, during sleep, the censorship is weakened, thereby rendering the analyst's task less arduous. I, myself, suspect that the resistance of the censorship is as potent during sleep as it is at any other time. The reason why dream analysis may seem easier than the analysis of other mental phenomena could well be explained more simply. The dream is, for the patient, experienced as an alien something that comes upon him and in relation to which he is a merely passive subject. Because he is not responsible for this particular psychical product, he can go ahead and analyze it with equanimity. Often patients feel similarly relaxed about the analysis of ego-alien symptoms. They do not, for example, hesitate to talk about and to study painful compulsion symptoms. But the story is quite different with regard to character traits or sexual activities such as masturbation. If such ego-syntonic traits or behaviors are discussed or analyzed, the patient is liable to be personally affronted—narcissistically injured—and to feel uncomfortable. It is as though the patient is saying, "Hey, that's *me* you're talking about!" In other words, the ego-alien quality of dreams renders them more tolerable as the subject of analytic scrutiny. I doubt that this has anything to do with any weakening of the censorship, despite Freud's opinion to the contrary. According to my reading of psychoanalytic theory, the censorship—the resistance—is ubiquitous.

I can only advise every student to read *The Interpretation of Dreams* (Freud 1900), apart from Chapter 1, which is a long-outdated literature review. Chapters 2, 3, and 7 repay reading over and over again. Chapters 4, 5, and 6 need not be read in full since Freud gives far more examples than are necessary nowadays. But the avalanche of proofs that Freud brings forward are of great interest, if only because one can see how determined he was that his readers should not be able to escape from his web of arguments.

I can also recommend to the reader Ella Freeman Sharpe's, *Dream Analysis* (1949) and Erik Erikson's article, "The Dream Specimen of Psychoanalysis" (1954). The latter is to be read in conjunction with Chapter 2 of Freud's dream book. Brilliant though it is, I have some difficulty with this article. Erikson's reification of the ego and his promotion of what he believes to be laudable ego achievements, are, as the reader is by now well aware, in marked deviation from the interpretive view of psychoanalysis to which I hold. But the article also displays Erikson's genius for interpretive work, on this occasion using as his subject Freud's own dream from Chapter 2 of *The Interpretation of Dreams.*

I also commend to the reader Chapters 13 and 14 from Jacques Lacan's *Seminar* (1954–1955). It is the work of yet another interpretive genius but, this time, an interpreter who is chaotic, provocative, and poetic. Do not expect to find coherent explanations but do note Lacan's flamboyant creativity.

10

Abstinence and the Analytic Attitude

Analytic treatment should be carried through, so far as possible, under privation—in a state of abstinence.

Freud, *Lines of Advance in Psychoanalytic Therapy*

Modifications of psychoanalytic theory inevitably seem to lead to abandonment of the rule of abstinence. Such technical changes, although seemingly benign, reflect, at best, misunderstandings of psychoanalytic theory and, at worst, discarding of the theory. An examination of such proposed theoretical innovations illustrates that, to a greater or lesser extent, all fail to preserve the keystone of the theory, namely, repression and the contradictory repressed. Instead the proposed innovations recommend behavioral techniques, a focus on consciousness, and the avoidance of arousing and disturbing material. Adherence to the rule of abstinence guarantees that practitioners do not unwittingly fall into nonanalytic therapeutic methods.

Psychoanalysis, of course, is the theory of the unconscious. What else could it be? Freud was never finished reminding us that "the theory of repression is the corner-stone on which the whole theory of psychoanalysis rests" (Freud 1914a, p. 16). In this chapter I propose that the second fundamental rule of psychoanalysis, the rule of abstinence, is an inevitable and invariant consequence of the theory of repression, the cornerstone on which Freud's theory rests. My claim is that the abstinence injunction can and should be paraphrased as "abstain from slipping into nonanalytic theories!"

Such an assertion depends on a particular version of psychoanalytic theory, a view that is conservative and is seen by some as old-fashioned. At other times the same vision of psychoanalytic theory is considered to be radical and subversive. The theory is grounded upon the notion of repression and therefore uses a methodology that inspects all psychological data in two registers. Manifest behaviors (including all thoughts, feelings, and actions) constitute one of these registers. Additionally, these behaviors are understood to obscure or hide a contradictory universe, the universe that we most commonly refer to as the repressed or as the unconscious. This second register in which behaviors are to be understood is considered to be of equivalent importance to that which is manifest.

This theoretical position is conservative insofar as it emphasizes Freud's early discoveries of the unconscious and of the "act of will" that leads to the warding off of dissociated psychical groupings (see, for example, Freud 1894 and 1914a). It is also in accord with Freud's application of the theory of the unconscious to dreams, parapraxes, and humor. But this stance on psychoanalytic theory is radical (but not at variance with Freud) insofar as it applies the notion of the unconscious to all behaviors and grants no immunity to behaviors that are frequently referred to as preoedipal, narcissistic, or as autonomous and conflict free. To this extent the proposed theoretical stance contradicts many currently popular theoretical positions. Freud's formulations on narcissism and libidinal development, especially, can be used to support theories that compete with the stance on theory that I am proposing.

What is the nature of the competing group of theories that I have in mind? It must be made clear that the second group of theories is highly diverse. Few readers would doubt that the theories of self psychology are fundamental revisions of psychoanalytic theory, especially since they place so little emphasis on the unconscious. Indeed, with regard to the unconscious, Kohut himself has said this quite straightforwardly: "An increase in the scope of consciousness does not always occur, and it is not essential" (Kohut 1984, p. 65). But some might be surprised that I would include some of the theories of ego psychology in the competing deviationist group. What characterizes the second group of theories is that they do not locate repression and the unconscious at the center of psychic functioning. In contradistinction to the repressionist thesis, these theories make the assumption that the psyche has a central core that is the instrument of repressive events. Repression, in this mode of theorizing, is a secondary rather than a primary phenomenon. Later I will argue that when analytic psychotherapists opt for the theoretical stance that I advocate—repression as primary and fundamental—the rule of abstinence is followed automatically.

Let me attempt to further clarify the distinction between the two stances on theory building that I have outlined. The conservative and radical doctrine that I propose claims that all mental functioning, in its very nature, is contradictory. This contradiction is located at the center of the psyche, that is to say, the subject of experience is the locus of a fundamental ambiguity. Plainly put, all manifest experiences, beliefs, and actions simultaneously obliterate (make unconscious) contradictory experiences, beliefs, and actions. That which is manifest forbids a complementary but opposite unconscious.

The opposing theoretical doctrines (whose adherents think me old-fashioned and who I, in turn, think of as revisionists) postulate a central psyche that is spared from contradiction. Those ego psychologists who emphasize the autonomy of the ego claim for those functions immunity from repression, from contradictions, and from unconscious motivations. Object relations theorists frequently postulate the internalizing of objects that serve stabilizing and grounding functions. The adherents of "repression-as-central" theories prefer to emphasize that psychological manifestations of such stable internal objects are analyzable psychological positions like any other. Finally, I would mention the self psychology group that, more explicitly than most, proposes that, under ordinary developmental conditions, a cohesive self is to be the central psychological construct of psychoanalytic theory. Under unfortunate developmental circumstances, a fragmented self eventuates but, nevertheless, that fragmented self is supposedly accurately perceived by the patient.

Pari passu, the self psychology group de-emphasizes the importance of repression and of the unconscious. The theoretical notion of a unitary self guarantees the existence of a nonconflictual, noncontradictory sphere of mental functioning; Freud's dualistic notion of "the ego and the id" guarantees the ubiquity of conflict and contradiction.

Philip Rieff (1966) has critically evaluated the attempts by Jung, Reich, and D. H. Lawrence to establish alternative methodological grounding for their theories (see also Lawrence 1971). One can add to their names that of Sartre (1953) and many others of a host of more recent analytic writers who seem to deviate from the standard theory.

It seems to me that in every case, those who offer theoretical revisions advocate synthetic rather than analytic positions. By "synthetic" I mean that they have in mind concrete behaviors that they consider to be nonconflictual, mature, or healthy, rather than, like Freud, examining the "why" of what it is that patients do. All analytic treatment attempts to break down into its components—to analyze— what the patient thinks and does. Those who wish to modify the theory, on the other hand, advocate preferred styles of thought and behavior that they count as healthy and that they therefore think that the patient should come to adopt. Freud himself never slipped into such unambiguous behavioristic enthusiasms. But two provisos must be kept in mind if analytic dissection is our sole goal.

First, the deconstructive activities of psychoanalysis (and every interpretation is a deconstructive act) is never to be carried out in the spirit of "nothing but." Obviously the analytic therapist never says nor wishes to imply to a patient that "your love for me is nothing but your way of disguising your hatred of me." Although we may find a hidden hatred, our reductionistic act is first and foremost additive. Love is never denied by the discovery of repressed hatred. The patient's experience is, it is hoped, enriched by a proper interpretation. Although analysis subverts naive acceptance of conscious experience, surely we never aim to *disallow* a patient's conscious experience. It might be added that every interpretive reduction dissolves away as we pursue a multiplicity of additional unconscious meanings. This means that an analytic discovery of hatred claims no substantiality for that hatred but simply subjects it, in turn, to analytic scrutiny.

Second, it must be kept in mind that the repressionist theory establishes that the unconscious is, in principle, eternal. All conscious psychological positions, especially belief systems and character styles, are universes of discourse—stances on reality—that deny and contradict other possible universes and realities. All other realities, so to speak, are negatively hallucinated. Those realities that are momentarily or temporarily oblated are said to be preconscious; those that are relatively permanently oblated are said to be unconscious.

The characterologically good man, by virtue of his "good" way of life, denies and contradicts his fears of his own wickedness. The rigid believer in free will thereby denies and contradicts his own helplessness and victimhood. It must be kept in mind that the analytic reappropriation of the repressed does not eliminate what is unconscious. It is more accurate to say that the manifest—consciousness—is rendered more complex by analytic work and the unconscious, contrapuntally, also is rendered more complex. In other words, the patient's conscious motives, after analysis, are less univalent, less arbitrary, and less stereotyped, but repression and the unconscious exist forever.

All of this can be summarized by stating again that the analyst abstains from only taking the patient's statements at face value. The rule of abstinence insists that conscious statements and claims are only part of the story and simple acceptance and gratification of them only can lead to participation in the patient's self-deceptions. Worthwhile comments on the rule of abstinence are to be found in Stone (1961), Menninger and Holzman (1973), and Schafer (1983).

What then is this abstinent method? What is this observational attitude? Although the analytic attitude is an ideal that we can only hope to achieve incompletely and inconsistently, my best answer is as follows: The analyst plants her feet, so to speak, "in between" and abstains from believing or judging what she hears. She hovers silently between criticism and acceptance, between sobriety and awareness of the ridiculous, between passion and indifference. If the patient speaks scientifically, the analyst, although she may be inclined to agree, also thinks poetically. When the patient speaks of hope, the analyst, although she may be equally hopeful, is inclined to also think of tragedy and despair. And vice versa. Always the analyst thinks vice versa. One can summarize this by saying that the analyst, as she listens, is simultaneously appreciative and wary. Paradox and ambiguity are the analytic therapist's lodestones. That is why I like to think of our field as the "ironic science."

Some analysts slide between certainties and uncertainties intuitively. Theodor Reik (1948) referred to this as "Listening with the Third Ear." Others are more skillful at uncovering psychological depths by way of logical application of the theory. I assume that most of us, at times, do both.

Commonly, the abstinent analyst becomes absorbed in the patient's manifest statement. She lets herself be more or less "taken in" by what the patient says. She respectfully believes that there is honor and dignity and value in every position. But sometimes sooner and sometimes later, she begins to think about what is denied, forbidden, contradicted (in short, repressed) by what she hears.

The rule of abstinence, the second fundamental rule,

requires us never to take the easy way and simply to reside with our patients in the universes they exhort us to join them in. If, for example, the patient pleads for reassurance, here is what the analyst does: although sympathetic and inclined to offer comfort, she has other reactions as well. By way of her considerable silence she is, for example, also reticent, reluctant, and reclusive. Her analytic attitude leads her to be in a state of reserve that disinclines her to offer reassurance. Although empathic like any other person, she hesitates and delays. This is done because of her analytic tendency to focus on what is *not* asked for and what is *not* said. It is not that the analyst ignores the manifest statements made by the patient. It is just that she realizes that the unconscious messages are difficult to discover and easy to miss. Among other things, the analyst has a curious obstinacy that doggedly implies that there is more to the matter at hand than meets the eye. "What else?" says the analyst with her silence. The analyst thereby encourages the elaboration of conscious contents in as much detail as possible. Only then can the construction of the unconscious be performed with analogous detail and accuracy.

Although the psychoanalytically oriented analyst typically abstains from explicitly gratifying desire, she does gratify the desire for analytic self-knowledge. Along the way she inevitably gratifies, or is understood by the patient to gratify, many varied wishes. *Pari passu,* she frustrates or is seen to frustrate a variety of other wishes. But the analytic therapist does not have in mind that she should eliminate the patient's conscious beliefs and wishes. If in the course of analytic work belief wanes, the analyst, in principle, has no particular reaction to this except to continue to reside in her thoughtful, interpretive world. She is neutral to every substantial claim made by the patient and to every reductionistic totalization. In principle, the analyst is forever skeptical, wistful, amused, and concerned as she contemplates her own and her patients' self-deceptions.

There are, I would say, refreshing consequences to analytic abstinence, since it allows for the possibility—albeit a possibility that is unattainable in practice—of a perfect tolerance of a veritable kaleidoscope of realities. Although we can do so only temporarily, when at our best we analysts can contemplate and participate in any belief system.

Patients live and act as they do, we think, because they are free and, in contradiction of this, we simultaneously believe that patients are deterministically caused to act as they do. When at our best we coolly and ironically occupy a truth-world in which patients are victims of fate and of astrological influence. Clearly, we may think, certain patients live as they do because it is the will of God. At times we realize them as being possessed by spirits and demons. All, we suppose, are reincarnations of Oedipus, of Emma Bovary, of Christ, and of Hitler, as are we, their analysts. They, our patients, are found to be unexpected reincarnations of us.

Such complex and unusual truths are components of every analyst's working world. She believes and disbelieves all of them. And although she strives to adopt that analytic attitude, she finds that she is also fated eternally to fail. The Divine, for example, is a perfectly admissible option in the analyst's world. On certain occasions the analyst may be inclined to believe in Him but, in keeping with the ironic spirit of psychoanalysis, the analyst thinks with equal ardor that God is both silly and dead. Psychoanalysis surrenders specialness to nothing. Nothing is afforded privilege.

It is not the mission of any analytic therapy to hold a brief for any fixed reality—be it material, psychological, or spiritual. Nor is it the mission of psychoanalysis to dismiss any particular reality. The one reality that the analyst stands by is not a fixed one. Her recurrent claim is that repressive forces always and forever lead us into illusion and that every reality claim is as false as it is true.

The reality that the analyst stands by also is not an ultimate reality. But it *is* the reality that psychoanalytic theory opts for. Therefore, the gratification of wishes that are claimed to be realistic, or to be based on needs, is a deviation from both psychoanalytic theory and practice. The rule of abstinence is the technical guarantor that the theory is not forgotten.

The majority of new technical modifications are based on theoretical changes such as those that I have described earlier. If one agrees with Freud (1914a, p. 16) that "repression is the cornerstone upon which the whole theory of psychoanalysis rests," then one must view the human condition as paradoxical. From such a view springs the abstinence injunction, since any principle of gratification must accept a corresponding substantial need and deny the inherent contradictoriness of the psyche. It seems to me that new technical and theoretical innovations typically advocate abandonment of the rule of abstinence. What, you might ask, is it that is advocated? Most commonly, it is advocated that the analyst should offer to patients a real relationship. It is hard to be sure what is meant by a real relationship since the analytic relationship is as real as is any other relationship. It is, however, different from many other relationships because of the analyst's analytic attitude, that is to say, her resolute pursuit of unconscious meanings. As a consequence of this pursuit the analyst follows the rule of abstinence and does not gratify the wishes of the patient apart from the patient's agreed-upon request for analytic treatment.

Advocacy of a real relationship contains theoretical premises that sometimes are not made explicit. The theoretical assumption seems to be that certain, if not all, patients require gratification of certain needs. The psychopatholgical lesion, it is said, is not due to repression, but is due to having missed certain crucial childhood experiences. Therefore, healing does not depend on self-understanding but, instead, depends on behaviors in the analyst that replace missed experiences. The analyst should be parental, kind, and caring. There is, in such a suggestion, a subtle implication that an analytic approach, that is to say, an attempt to discover hidden motives, is unkind or in some way not good. An analytic attitude is seen as harsh, demanding, or confrontative. Certain patients make similar claims. The analytic attitude, they say, is heartless and cold. But every analyst knows that other patients, probably most other patients, say otherwise. They claim that the analyst is wise, good, patient, and sympathetic. If indeed we are wise, we take neither the complaints nor the compliments at face value.

The called-for goodness and kindness is part of a wider current of affirmative therapeutic enthusiasm. By affirmation, such analysts mean the affirmation of the patient as good, as needy, and as lovable. If the word *affirmation* is applied to analytic psychotherapy, it could only be said that the analyst affirms that the patient is complex, self-deceiving (as are all persons), and worthy of analytic scrutiny.

A romantic term used to refer to the wholesome attitudes recommended is *authenticity*, a mode of interpersonal relationship recommended by, among others, some existentialists or quasi-existentialists. A noncontradictory existence or *Dasein* is, of course, an unsatisfactory grounding for a theory of contradictoriness—of the unconscious. Either persons are contradictory in their psychological essence or they are not.

There are other popular terms that are synonyms for the state of authenticity that is advocated. North Americans, especially, are exhorted to *share, be with, validate, acknowledge,* and *communicate.* These terms recommend that the parties to the dialogue in question can and should achieve an identity of experience. The theory of repression guarantees, of course, that such an identity of experience is eternally elusive. In this regard psychoanalytic theory is highly inconvenient. Freud himself wistfully described his theory as "the plague" and as "disturbing the peace of the world" (1911, pp. 32–33).

All such modifications, it seems to me, are anticipated by Ferenczi (1929) who suggested to us that

> [some] persons have remained almost entirely at the child-level, and for them the usual methods of analytic therapy are not enough. What such neurotics need is really to be adopted and to partake for the first time in their lives of the advantages of a normal nursery. [p. 124]

One can see that repression and the unconscious are neglected by such an assertion. In contrast, psychoanalytic theory claims that no matter how traumatized or neglected a patient has been, his manifest and conscious state oblates an unknown contradictory repressed.

It seems to me that most attempts to modify psychoanalytic theory are variants on what Ferenczi advocated many years ago. Stable, empathically responsive, and 'good enough' parental substitution are deemed to be the crucial therapeutic ingredients.

All such innovations depend on theories of self-actualization or on theories of environmentalism. With regard to self-actualization, the patient is believed to have a potential for development that is, so far, unrealized. To the extent that they share this belief, revisionist theorists are partners in the widely popular human potential movement, even though they couch their theories in language that is less romantic and less strident. In the case of environmentalism, wholesome and beneficial effects are attributed to the outer world. It joins the patient in believing in "the logic of soup with dumplings for arguments" (Freud 1915, p. 167), that is to say, that substantial acts lead to healing. Usually these two theories are combined: self-actualization is dependent on proper environmental effects. It is important to note that such theories are plausible. But it is even more important to remember that they are not psychoanalytic theories. Psychoanalytic theory is the theory of the unconscious. The theories under examination are in competition with psychoanalytic theory.

In the service of theoretical thoroughness, one might add that even the notion of the expansion of consciousness can be viewed skeptically. Ultimately psychoanalytic work is not only consciousness *expanding* but, in addition, is consciousness *subverting.* A multiplicity of popular psychotherapies aim to raise, increase, or expand consciousness. Only psychoanalysis searches for a contradictory repressed. Here is a brief analytic vignette that exemplifies this point:

> "Last night I dreamed about Phyllis Leavy. Why, I wonder, would I dream about Phyllis Leavy? I hardly know her, after all."
> "Phil is leaving", said the analyst.

There was a pause. "What do you mean by that? Why can't you be clearer, less elusive, less cryptic?" And then suddenly the patient realized that the dream is a pun and refers to the pending vacation of his analyst—whose first name is Phil.
Phyllis Leavy . . . Phil is leaving . . . Phil is loving.

Phil means *philas*—loving—and also means *filius*—the son. The dream is about sadness and about the patient's love for his analyst. The part, "Phyllis Leavy," is compared with the whole, "Phil" the analyst, and the analyst's vacation. This integrative act causes consciousness to be expanded. The patient's subjectivity is now more complete than it had been and the analysis represents what is done in many, if not most, dynamic psychotherapies. It is, however, only a preliminary part of an analytic study of the dream. In fact the analyst and patient spoke further:

Phil is loving . . . Phil is living . . . Phil is dying,

or, as the patient said on a later occasion, "I wouldn't give a damn if your plane crashed and you never came back."

In other words, the first interpretation of the dream is only an elaboration of the manifest content. It is a wish that between analyst and patient there should only be wholesomeness and affection. The repressed contradictory turns out to be concerned with the topics of hatred and death.

To rest at the point of full speech and to believe in the completion of self-knowledge—the Lacanian belief characteristic of many psychotherapies—contradicts Freud's aim of showing that the meaning of every text can only be discovered through a labor that overcomes an active resistance. In contrast, these approaches treat the text affirmatively rather than negatively. Such practitioners thereby contradict the psychoanalytic assertion that unconscious contents are ubiquitous, if not eternal.

Theoretical and technical modifications typically spring from the conviction that they are required when one treats and studies profoundly disturbed patients. This despite the fact that anecdotes of favorable outcomes are told by analysts and therapists of many theoretical persuasions. The research literature even suggests that "all must receive prizes" (Luborsky et al. 1975, p. 995, see also Luborsky and de Rubeis 1984), that is to say, there seems to be little or no demonstrable difference in treatment results when different theories and techniques are applied.

Those patients designated borderline and narcissistic particularly seem likely to stimulate theoretical and technical revisions. Why should this be? After all, a psychological theory of human behavior should be applicable to all human functioning. Ad hoc shifts of theory, dependent on the kind of patient being studied, guarantees that we are working with no theory at all. Freud was very clear about the fact that he interpreted psychopathology as not fundamentally different from the ordinary psychology of any person, including the analyst (Freud 1933, Ornston 1978, 1985). Kaufmann (1980), in his study of the intellectual foundations of depth psychology, counts this as one of Freud's enduring contributions to the study of mind. As we all know, Freud had no hesitation in using his own dreams and mental processes as illustrations of his theory. Brenner (1976) is perhaps the best-known modern theoretician who explicitly denies that there is any essential difference between the psychology of psychosis, of character abnormalities, and of neurosis. He decries

> the idea that psychotic symptoms are different from neurotic ones, that they are not compromise formations at all, but true "endopsychic perceptions" and are therefore to be taken at face value rather than analyzed as a neurotic symptom must be. [p. 12]

Insofar as he asserts this, Brenner stands with Freud in believing that repression is the key notion in psychoanalytic theory. I would agree.

One can only speculate about why some analysts—and all of us do it from time to time—are inclined to believe the patient's exhortations and rationalizations. Like all psychoanalytic explanations of human behavior—be it of the actions of the patient or of the analyst himself—the most important reasons are unconscious. This particular analyst behavior— taking the patient's statements at face value—is no different. Our dread, fear, rage, and lust, inevitably inspire us to deceive ourselves because of our wish *not* to know all that is in the soul of our patients. We do this despite our conscious intent to obey another of Freud's injunctions.

> [It is] a fundamental principle that the patient's need and longing should be allowed to persist in her, in order that they may serve as forces impelling her to do work and to make changes, and that we must beware of appeasing those forces. [Freud 1915, p. 165]

There are many profound analytic issues here. I will raise only one. How, I might ask, can one come to know the evil in the soul of the patient? From listening to colleagues who advocate goodness, parenting, or empathic responsiveness as therapeutic modalities, I find it difficult to believe that they would discuss frankly with patients the evil, the selfishness, the cowardice, and the corruption that all of us shrewdly deny in ourselves. The impression I have is that such unwelcome qualities would only be talked about in a context that explains away or excuses. I would say that these unattractive qualities are part of all of us. Although an exploration yields a multiplicity of motives for evil behavior, it is important that we not avoid a particularly distasteful explanation, specifically explanation in terms of the patient's personal desire and personal responsibility. The latter explanatory statements are truths—but not the only truths—that analysts attempt to face. The avoidance of these issues is achieved only by abandoning the rule of abstinence, that is, by gratifying the patient's desire not to know his own disagreeable qualities. The same principle holds for patients who are eternally cranky and argumentative. They decline to know of anything good or wholesome in themselves.

A most serious deviation from the rule of abstinence is when the analyst and patient become sexually intimate. Such sexual misbehavior by an analyst is, of course, not considered to be a simple breakthrough of a repressed desire. Like any other behavior it is considered to be compromise formation, ingeniously designed to ward off unconscious contents. In this instance patient and analyst typically claim that, by way of their intimacy, they "commune" with one another, that is to say, they share the self-deceiving illusion that the fulfillment of conscious desire constitutes a therapeutic experience. From an analytic point of view, such analysts participate in conscious acts that unconsciously are also a self-damaging trick: they invite their own professional downfall.

Conscious agreement that abstinence is not warranted and that gratification is to be given is always a conspiracy between analyst and patient by way of which both parties avoid unpalatable truths. Needless to say, all the complexity and richness of psychological functioning is thereby rendered opaque.

If one begins with a nonpsychoanalytic methodology—one that does not resolutely strive to discover the unconscious by way of analytic abstinence—the procedure is not analytic psychotherapy. Alternatively, if one shifts methodologies in midstream, one can anticipate only avoidance and chaos. It is to be expected that shifts of theory will occur at those points where analytic labor is heaviest. Typically this will happen when patient and analyst are most frightened or most aroused. Ad hoc shifts in theory are analogous to changes being made in a legal code according to whim, or to rule changes in a game whenever this is opted for by a player. Freud illustrated this point as follows:

> What would happen to the doctor and the patient would only be what happened . . . to the pastor and the insurance agent. The insurance agent, a free-thinker, lay at the point of death and his relatives insisted on bringing in a man of God to convert him before he died. The interview lasted so long that those waiting outside began to have hopes. At last the door of the sick-chamber opened. The free thinker had not been converted; but the pastor went away insured. [Freud 1915, p. 165]

The rule of abstinence can be weakened and discarded. We live, as we say, in a free country. But those who do so thereby acknowledge that they have discarded psychoanalytic theory and its grounding tenets.

The idea of analytic neutrality and analytic abstinence is always in the back of the analytic therapist's mind. At the very least it is an idea that constantly influences her. It is an ideal—albeit an ideal never attained nor even approximated. But it is an ideal that, if the analytic therapist has grasped its importance and profundity, will forever influence her.

She will, for example, not be able to make up her mind about the question of whether her patient is sick. She will often slide between recognizing that the patient's suffering is evidence of unwellness, and an equally firm recognition that his so-called illness is an urgent posture designed, in part, to cast himself into a role of inferiority. The analyst will, there-fore, decline explicitly to agree that her patient suffers from psychopathology. Instead she will think to herself that there are many ways to skin a cat and many ways to live a life. And she will fear that her agreement that the patient is sick, regressed, infantile, narcissistic, or borderline will be an enactment with him of a self-defeating enterprise that he has invited her to join him in. Thus Thomas Mann:

> Rejection is as honorable a destiny as any other. [*Joseph and His Brothers*]

The analyst will also know perfectly well that diagnostic and psychopathological statements will be required of her in her records and reports, but she will not ascribe to such usages essential or substantial truths. She will use such terms for practical reasons and may well have a twinkle in her eye when she does so.

The notion of penis envy may illuminate this idea fur-ther. Freud's idea about penis envy was that women have a belief that they are inferior to men because their lack of a penis is interpreted by them as "missing something." This flat-out assertion was characteristic of Freud at times. But much more characteristic of him was the idea that everything is tentative and that every psychological position serves a purpose. The stance of female inferiority—of penis envy—serves the purpose of asserting the superiority of men for dynamic reasons. In other words, women who demonstrate this trait have a psychological stake in maintaining that the patriarchal social structure is intact. They are resolutely affirming the potency of men because they have a dreaded fear that, in fact, men may be fallible, weak, or impotent. The unconscious fear of such women is a fear of their own powers. This penis envy position (although multidetermined like anything else) is perfectly analogous to the inferiority claims of those who understand themselves to be sick or damaged.

I cannot recommend that the analytic therapist promote the development of a relationship between analyst and patient. Such a recommendation would surely be a waste of breath since a relationship exists from the beginning and takes a particular course as times goes on. The analyst's interest is in the *nature* of the relationship in order that it can be analyzed—that is to say, so that it can be verbally dissected, teased apart, and played with. The analyst may well be amused, sobered, or disturbed by the relationship. Ultimately, she will, with the patient, turn it inside out and outside in.

The analyst likes it when her patient trusts her and works cooperatively with her. But in her somewhat quirky way, the analyst holds no brief for such positive transferences and analyzes them as well as she can. When asked whether she believes the therapeutic alliance is important she is at a loss as to how to answer and probably murmurs something like "Yes, but . . ." The topic makes her uneasy but at the same time she wonders about her (defensive?) uneasiness and wishes she could be in a state of bemused indifference about the matter.

Here is the kind of problem she is worried about. What if this therapeutic alliance business is just a subtle but unmistakable attempt to get the patient to be good? And what if this is at least as worrisome an idea when one turns to the topic of psychotherapy research? What if:

1. Patients are accepted for therapy because they show promise of developing a therapeutic alliance?
2. Patients who count as being improved are those who have a positive reaction to the treatment?
3. Objective measures that we apply also have to do with such positive attitudes?
4. Therapeutic alliance, positive transference, and positive therapeutic outcome are the same thing?
5. We refer for therapy patients who already have an attitude that later will be counted as improvement?

Despite the analytic therapist's abstinence, tentativeness, and irony, she also observes her patient with great earnestness and serious human concern. I expect that most analysts possess such qualities when they begin their training. That laudable human concern is typically a good quality that, with training, can be made enormously more complex and finely tuned.

11

Yielding to the Pressure to Deviate

Give me chastity and continence, but not just now.

St. Augustine

My definition of the model technique for psychoanalytic psychotherapy is simpler than some, albeit more long winded than some. I would say that this form of treatment is

> a psychological treatment based upon a particular attitude and a specific interventional method. The analyst's attitude is one of neutrality, that is to say, she has no goals for the patient apart from self-knowledge. The analyst radically abstains from belief or disbelief in what the patient says, and equally abstains from judging as good or bad, as healthy or unhealthy, or as mature or immature, that which the patient says and does. Although as compassionate and as moral as anyone else, the analyst, insofar as she is practicing analytic therapy, adheres to the idea that she should abstain from judgment and suggestion since she ardently believes that she has no privileged knowledge of how to live a life.

The interventional method is interpretation alone, that is to say, the identification of the patient's behavioral, cognitive, and affective patterns, and the methodical pursuit of the unconscious motivations for those patterns. Clarifications, questions, confrontations, and other noninterpretive methods are perfectly legitimate if used for the purpose of preparing the ground for interpretations.

There are, of course, many other forms of psychotherapy, all of which are at great variance with the above. Forms of psychotherapy that set goals, such as behavior therapy, assertiveness or cognitive training, or straightforward counseling, are supportive psychotherapies. But there is a form of psychotherapy that claims to be psychoanalytically informed but deviates from the definitional demand that I have outlined. This is usually referred to as supportive psychotherapy or its modified form, supportive-expressive psychotherapy. I might add that interpretive psychotherapy in general, when it is not classical psychoanalytic treatment, is all too often subjected to deviations from the model technique. Brief therapy, too, is a frequent candidate for nonanalytic supplementation.

The definition that I have put forward does not see formal psychoanalytic treatment as the model technique. Instead, I have located the kernel of analytic psychotherapy in the attitude of the analyst and the use of interpretation as the sole interventional instrument (apart from interventions that prepare for interpretation proper). This means that the use of the couch and the great frequency of meetings in formal psychoanalysis are not defining characteristics of the analytic method. This is in no way intended to call the formal psychoanalytic method into question. Indeed, my own practice consists in large measure of formal psychoanalytic work. It is just that the couch and the frequency are not essential features of analytic psychotherapy. The value of my definition is that it permits the expansion of the analytic approach to psychotherapies of lesser frequency, including brief therapies, and even to single-interview contacts with patients.

I aim now to critique—and by that I mean to say that I will critique and find wanting—the whole idea of supportive psychotherapy. I must begin my critique by recording for the reader a number of techniques used in psychoanalytically informed psychotherapy and some of the reasons why its practitioners intervene as they do.

A much favored intervention is persuasion and instruction. The analyst, being wiser in the ways of the world and more psychologically stable than is the patient, is understood to be in a position to give such counsel. The analyst will reassure and may persuade the patient that his fears are unfounded. Such interventions are certainly a form of psychotherapy and often an effective therapy at that. It is also something that patients ask for and, when the analyst does not offer it, some patients may complain bitterly. Effective though it may be and, desirable though it may seem, this is not an analytic form of intervention. It is not the service that the analytic therapist is "selling," so to speak. She is, as I have said, unwilling to believe that she knows better than her patient; nor does she believe that her reassurances are something her patient cannot do for himself. Besides, she suspects that reassurances are usually clichés and have been given to the patient by many persons before her.

But if it is effective, you might ask, why would one not go ahead and give such support? The answer to this question is that the analyst is convinced that her method is at least as effective as is the supportive psychotherapy of her colleagues. She is also convinced that her patients have more thoroughgoing benefits, but, convinced though she is, she declines to use this argument. Her conviction, as she is well aware, might be a matter of vanity and, besides, she knows perfectly well that her own convictions, like everyone else's, are based on a host of unconscious motives.

The exception to the banishment of persuasion as an analytic intervention is its use in the service of interpretation. Since this will be discussed at greater length in a later chapter, I will only say now that interpretations are not magically effective and, with due respect for the patient's opinion, the analyst must be prepared to make her interpretive case with enough force that the patient will seriously consider what is being argued. This is not to suggest that the analytic therapist knows exactly what the patient's various motives are but only means that she works hard to make sure that her points are seriously considered.

Nevertheless she declines to advise, instruct, or give reassurance about behavioral matters. This is because she has a great uneasiness about establishing a hierarchical situation in which she, the analyst, is ranked higher than is the patient. Advice givers, by virtue of giving their advice, claim to know better. The analytic therapist holds to the position that she must not do this and that she must hold to this position on moral grounds. But in a funny way she wants to make the argument that her moral position has a solid scientific grounding. What could the analyst mean by such a statement? She would like to emphasize the fact that all ways of understanding the world are interpretations of the world. This means that should she advocate to a patient one or another way of living or behaving, she would be asking the patient to live according to her interpretation of the world. She declines to do this even if her interpretation of the world is in conformity with the social conventions. Since she has no substantial facts about how a person ought to live, advice giving and the like could only be a moralistic position to take. A moral position, to the analytic psychotherapist, would be to assiduously avoid all moralistic positions. She finds that, consequent upon such deliberations, she has become less certain about what is proper and what is improper, and less clear about what constitutes psychological health and psychological disorder.

She is well aware that, as she does her analytic work, she herself introduces moralistic and personal preferences all the time. Despite her blindness to her own foibles, she tries to counterbalance such subtle attempts to coerce patients by pronouncing herself a fascist whenever she manages to catch herself doing so. She regrets that her most malignant fascisms are unconscious and therefore she, the analytic therapist, worries a good deal. Nevertheless, she finds such contorted analytic thinking to be self-indulgent, comic, and necessary. She insists that she says such things both tongue-in-cheek and with great earnestness.

The second ingredient of supportive psychotherapy, as I was taught it, is guilt induction. The analyst says things like,

"You have a responsibility to that girl."

"The behavior you are intending is, if you think about it for a moment, reprehensible."

I can barely bring myself to comment on such guilt-inducing interventions. The patient already knows his responsibilities to the girl, and the other patient knows perfectly well what constitutes reprehensible behavior. The analyst cannot possibly be as guilt inducing as is the patient's own superego and the intervention is therefore not at all psychoanalytically informed. Indeed, the patient's guilt is precisely aimed at getting the analyst to respond in the judgmental way that I have noted.

A third supportive mode is for the analyst to act on the side of the patient's defenses. For example, the analyst, for the patient's benefit, may enact the role of the idealized hero. The supposition here is that the patient needs an idealized hero in order to function properly. But, since analysis of such needs reveals the patient to be enacting a resolute self-denigration— casting himself in an inferior role—the pretense by the analyst that she is an ideal figure can only perpetuate the neurosis. Similar supportive methods suggest, for example, that one should scold a teenager who, supposedly, needs a powerful parent. "Turn down that music immediately!" one might say. I have no worthwhile comment to make about this either.

Therapists also, I am told, instruct obsessional patients to do crossword puzzles or paint-by-number kits, which, it is said, will strengthen their compulsive defenses. I suspect that the therapist's endorsement of compulsivity would only confirm the patient's preexisting fears of spontaneity, passivity, and affectivity. The same goes for the advice to hysterical persons that they should learn acting and dancing and that they should buy attractive clothes. They would, of course, only thereby be invited to fear rational knowledge more than is already the case.

I find no convincing rationale for supportive psychotherapy and therefore advise the use of the model technique, the essential ingredients of which are the analytic attitude and interventions that have an exclusively interpretive intent.

Despite what we might wish, from time to time some of us find ourselves required to conduct research-related brief analytic therapies (which I would prefer to call "psychoanalytic brief therapy" or even "brief psychoanalysis"). Such an eventuality, I would say, should not lead us to abandon our analytic stance. Such external constraints often make patients uneasy but, perhaps to an even greater extent, they make analysts uneasy. Both parties concerned generally expect the treatment to be an extended give-and-take situation. Some of us expect that, if all goes well, self-analysis should continue even after formal meetings have ended. Small wonder that many analytic therapists have misgivings about brief therapy. But for purposes of research, for example, the adjustment must be made.

In point of fact I have been unable to find in the literature reasons why, in brief therapy, our methods should change. Therefore, I have concluded that the time limitation placed on the treatment presumes no need to change our resolute analytic approach to patients. Nor do I believe, as do some, that as termination approaches, a tapering of meetings to once per month is advantageous. In my opinion, this is an external expectation placed upon us by some research protocols, and to which analysts will be expected to conform. If they have reactions to these constraints other than benign indifference—and most of us do and will—they will be expected simply to treat that reaction as another countertransference that will be of interest to them as they work with their patients.

When I originally embarked on writing this book, I considered including a chapter on the method of unmodified brief analytic therapy. But in thinking about that enterprise I realized that if the brief form of therapy is indeed to be an unmodified and analytic therapy, the chapter would have to be, simply, about analytic psychotherapy. My argument is that analytic principles apply to full-fledged classical psychoanalysis, to all forms of the usual expressive, dynamic, and analytically oriented psychotherapies, and to brief analytic therapy. I have even argued that these principles can be used in a single consultative interview with a patient.

Many who write about brief analytic therapy have recommended that the method be modified, for example Klerman (1984) and Kernberg and his associates (1989). I now find it hard to understand why such modifications are felt to be desirable. Surely, what is sauce for the goose is sauce for the gander! Deviations from an analytic approach deprive patients of in-depth self-knowledge that they might otherwise acquire.

One suspects that the prospect of a limitation on their time may spur some analysts to attempt to speed up the treatment process. To me this resembles attempts to speed up the sunrise—a kind of incomprehension of the nature of human psychology. If, for example, psychotherapeutic change is slow—and it often is—why would one deprive a patient in long-term therapy of interventions that speed up treatment? And if interpretive/analytic interventions benefit long-term patients, why would those in brief treatments be deprived of them? Even in *one* analytic interview it is sometimes possible to achieve profound insights into oneself, including awareness of transference patterns and childhood antecedents of such patterns, and to see how such patterns appear in day-to-day life. In profitable one-time interviews, constructions of unconscious motivations are at least possible, and on some occasions are quite straightforward. It is therefore hard to understand why analytic insights are to be limited by some of the measures advocated by the above authors, for example, by the avoidance of transference observations, by the encouragement of advice-giving, and the like.

The most characteristic thing about brief therapy is its time limitation. That limitation may be imposed by insur-

ance constraints, by the preference of the analytic psychotherapist, by the desire of the patient, or by the demands of
research. If there is any factor that could affect the method it
is, I suppose, that arbitrary time limitation. Yet, why should
this be so? There are other limitations placed upon the
psychotherapeutic situation and this, I claim, is simply another limitation. The patient, for example, can attend only if
he takes responsibility for the payment of the therapeutic fee.
He is not permitted social access to the analyst, nor is he
permitted to violate certain social proprieties regarding the
analyst's person or the analyst's premises.

Such limitations frequently enter into the therapy one
way or another. The analyst deals with these as analytically
as she can. Cannot the time limitation imposed by brief
analytic therapy be dealt with in the same way?

There is however, one nonanalytic thing that she *can* do,
but it is something that she can only do outside of the
therapeutic situation. After the brief therapy is done, and
after she has said in the final appointment that "The time is
up," she may, if she knows or senses that the patient wishes
it, discuss with the patient the possibility of further treatment. But under no circumstances should this be anticipated
by the analyst. For example if, during the therapy, the
patient voices his desire to continue beyond the preestab-
lished ending, the analyst should respond only analytically.
She should not even say something as benign sounding as,
"We can discuss that after this therapy is done" because, if
she does so, she interrupts the tension of the therapeutic
situation and deflects the state of desire embedded in the
patient's request. The patient's unconscious motives would
thereby be rendered less accessible.

But why can the analyst, on her own initiative, bring up
or discuss a more extended therapy after the last appointment? First, the analyst perfectly well knows the patient's
wish and no silly game of avoidance of the topic is indicated.
Second, after the therapy is done, a further diagnostic discussion, including further treatment recommendations, is perfectly legitimate.

If I have such a discussion with a patient after the

termination of a brief therapy, my most typical recommendation is to say,

> You may well be right and a period of longer-term therapy may be the right thing for you. But why don't you take a couple of months to think it over? It may be that at that time you will feel differently. If you then still feel a need for further treatment, give me a call and we can discuss it further.

My hesitation about helping the patient to get back into treatment is because I always fear that patients will define themselves as needy, on this occasion as needing more therapy, and I do not want to give the patient the message that I agree that he is needy in this way.

In summary, I have argued that the model technique advocated by me is indicated in all instances of analytic psychotherapy. It applies to psychoanalysis, to brief psychotherapy, and the usual once or twice weekly therapies. It requires no modification in any of these venues.

For physicians who practice analytic psychotherapy, the alluring problem, that is to say the temptation to deviate from the analytic method, can center on whether or not to prescribe drugs. This temptation should be trivial or nonexistent when a patient during the process of assessment asks for a prescription for minor tranquilizers. The analyst may simply decide to take an interpretive approach to such a request and, in an ideal world, that would be the only approach contemplated. But, since the therapy has not yet begun, this is not mandatory. In practice it is sometimes simpler to say, straightforwardly, "Since psychotherapy is what we are discussing, perhaps it would be better to just go ahead with the psychotherapy." In effect, one says that psychotherapy is the service that is for sale.

Some patients will persist in their request. If this happens one has no choice but to approach the request analytically. In doing so one quickly begins to deliver information to the patient about the analytic attitude even though the analytic therapy has technically not yet begun. The analyst thereby begins to indicate to her patient that she neither prescribes nor proscribes. She reveals as well that she has a particular set of attitudes toward time. For example, although she is steady and reliable about the beginning and end of appoint-ment times, about most other matters she has a relative indifference to time. She sees no need to solve the problem of prescribing or not prescribing, and simply defers to her greater interest in the therapeutic dialectic.

Still other patients announce that they are already taking a minor tranquilizer and their request is that the analyst will take over the renewal of their prescriptions. I suggest that analysts should tell patients that they should continue to deal with the person who has, up until then, been taking care of the matter. "But", they might say, "she has declined to write me more prescriptions because she knew I was coming to see you." Additionally, the patient might imply that he is prob-ably somewhat addicted to the drug and that, if the analyst does not give him prescriptions for his medications, she is placing him in a state of medical risk. The beginner and the nervous analyst may have to insist that the patient return to the physician who wrote the prescription originally. More experienced analysts probably have to do this less often. I know that my patients seem to sense that my interest is not specifically in their medication, and they nowadays seem not inclined to pressure me about it. They recognize that what I am gently but persistently interested in is, first, why they take the drug and, second, why the interview has taken on its drug-focused content.

My lack of interest has nothing to do with any doctrinaire antipathy to the use of drugs. On the contrary, I suspect that many analysts themselves would not hesitate to take a Valium tablet from time to time. It is just that I have a sense that, since I am a psychoanalyst, God or Destiny or some-thing has parachuted me into the consulting room to do something other than to prescribe drugs. As far as I can tell, if patients need prescriptions they can easily get them from their family doctor. And should they do so, I will attend to those acts in my analytic work without implication that they ought not to consult other doctors. Nor do I imply that the patient ought to stop taking the medication or that they are misbehaving by taking them.

The perfect analyst will, with regard to drugs, do what I have suggested in the preceding paragraphs. But since the perfect analytic psychotherapist is also a perfect fiction, it must be admitted that many analytic psychotherapists occasionally, usually *very* occasionally, do prescribe for patients. I can think of two such cases in my own practice. Both these patients took Valium in small doses on infrequent occasions but, about twice a year, would announce that they had run out of pills and requested that I renew their prescriptions. Consciously I told myself that this was a trivial matter and had thoughts such as "Who cares? What's the difference?" Once or twice I imagined myself to be Alfred E. Neuman of *Mad Magazine* voicing his mocking yet benign motto, "What, me worry . . .?" Occasionally I thought that, like Goethe, I should say to myself, *"Mach es kurtz. Am letzten Tag ist's nur ein Furtz."* (Make it quick. On Judgment Day it has no more importance than a fart.)

One of these patients was a highly successful and attractive businesswoman. She and I got on famously. I dream very rarely about patients but one night I, in fact, did dream about this woman, more specifically, that I was involved in a sexual encounter with her. When I awoke in the morning I found that I was in a peculiar state of mind. I was, I thought, slightly stunned and, to my chagrin, was . . . slightly . . . sort of . . . in love with my patient. It was, as I have said, peculiar to feel so unexpectedly enthralled. This feeling of love passed after a few hours. Suffice it to say that I had certain associations to my state of "being in love." The associative word which I remember was *shark*. How I reached that particular word became an example of "successful repression," as it has been lightheartedly called. In short, I realized that I had a fear that my patient was dangerous—a shark—and that I must not cross her. That is why we always got along so well, why I had "fallen in love with her" and, to get back to the point, why I had repeatedly renewed her prescriptions. That experience of the dream led me to focus on the patient with an altered frame of mind. She and I discussed the prescription in a new way, and she never requested a prescription again. But we did talk much more about her as a "ball-breaker" and about men as "weaklings" and "wimps."

The second patient, a high-ranking professional man, was much preoccupied by the corruption and petty failings of senior members in his profession, that is to say, male members of his profession. In fact he had the same disquietude with regard to senior men outside his profession. He had been much disappointed as a child by his father's weaknesses. But, although I was his fourth psychoanalyst, he could find little occasion for disappointment in the various psychiatrists who he had seen. He seemed puzzled when I speculated about this and, in an extraordinarily concrete way, wondered why on earth I would raise such a topic. Although he was highly sensitive to theater and aware of the psychological nuances of literature and art, he was, with regard to the transference relationship with me, a psychological "lummox." A "lummox"? What a nasty word to apply to one's patient. The patient, a young heavyset man, would not take kindly to any reference to himself as being a lummox. Would he punch me? Would it therefore be best to keep our therapeutic relationship manifestly analytic but always to maintain a fragment of cordial collegiality? Perhaps best to pay only lip service to analytic work with regard to his requests for prescription renewals? And should he and I therefore regard our therapeutic scenario as something that is just "between friends." Despite these insights my analytic efforts realized no change in his prescription request behavior.

The problem of drugs is more troubling with regard to antidepressant medications for seriously depressed patients. The situation is troubling because there is a large community of belief that drugs are the treatment of choice for these patients and, to make our difficulties greater, some colleagues insist that not to use these drugs is medically negligent. I happen to think that such opinions are at best extreme and at worst downright silly. But living with such problems is part and parcel of psychotherapeutic work. Although our uneasiness may be greater with regard to these drugs and their possible use with the depressed patient, the principles of psychotherapeutic management do not differ from what I have already outlined regarding other drugs.

> The melancholia of everything completed.
>
> Nietzsche, *Beyond Good and Evil*

For some, it is tempting to modify the analytic method at the time of termination. Perhaps, they wonder, one should become "more real" toward the end. Or perhaps one should taper off the appointments. Some insist that it is necessary to set a termination date well in advance. I personally am not sure that any of this matters. It is hoped that the fact of the eventual end to the analysis, and the patient's reaction to this, would have been periodically analyzed right from the beginning of the treatment. Patients who scrupulously avoid the idea that the analysis will some day end will, from time to time have had this drawn to their attention. And, I expect, patients who have been obsessionally preoccupied by the ending also will have had ample opportunity to analyze *that* reaction to termination.

Menninger and Holzman's (1973) idea that the therapy seems to "wear out," calls up for me a sense of recognition. Patient and analyst have diligently carried out their work but slowly come to realize that the analytic work seems less and less necessary. In some cases this can happen after as short a period as six months but more often the awareness of lessened necessity comes only after several years. I have an inclination to caution the reader and to say that after five or six years one ought to worry that the treatment has gone on too long. Despite my practical wish that treatments not go on forever, I know perfectly well that after five years it seems important in some cases that the analytic therapy should continue.

When thinking about termination we certainly do not have in mind that the patient's conflicts should have disappeared. I have been at some pains to clarify the fact that conflict is an inevitable and permanent consequence of the human condition. Personal desire is offered avenues of gratification by all societies. These modalities of gratification are, however, more or less arbitrarily specified. In effect this means that personal desire is to be restrained. Society's demand, internally represented by the superego, is the guarantor that conflict is eternal. Therefore, the analytic therapist's goal is only to achieve a shift in the balance of forces, a shift that, under favorable conditions, allows for less personal suffering and more personal satisfaction. More than that we should not hope for.

Menninger and Holzman (1973) attempt to establish guidelines that would offer a more objective method for determining when a patient is ready to finish. Although their proposed guidelines are eloquent and even inspiring, they are, I fear, unconvincing. The criteria all refer to socially approved, and therefore conventional, value systems. The goal of analytic therapy is not that patients should conform and have, for example, good object relations. Most of us do, of course, secretly applaud when our patients make seemingly good marriages and have children. But it is not our goal for them. Some patients may be best off living alone and others may be best off divorcing. They, the patients, must determine the course of their own lives. We, the analysts, can only stand by even though we know that they determine their lives less than they may think. And, at the time of termination, the patients also (we hope) will know that they are less self-determining than they once thought. At the end of their analytic treatment patients will only be what they will be. They usually will feel little need for further treatment and, for most, they will feel their lives to have been bettered. Many will have fewer symptoms but, paradoxically, others will have symptoms they did not have before. For example, some patients may have more anxiety after analytic treatment than they had before. This may be unexpected and unwelcome but be acceptable nevertheless. Perhaps, in his new status as a person who, at times, suffers from anxiety, we might be able to say that the patient is "a better man for it." For more than this we cannot hope.

Apart from these considerations, the analyst simply continues to analyze. Some things she will have analyzed well and others, not so well. Some matters she will have neglected. Some analysts will have neglected issues of termination, whereas others will have compulsively overemphasized matters of ending. Despite her neglect, that analyst's patients will also, sooner or later, come to a time of termination. She will analyze, without deviation from the model technique, until the very end. Like my analyst and like me, at the end of the final appointment she will say "The time is up." At the door she may shake hands with the patient and murmur "Good luck"—if that postanalysis farewell looks to be a comfortable way for the patient. The parties to the analytic treatment will part company with mixed emotions. The analytic psychotherapist will consider that she should be available for further consultations should these be necessary but, in keeping with her continuing analytic attitude, she would never say such a thing to her patient. Such an assurance would be seen by her as a rather empty or even a patronizing statement. The analyst, should she make such an offer, would feel that she was betraying the dignity and seriousness of what had gone on before. Besides, by then the patient knows her well enough that he knows perfectly well that he can call.

A small percentage of patients return requesting further treatment. Usually they will have had a satisfactory outcome when the original treatment ended, although a few, at least in the analyst's opinion, will have stopped prematurely. The analyst will accommodate such patients if she can and, if she cannot, will help them to find someone else.

From time to time the analytic therapist will meet her patients socially. It is probably best to keep such contacts courteous and carefully circumspect. The analytic therapist often would like to let go of her cautiousness in such matters but feels duty-bound to remain subtly professional and therefore assure that she will continue to be professionally available. Who knows when she might again be needed? Despite this counsel, friendships between analyst and onetime patients sometimes develop. This is human and understandable. To forbid such friendships is silly, small-minded, and lacking in common psychological awareness. It is infantilizing to assume that treatment can never be over—a wish, perhaps, of those who deny that nothing lasts forever.

12

The Problem of
Developmental
Change

It is only charlatans who are certain . . . Doubt is not a very
agreeable state, but certainty is a ridiculous one.

Voltaire, in Robertson 1922, p. 122

In these final chapters I argue that there are two major groups
of theories concerning analytic change. The first of these
springs from the very great interest that psychoanalysts have
come to devote to developmental theory. Since I worry about
certain aspects of the developmental approach, I propose to
subject some of the developmental theories to an extended
critical discussion. To me, the proper focus of a psychoanalytic developmental theory is not a predictive one, that is to
say, a theory that could lead us to anticipate the ordinary
course of normal development. At best, such predictions are
statements about how the average child develops and, being
about normative behavior, have more to do with demography
than with psychoanalysis.

An even greater danger is that such predictive theories
can become announcements of how the developing person

ought to behave. This is a danger of great importance and its potential to deflect psychoanalysis from its mission cannot be overemphasized. Its inherent message is an advocacy of particular behaviors that can only be described as conventional. The analytic therapist is, of course, at great pains never to be an advocate of particular behaviors because, to her, this is, at best, a form of behaviorism and, at worst, an unattractive authoritarianism. I fear that when we speak in a congratulatory manner of someone who has good object relations, we are speaking as behavioral advocates rather than as psychoanalysts. I have already argued that analytic neutrality is a centerpiece of analytic behavior and, indeed, of all analytic thought.

The second group of analytic theories—the theory used in analytic practice—is *post*-dictive, that is to say, aims to illuminate how, in fact, an individual *did* develop. This has, I would suggest, nothing whatsoever to do with how a person *should* develop. Szajnberg (1992) has suggested that psychoanalytic developmental theory is in the nature of an autobiographical genre, a suggestion that clearly reminds us of the specific nature of our developmental interest. Here is Szajnberg's felicitous way of putting this idea:

> Psychoanalysis, like post-eighteenth century autobiography, is a journey, albeit a journey inward. It is a temporal journey backward of persons (oneself and others) mostly familiar but occasionally foreign-feeling . . . Like accounts of outer journeys—ethnographies . . . this inward journey is fraught with excitement, apprehension, danger, unexpected circumstances, the hope of finding oneself or discovering another and sometimes learning about oneself through another as did Ishmael through Queequeg. [p. 376]

Such a developmental genre is akin to the traditional *Bildungsroman*, that is to say, novels that trace the development of the protagonist. The point of such novels is the flowering of individuality or, education through life. Every one of Freud's case histories is written like a *Bildungsroman*, a fact that Freud himself commented upon wryly (Freud 1893–1895). Examples from literature would be Joyce's *Portrait of the Artist as a Young Man* and Goethe's *Faust.* Like every psychoanalytic case history, these stories emphasize individuality and eschew any implicit or explicit normative goal for their heroes.

What I have called a second group of developmental theories understands analytic change to be a product of shifts in the patient's preferred psychological posture and not as the release of an innate biological schedule. This way of understanding psychoanalytic theory avers that change can be understood in terms of an alteration in the pattern of defensive behavior, as a modification of the superego, or as a shift in the balance of mental forces. None of these metaphors, of course, are to be taken literally. This position—the one that I prefer—is easy to criticize. Some might point out that it comes precariously close to saying that people change because they change or that they make psychological shifts because they make psychological shifts. Even worse, they might say, it comes precariously close to saying that the patient changes because the analytic therapist invites or persuades him to change. In other words, the analyst effects change by the way of suggestion.

Some have found it safest to say that the analytic therapist claims only to exhaustively describe what happens during the analytic treatment. Ornston (1985) documents in great detail how Freud himself intended a "describing psychology." Explanation, after all, is only one of the rational paradigms available to us. The distinction between explanation and description is that of the old philosophical conundrum between causes and reasons. To rehash that debate is a bit too scholastic—even for my taste. I suspect that most of us are content to allow both causes and reasons to count as explanatory notions. Adolf Grünbaum (1984), a psychoanalytically informed philosopher, suggests, simply, that if something "makes a difference," that it can then count as "explanation."

Even if one decides to opt for the idea that psychoanalysis is a descriptive discipline, one need not trivialize description by dubbing it mere description. That would be to forget the poetic and artistic aspects of the analyst's theories of change. What such theorists have in mind is not simple description but, instead, what has been referred to as "thick description" by the late philosopher of mind, Gilbert Ryle. What he calls thick description sounds to me like a perfectly satisfying explanation. I cannot do better at summarizing this idea than to quote Clifford Gertz (1973):

> Consider . . . two boys rapidly contracting the eyelids of their right eyes. In one, this is an involuntary twitch: in the other, a conspiratorial signal to a friend. The two movements are, as movements, identical; from an I-am-a-camera, "phenomenalistic" observation of them alone, one could not tell which was twitch and which was wink, or indeed whether both or either was twitch or wink. Yet the difference, however unphotographable, between a twitch and a wink is vast; as anyone unfortunate enough to have had the first taken for the second knows. The winker is communicating, and indeed communicating in a quite precise and special way: (1) deliberately, (2) to someone in particular, (3) to impart a particular message, (4) according to a socially established code, and (5) without cognizance of the rest of the company. As Ryle points out, the winker has done two things, contracted his eyelids and winked, while the twitcher had done only one, contracted his eyelids. Contracting your eyelids on purpose when there exists a public code in which so doing counts as a conspiratorial signal *is* winking. That's all there is to it: a speck of behavior, a fleck of culture, and *voilà!* a gesture.
>
> That, however, is just the beginning. Suppose, he continues, there is a third boy, who, "to give malicious amusement to his cronies," parodies the first boy's wink, as amateurish, clumsy, obvious, and so on. He, of course, does this in the same way the second boy winked and the first twitched: by contracting his right eyelids. Only this boy is neither winking nor twitching, he is parodying someone else's, as he takes it, laughable attempt at winking. Here, too, a socially established code exists (he will "wink" laboriously, overobviously, perhaps adding a grimace—the usual artifices of the clown); and so also does a message. Only now it is not conspiracy but ridicule that is

in the air. If the others think he is actually winking, his whole project misfires as completely, though with somewhat different results, as if they think he is twitching. One can go further: uncertain of his mimicking abilities, the would-be satirist may practice at home before the mirror, in which case he is not twitching, winking, or parodying, but rehearsing though so far as what a camera, a radical behaviorist, or a believer in protocol sentences would record he is just rapidly contracting his right eyelids like all the others. Complexities are possible, if not practically without end, at least logically so. The original winker might, for example, actually have been fake-winking, say, to mislead outsiders into imagining there was a conspiracy afoot when there in fact was not, in which case our descriptions of what the parodist is parodying and the rehearser rehearsing of course shift accordingly. But the point is that between what Ryle calls the "thin description" of what the rehearser (parodist, winner, twitcher . . .) is doing ("rapidly contacting his right eyelids") and the "thick description" of what he is doing ("practicing a burlesque of a friend faking a wink to deceive an innocent into thinking a conspiracy is in motion") lies the object of ethnography: a stratified hierarchy of meaningful structures in terms of which twitches, winks, fake-winks, parodies, rehearsals of parodies are produced, perceived, and interpreted, and without which they would not . . . in fact exist, no matter what anyone did or didn't do with his eyelids. [pp. 6–7]

Ludwig Wittgenstein (1967) had a considerable interest in psychoanalysis and, in conversation with students, referred to himself as a "disciple" (p. 41) of Freud. He therefore felt it legitimate to argue for its "descriptive" as opposed to its "explanatory" powers. Like philosophy, psychoanalysis was, to Wittgenstein, a matter of linguistic analysis, respectful persuasion, and (thick) description.

If someone says: "There is not a difference," and I say: "There is a difference" I am persuading, I am saying "I don't want you to look at it like that." . . . I am in a sense making propaganda for one style of thinking as opposed to

another. I am honestly disgusted with the other. Also I'm
trying to state what I think. Nevertheless I'm saying: "For
God's sake don't do this." [pp. 27–28]

Developmental theories have come to dominate the theoretical thinking of many practitioners and, especially, of
many students. In some ways, Freud himself was the first
offender in this regard, thereby inviting revisionists to use
Freud's own developmental notions to obscure what were his
actual revolutionary discoveries. Since I, myself, am a
Freudian apologist, I would say that Freud himself never
attempted to place his developmental theory at the center of
the psychoanalytic edifice and instead insisted that repression and the unconscious were the cornerstones of his theory.
Libido theory, Freud's developmental oeuvre, was precious to
him insofar as it was the grounding location for the Oedipus
complex. But insofar as libido theory is his theory of drives or
instincts, Freud at times was quite prepared to discuss that
theory as "our mythology."

Freud's link between the Oedipus complex and libido
theory was never insisted upon by him and the embedded-
ness of the oedipal dilemma in a drive theory is by no means
obligatory. I have already argued in Chapter 7 that the
oedipal drama is part and parcel of the child's existence as a
person psychologically embedded in a culture, and that the
oedipal dilemma is inevitable and eternal. It is not arrived at
after a period of psychological residence in a preoedipal
world, nor is it ever superseded and emerged from. There are,
I argue, only shifts and shadings about how a person positions himself in a world structured by the oedipal-cultural
law.

Naturally enough, those who wish to emphasize developmental processes in their theory of analytic change seize
upon Freud's hypotheses concerning preoedipal stages, especially the stages that he called narcissism. I fear that Freud,
by writing the (perhaps mischievous?) article "On Narcissism: An Introduction" (1914b), was himself the author of
much of the misfortune that has fallen upon his theories.
Since Freud is already so much maligned by many theorists,

I would prefer to spare him my comments on that article but, as is obvious to any thoughtful reader, it is jargonistic and a somewhat scholastic and unnecessary flight from psychological theorizing to the uncertain safety of metapsychology. The reader surely knows of the many contorted debates in the literature about primary and secondary narcissism, about the reflective and prereflective *cogito,* about autistic and symbiotic modes, and so on. What these developmental theorists have done is to embed the idea of analytic change into their developmental theories. What I mean here is that they postulate that, in essence, change consequent upon analytic treatment, stems from a resumption of normal psychological development. As I hope to clarify, these developmental theories are diverse and sometimes mutually contradictory. I, of course, have doubts about conceptualizing analytic change in this way and, when in a mischievous frame of mind, accuse these contributors of being deviationists and revisionists.

There are two large groups of theories that I will examine. The first of these, characteristic of writers such as Melanie Klein, Kohut, Eissler, Lacan, and Mahler, postulates that infants, to a radical extent, are incomplete, chaotic, and undeveloped, and that the understanding of proper development requires us to acknowledge, first, that infants are only complete in conjunction with an adequate parent, and second, these competent parents must modulate and correct the child's various deficiencies. Furthermore, the parents must facilitate the child's negotiation of, and emergence from, this primitive state. *Pari passu,* patients who undertake analytic psychotherapy are considered by these theorists to be in an equivalent or identical underdeveloped state. During their treatment, patients must also have such deficiencies modulated and corrected and, just as with infants, must have their egress from that unsatisfactory state of affairs facilitated by the analyst.

The second large group of developmental change theorists, in effect, have gone "through the looking glass." The chief theorists in this group are Winnicott, Wilhelm Reich, and some others who I will refer to as the emancipatory theorists. Most of the latter are linked with the so-called Frankfurt School, the members of which were much influenced by Marxism. Not all are psychoanalysts but some names with which the reader will be familiar are Fromm, Habermas, and Adorno. The primary assumption of these contributors is the perfect opposite of the assumptions of the first group of developmental theorists. Young children, according to them, are in a pristine and intact state. This fundamental state of wellness is liable to injury, in large measure due to the inept ministrations of parents. Others in this group emphasize the ungainly influence of the culture and its agents, an influence that corrupts or, better, stifles an authentic and wholesome natural state.

I will begin with the views of Melanie Klein. As is well known, she conceived of infants as being in a complex and disturbing psychological state (Klein 1946). Klein is at some pains to emphasize that, in this regard, she not referring to what is usually referred to as the *infantile neurosis*. This term, to her, is a misnomer. Proper terminology, to Klein, should refer to a *childhood neurosis*. For the infantile state she suggests that *infantile psychosis* would be a more appropriate term. This infantile state is said to be characterized by intense paranoid and persecutory fantasies in which the child perceives the world as filled with attacking and devouring part objects. Such part objects are fragments or aspects of people in the infant's psychological world—aspects that the child has not yet integrated into more complete or more realistic whole objects. Such part objects are at least partly a product of intense splitting mechanisms but are also simple fragments of thoughts that the child applies to the world. The splitting actions that I have mentioned are conceived of by the child as evidence of its own ruthless and destructive attacks upon various persons in its world. It is important to note that Klein believed this to be characteristic of all infants. All infants, in effect, live in a psychotic world.

What can one say about such a claim? One can acknowledge that Klein took very seriously the notion of psychoanalysis as a depth psychology and her writings are a window upon her passionate pursuit of what lies in the depths of the mind. On the other hand, one can only feel uneasy about her literalization and concretization of the unconscious that, to her, can rupture into consciousness, can be seen, and can be interpreted. What is ordinarily called the manifest content is treated by her as a direct revelation of something unconscious. Klein sometimes slips, it seems, and fails to understand that the unconscious is unconscious with a vengeance and is kept so by way of a thousand subtle and complex maneuvers. She seems unaware that the unconscious is always just that—it is deeply unconscious and never manifest.

And what can one say about the violent psychotic world in which she claims infants live? Certainly the infants I have known do not appear to me to inhabit such worlds. I would hasten to agree with her that all persons with whom one can communicate show us that they live in a psychological world populated by a kaleidoscope of archetypal figures. All of us know that mothers are wholesome and that fathers are strong. And women clearly are bitches and men obviously are wimps. On some occasions, women are to be discovered as angels, seductresses, mental lightweights, and so on, whereas men are to be discovered as tyrants, heroes, sissies, and whatever. These categorizations are both believed in and not believed in by all of us. When we entertain thoughts such as "Gypsies are likely to cheat you," it does not mean that we are psychotic, nor does it necessarily mean that we are racist. It means only that we know the cultural stereotypes and, moreover, are constantly at risk of participating in them unreflectively. I do not mean to suggest that such archetypes (stereotypes, templates, internal objects, part objects) are nothing but learned cultural events. All of us are psychologically served by such imagery and live with a cast of images that is personal and unique to us. He who ardently believes that men are brutal sadists lives in a culture that is familiar with this particular part object, and such a man gives this archetype a special preference. From an analytic point of view it would be claimed that he has an array of unconscious motives for holding to this belief.

My point is that abstraction, generalization, reductionism, and isolation are ubiquitous in human beings and that
these mechanisms are our means of creating such archetypes. And I also claim that it is pure folly to call this
psychosis. It is a parallel and equal folly to call the thoughts
of infants psychotic. All such imagery is embedded in what,
after all, is just another person—be it adult, child, or infant.

This is the working assumption with which Melanie Klein
begins when she works therapeutically with her patients. Her
theory reminds me of the theory of child rearing that I grew
up with. The idea was that children are born lazy, dirty, and
overly interested in sex ("psychotic" in Klein's terms?), and
that the task of child rearing was to rid the child of these
flaws. In a similar vein, Klein's theory of therapeutic change
has to do with ridding the patient of his psychotic inner world
or, at least, to bringing his psychotic inner world under
control. In normal development (and in psychoanalytic treatment), she says, a competent parent (or analyst) offers an
experience good enough that the child's primitive world gives
way to a realistic world. In considerable measure this takes
place because the good parent or analyst does not participate
in the madness of the child or the madness of the patient.
Kleinian analysts doubt whether parents, on their own, can
very often achieve this—or so I am told. Therefore, they say,
it is very worthwhile for every child to have personal analytic
treatment. Since I doubt the proposition that all infants are
psychotic, I could hardly agree. And, as the reader knows by
now, I am inclined to have doubts and contradictory ideas
about the notion of psychological pathology in general.

Klein cannot be faulted for advocating nonparticipation
in the patient's preferred psychological world (which she
would call his psychotic or paranoid-schizoid world). All
analytic therapists, of course, do this. Properly, she also
advocates that the analyst must take an interpretive approach to what is going on. With this, one also can only agree.
Even if some of us feel uneasy about her rather dogmatic and
reductionistic style, further comment on that score is irrelevant to my critique of Klein's development theory of analytic
change. The essential point here is the explicitness of the

developmental theory that explains change for her. The patient, in the toils of a psychotic inner world, comes into the care of the competent and interpreting analyst, and can then move into the developmental stage known as the depressive position. She argues that the patients' psychotic projections, introjections, rage, and terror are worked through as he becomes aware of the analyst as a real person. Development and recovery are one and the same thing.

I now turn to Jacques Lacan because there is a theoretical sympathy between him and Melanie Klein. In one of his seminars, "The Topic of Imaginary" (Lacan 1953–1954). Lacan specifically discusses the mental state of the infant. He characterizes that mental state in his own words without specifically using Kleinian terminology. But the state he describes is perfectly analogous to the psychotic state described by Melanie Klein. Lacan refers to this infantile condition as primitive, primal, chaotic, absolute and as being made up of "ids, objects, instincts, desires" (p. 79). Since he uses as his clinical example a case of Melanie Klein's, one can only assume he is referring to the same infantile condition that Melanie Klein has written about.

But there is another intriguing and puzzling idea that Lacan introduces here. This state—the one that he has just described—is characterized by him as "reality pure and simple then, which is not delimited by anything, which cannot yet be the object of any definition, which is neither good, nor bad, but is all at the same time chaotic and absolute, primal" (p. 79).

This is Lacan's "Real." A chaotic and psychotic state is conceived by the mischievous Lacan as worthy of a paradoxical title. Hence its designation as the Real.

The aim of analytic treatment is to help the child emerge from its psychotic state—the Real—and to enter into the depressive position—the Symbolic. I will come back to the Real and the Symbolic in a moment since, at this point, I wish only to point out Lacan's theory of analytic change. It is a theory identical to that of Melanie Klein insofar as it, first, is developmental, and second, refers to an emergence from chaos into the world of human order. The difference from Melanie Klein, among other things, is Lacan's designation of the primal chaos as the Real. That infantile state, for Lacan, is to be ambivalently viewed. Insofar as it is madly chaotic, it is something to be overcome. But insofar as it is the Real, one must grudgingly give that mental state a certain credit for authenticity and genuineness. I take note of this latter idea, mentioned by Lacan only in passing, because, as I will discuss later, echoes of this idea appear in Winnicott's notion of the "true self" and in the work of existentially inclined analysts who pursue and advocate a return to a primal authenticity.

Before looking further at Lacan's theory of analytic change (and developmental change), let me digress briefly and add a few more comments—philosophical comments— about the state of chaos to which Lacan refers and that he conceptualizes in such literal and concrete terms. As analytic psychologists, we should always keep in mind the dichoto- mous character of all our thinking. Good can only be con- ceived of if we have a notion of bad. There is no notion of bigness without an idea of smallness. In other words, there is no conceivable one-term universe. For any universe of dis- course to come into existence, at least two terms are re- quired. And this holds true for Lacan's supposedly primal chaotic mental state. There can be no chaos without organi- zation. The infant cannot know disorder unless it knows orderliness. The Real that Lacan postulates is a reductionistic idea uncharacteristic of him but, like all of us, I suppose that he longs to find a solid place to plant his feet. In this instance he resorts to an ontologization of a chaotic Real. In disagree- ment with Lacan, I, myself, suspect that infants enter into psychological positions swimmingly, or hazily—that uni- verses float ephemerally into being. And I insist that to inhabit the world of personhood it is necessary that the infant apprehend and conceive organization of some sort.

And now, with those preliminary remarks made, we can look at how Lacan (1953–1954) understands analytic change to take place. As I have already suggested, his model is a developmental one and I will begin by describing his formulation regarding the infant's emergence from the chaotic Real into the world of psychological competence. This takes place, says Lacan, by the imposition upon the child's chaos of the symbolic order. With regard to the case of Melanie Klein that Lacan is using as his example, he states,

> Here is a case where it is absolutely apparent. There is nothing remotely like an unconscious in the subject. It is Melanie Klein's discourse which brutally grafts the primary symbolizations of the Oedipal situation on to the initial ego-related *(moïque)* inertia of the child. [p. 85]

Lacan's developmental sequence goes from the Real, to the Imaginary, and finally, to the Symbolic—although this may not be perfectly clear in the quotation. Nor is this perfectly clear in Lacan's writings in general. I suspect that Lacan himself would object to my rather reductionistic scheme of Real—Imaginary—Symbolic. He would prefer to keep his formulations ambiguous and tentative and, in large part, this is precisely (or imprecisely) how Lacan delivers his message to us. However, there is no doubting that his Real is primordial and that, by way of the Imaginary, the child achieves competence once it enters the world of the Symbolic. His theory of analytic change is clearly developmental. It is the same theory used by Melanie Klein except that, rather than development being a product of stable and adequate parenting, change is due to a donation to the child of a symbolic ordering or structuring. It is a theory of linguistic competence.

You will recall that in Chapter 7, in my discussion of the Oedipus complex, I, too, held to a view that placed great weight on the child's existence in a symbolic order. But I would prefer not to think of this as a developmental step. From the moment that a child is aware of itself as a person, it inevitably is aware of itself as being located in a culture, which means that it is acting within a set of expectations or, in other words, within a set of rules. No person, child or adult, functions in a vacuum. Thus, every thought or action harmonizes with its morally expectant surround or, under other circumstances, is dissonant with that surround. No psychological stance can be immune from such a positioning. Hence the title of Philip Rieff's *Freud: The Mind of the Moralist* (1961).

This means that, in contrast to Lacan, I would argue that the child does not exist as a psychological creature except insofar as it is part of a symbolic order, that is to say, structured by the oedipal-cultural law. My view is nondevelopmental in this sense. It denies precultural or preoedipal primitiveness and acknowledges only different modes of existing within the symbolic order. In this way of thinking, a child is not to be thought of as primitive but, instead, is merely youthful. Psychologically speaking, child-like behavior can be unattractive in an adult or, contrariwise, can be judged as charming. But in either instance, it is unattractive or charming behavior within a social context, that is to say, within the oedipal-cultural law.

Rather than identifying any progress toward maturity or health, we can discern only that some persons behave normatively and do so for a host of reasons and motives, both conscious and unconscious. About those who do not behave normatively one must say the very same: they do so for a host of reasons and motives, both conscious and unconscious. Normative and nonnormative behaviors, for me, do not refer to developmental stages. The infant is as normative or nonnormative in its behavior as is the adult.

To live within a symbolic order is to achieve personhood. Unexpectedly, to be a person does not require that one be human. One need only think of our ability to attribute personhood to a Martian. The conditions under which we attribute personhood are many and varied and I can recommend Daniel Dennett's (1978) discussion of this matter in *Brainstorms.* Once again Ornston (1985) has drawn attention to Freud's own frequent use of the word *person,* albeit often (mis)translated by Strachey into more jargonistic Latin-based words—words that to him seemed more scientific. By doing so, Strachey lost the evocativeness of the plain German that Freud himself preferred. For my purposes, to study and understand a person qua person, requires that the object of study have at least a rudimentary capacity to use a natural language. Using a language includes an awareness of the value system embedded in such a language. In a certain sense, one could say that this is precisely the function served by language—to assign value and quality. Everything is good or bad or, more subtly, better or worse. The world is warm or cool, bright or dull, calm or agitated. All depends on language. I can easily change the meaning of *bright* or *dull* by modifying the language to *glaring* or *subdued*. This is the kind of value assignment that Lacan is making when he notes "progression" from "primitive" modes to "competent" modes of living within the symbolic order.

Psychoanalysis, in contrast, claims only that there are different modes and denies that one mode is better than another. For us, that difference usually has to do with degrees of suffering. This is an example of the kind of theorizing that Freud preferred because it is plain talk and avoids the additional theoretical step of attributing that suffering to developmental deviation. Such suffering is to be understood as coherent and, in principle, understandable. It is motivated and self-devised by the patient in question.

When we treat an infant as an object of psychoanalytic study we attribute to it an array of desires, tastes, and intentions. We do so because, as psychoanalysts, we have made the a priori resolution that the child's behavior will be treated as a form of communication, that is to say, as language. From a theoretical point of view, whether or not the child, even in a rudimentary way, can use a natural language is beside the point. The only thing that matters for the theorist is whether such a model has practical consequences—even if the practical consequences are limited to our increased sense of understanding. After all, we attribute such intentions to inanimate things all the time. For example, I do this when I say that my automobile "wants to pull to the right." It might be argued that this is just a colorful metaphor but, in certain circumstances, we must attribute intentionality to inanimate things. For example, when playing chess against a computer, we can do so only if we treat it as an intentional system, that is to say, treat the computer as though it wants to win, as though it wants to mislead us, and as though it wants to capture our pawn. But although a computer can be treated as an intentional system, we have difficulty treating it as a person, lacking as it does, crucial features of personhood. A computer is not sensuous, desirous, guilty, or conflicted, as are persons. Nor can it speak a natural language.

The point of all this discussion is that in our day-to-day lives we treat infants as linguistic and desirous and, in addition, believe that it is legitimate for the analytic theoretician to do so as well. As analytic theorists or as analytic practitioners, we always treat patients as persons. The study of people as biological systems we leave to others. Our focus is not on transitional developmental events, especially not on peculiar developmental events such as those that Lacan describes. I call them peculiar because he seems to suggest that our analytic attention is upon a transition from a primordial biological state to existence in a psychological world. I suggest, instead, that the analytic focus is always on persons and, more specifically, on persons as desirous creatures living within a symbolic order that they apprehend and negotiate.

Lacan, despite his brilliantly associative texts, seems to be surprisingly disinterested in recovering the contradictory repressed. Instead, he seems intent on performing an educational task (a development-facilitating task) whereby he teaches his patients to upgrade their linguistic abilities. To him, patients suffer from an impoverished participation in the linguistic system and the analytic therapist's task is to display associative genius in which patients can come to participate. It suggests to me that reading James Joyce's *Ulysses* or *Finnegans Wake* is the equivalent of an analytic therapy. Both Joyce and Lacan are, after all, associative geniuses. I fear that, ultimately, Lacan's brilliant reading of Freud is also a misreading of Freud's analytic idea. Linguistic completion and linguistic competence have less to do with the reappropriation of unconscious contents than Lacan thinks. I can only add that reading Joyce is rewarding and enriching and one might well say the same about reading

Lacan. But this is a form of "literature therapy" and not an analytic therapy.

To Lacan, the promotion of linguistic competence means that the patient has come to more fully inhabit the social or symbolic order. More specifically, he means that the patient has come to accept the law of the father. He says this repeatedly and by doing so reveals himself as a revolutionary who, at heart, is a moralist. Freud, in contrast to Lacan, hoped that, after analytic treatment, the patient would be somewhat freed from the "law of the father," that is to say, freed from arbitrary enslavement by his own superego. The patient could then, Freud hoped, lead a prudent rather than a law-bound life.

The theorists known as ego psychologists by and large have maintained an analytic focus upon conflict and on the unconscious. But in their theoretical formulations they have introduced ideas that open the door to psychoanalytic impoverishment. In large measure this was done in order to pursue the bootless goal of transforming psychoanalytic theory into a general psychology. What they attempted to do was to graft onto analytic theory the objects of study of academic psychology. These grafts were dubbed "ego functions" or, more injurious to analytic theory, "autonomous ego functions." Suddenly the theory was asked to ingest exceptions to its fundamental tenets. No longer was the human subject to be apprehended as the locus of a fundamental contradiction but, instead, certain aspects of the subject, the autonomous ego functions, were found to be exempt from contradiction.

What a pity! I sorely regret that important contributors such as Hartmann, Rapaport, and many others, lost their focus on the analytic idea. I have already considered at some length how Kurt Eissler (1953) participated in this aberrant line of thought and advocated the use with certain patients of the so-called parameters of technique. These are the patients who had come to be referred to as having damaged, absent, or distorted ego functions. For this delimited group of patients, analytic change seems to be conceptualized in developmental terms. Like Melanie Klein and Jacques Lacan, Eissler sees certain patients as developmentally impoverished and, to him, a necessary ingredient in their treatment has to do with some form of reparative effort. It is none too clear how the ego psychologists explain the occurrence of aberrant ego functions, although attempts have been made, notably by Loewald (1960). Nor is it clear how the use of parameters corrects the deficiencies in an ailing ego function. When one reads between the lines it seems that the analyst is to act in place of the damaged ego function, or to persuade and suggest to the patient that he should try to use his ego functions in a particular way. All of this has nothing to do with analytic theory as I understand it. As I have already argued, it seems to be a reversion to the pre-Freudian theory of mental degeneracy.

Perhaps I could use as an example, the psychological action—the ego function—known as *judgment.* If a person repeatedly spends more than he has and, as a consequence, is constantly in financial difficulties, we typically say that he has bad judgment. But certain ego psychologists would, I fear, treat this behavior in a nonanalytic way. They would, as I understand it, apprehend such behavior as a straightforward cause-and-effect result of a deficit in the patient's judgment function and, like Klein or Lacan, would act to repair or substitute for that absent function. I heartily disagree. The psychoanalytic assumption is that such acts of bad judgment are motivated and serve unconscious purposes. The behavior is to be analyzed as is any other. The same principles apply to insight, motivation, cognition, and affect—all of which have been redesignated as ego functions by the theorists in question. I conclude again that analytic change is not developmental.

Such formulations are reversions to a form of theorizing known as *functionalism.* Functionalism is description pure and simple but, I hasten to add, exhibits none of the exhaustive descriptive detail of thick description. Properly used, functionalism simply refers to an abstract categorization of actions that can be brought together in the class of, say, judgment—or of affect, or cognition, or of any other behavior. In psychiatry it is called upon in so-called functional cases wherein no causal elements can be identified. Improperly used (and I fear that many ego psychologists do, indeed, use this quasi-explanatory term improperly), functionalism has resulted in unhelpful tautologies such as "judgment is due to the judgment function," or "cognition is due to the cognitive function." Worse, these tautologies seem to deceive some authors into believing that they have explained something when they speak of weak or absent ego functions.

The most misleading misuse of functionalism that I know of is when theorists claim that the behavior of those diagnosed as antisocial personality disorder is caused by the absence of a superego. This idea would be merely pathetic were it not taken so seriously by many students and, indeed, by some colleagues. Such a theory is pathetic because it fails to recognize that the superego is an inevitable attribute of being a person. Awareness of oneself is what makes persons conscious since, to be conscious, one must reflect upon oneself. Such reflection-upon-oneself is the essence of conscience or of superego. Self-observation is a critical examinational act that is the underpinning of both *consciousness* and *conscience*—these two words having, in fact, the etymological link that is suggested by their resemblance to one another. Superego manifestations turn out, upon analysis, to be far more complex than this, especially insofar as they turn out to be powerful identifications of one sort or another. For the purpose of the point that I am making, it is enough to reaffirm that guilty and self-defeating behaviors are ubiquitous and cannot, in principle, be absent.

Kohut and his followers—the self psychologists—are the fourth group of theorists for whom developmental change is equivalent to psychoanalytic change. There are two major differences from the ego psychologists: first, self psychologists locate the deficit in what they call the self. Second, they claim that patients with "self pathology" constitute a very large proportion of patients who come for psychoanalytic treatment. Some self psychologists go even further and claim that self pathology is the characteristic pathology in all patients.

In response to such formulations I can only reiterate what I have already said. These theories are permissible. They are even plausible. But such theories are *not* psychoanalytic. To me, they render humans as impoverished homunculi, devoid of complexity and paradox, who lack the fascinating secret cleverness that the psychoanalytic view turns up in all behavior.

The psychic deficit postulated by these theorists is that of self-fragmentation. One can immediately recognize the analogy with the psychotic world in which Melanie Klein imagines infants to reside. Klein has even talked of a "shattering of the ego," or of internal objects being "smashed to bits." Such notions are renamed by Kohut as a fragmented self. This idea is equally reminiscent of Lacan's primal chaos and is somewhat reminiscent of the weak or damaged ego functions postulated by Eissler. Such theories of fragmentation have a long history in Christianity, a history that again and again reveals doctrines in which movement from chaos to "wholeness" are central (Bynum 1992). Development toward a more adult functioning is the theory of change preferred by all of these writers.

Kohut's theory has a remarkable resemblance to ethology. Many self psychology writers refer explicitly to infant observation studies and to the ethological writings of Daniel Stern (1985). Ethology, as I understand it, is the study of innate behaviors, universal to the species, evoked by specific sign stimuli. Here is how self psychology fits with the theory of ethology. The patient begins in a state of self-fragmentation. In the analytic situation, the analytic therapist responds with empathy. This empathic response is the specific sign stimulus and, in response to it, the patient emits an innate behavior, universal to the species. That behavior is self-cohesiveness. Fragmentation is transformed into cohesiveness according to an innate developmental program when the empathic sign stimulus is administered. The theory is identical when applied to infants. They, too, begin in a state of self-fragmentation that is systematically transformed into self-cohesiveness by the empathic parent. This is not a theory of motives, desires, beliefs, fears, and strategies; that is to say, it is not a psychological or psychoanalytic theory. Instead, it is a development theory that gets away from the psychoanalytic notion of repression and self-deception.

The empathic responsiveness advocated by self psychologists is also referred to by them as mirroring. I have already argued that, in responding to patients, we always mirror and rethink what has been said. For purposes of my argument I will point out that these theorists seem convinced that, first, it is desirable and possible to univalently mirror what a patient says, and, second, that such mirroring activities are agents of therapeutic change. Jacques Lacan holds to a diametrically opposed position. His claim is that mirroring leads to false identifications that stultify rather than enrich the analytic patient's life. The result of such mirroring, he says, is the development of an ego (self psychologists might say the development of a self). The creation of such an ego structure, to Lacan, is an unfavorable, false, and limiting eventuality. In other words, some consider mirroring to be beneficial whereas others consider it to be damaging. In parallel, I would point out that some patients find mirroring behaviors by the analyst to be comforting, whereas others find them to be patronizing and offensive. Neither reaction is a true or genuine one; both reactions are analyzable psychological configurations.

It goes without saying that Margaret Mahler's theories are explicitly theories of child development (Mahler et al. 1975). The theories, however, like the previous theories, are also applied to therapeutic ends. I cannot here detail the vicissitudes of child development as she understands them but will only make the analogy between her conceptions and those of the developmental theorists I have already mentioned. As I have done with the other theories, I will try to keep Mahler's theory at arm's length from what I call psychoanalytic theory proper. Mahler's early developmental stages, those of autism and symbiosis, differ from the primitive and chaotic infantile experiential world postulated by Klein, Lacan, and Kohut. To her, early infancy is radically different from adulthood only insofar as the child lives in its own world or in a blissful psychological union with the parent. That world, according to Mahler, is neither chaotic nor terrifying. But it is an infantile world nevertheless and, she says, its persistence into adult life causes difficulty. To the extent that autistic and symbiotic modes interfere with adult functioning, such modes deserve to be superseded and, to a certain extent, analytic treatment aims to achieve this. Mahler's claim clearly places her theories of analytic change into the realm of developmental theory.

Fairness dictates that I clarify the fact that the followers of Mahler have never claimed that this is anything but an aspect of change. Typically they have the same concern as do other analysts, that is to say, they keep a major focus on repression and on the notion of the unconscious. But insofar as they drift toward developmental theories of change, they enter into my category of analytic heresy. That heresy, of course, is the notion of the patient as primitive or developmentally retarded—thereby requiring assistance in personal growth.

There is another angle to this that has not been mentioned in this chapter. The angle I have in mind is the intolerance of human variety that enters into every developmental theory of change. All behavior, in such a theory, is necessarily categorized as infantile or adult, as primitive or mature. In other words, all behavior can be categorized as pathological or as normal. I suggest, as I have already suggested many times before, that the analytic stance of neutrality may note that behavior is normative or not normative (or note it to be conventional or nonconventional), but it never equates this with pathology and health. Consideration of this matter makes it clear that life teaches us otherwise. For some people, normative behavior is the pathway to psychological suffering. For others, nonnormative behavior is the pathway to suffering. Contrariwise, life also teaches us that normative and nonnormative lives, for some, are happy lives.

Margaret Mahler's theory offers an instructive example of such unexpectedly judgmental conclusions. Again and again, I hear from students that patients are enmeshed or symbiotically involved with their parents, with their spouse, or with someone else. But surely, this is an ego-centric (or theory-centric) judgment that such students are making. What I call enmeshed behavior may well be called socially responsible behavior by someone else. All too often such statements are simple cultural biases, without actual pathological significance. Those who are enmeshed and symbiotically involved may be as happy as can be. Those who are highly individuated may be correspondingly unhappy. Individuation and enmeshment, therefore, are descriptive statements only and have nothing to do with mental health, nor do they have to do with happiness or suffering.

Donald Winnicott is a theorist widely admired for his imaginative analytic contributions. They were once characterized as a "poetic evocation of child development and maternal experiences in an individual language difficult to link with other approaches" (Dare 1976, p. 264). I wish again to find fault, on the grounds that all developmental theories interfere with analytic neutrality. Invariably, the analytic therapist is required to adopt some behavioral goal couched in the language of maturity.

Winnicott's developmental theory is somewhat different from those that have gone before. He postulates, as do most other developmental theorists, an early primitive stage that he, Winnicott, refers to as a period in which the infant has a weak or fragmentary ego. But the stage of ego weakness ends, for Winnicott, with the emergence, already in infancy, of the self. But this self is no longer described as weak, fragile, or as being in any way tarnished. In point of fact, this self is described as pristine and as having qualities of authenticity and wholesomeness. If one disregards for a moment Winnicott's preliminary stage of ego weakness, we discover a developmental theory that turns on its head the theories that I have criticized already.

Two examples will illustrate this. First, I will quote

Winnicott himself on an occasion when he refers to "the native honesty which so curiously starts in full bloom in the infant, and then unripens to a bud" (Winnicott 1942, p. 146). The second illustration is Winnicott's theory of the true self and of the false self. What we ordinarily see, according to the theory, is merely the false self. Within, and hidden by the false self, is the true self. One can recognize that to Winnicott, a healthy self is present from the beginning and that, through the exigencies of life, this true self is suppressed, repressed, and hidden, plastered over by a corrupt false self. The theories of Klein, Lacan, and Kohut have been turned upside down. With regard to Winnicott's reference to an early stage of ego weakness one must note that this seems to be a tip of the hat to conventional theorizing and plays no significant role in Winnicott's actual theorizing.

There is, I agree, something delicious about Winnicott's recognition of "the native honesty" of the infant, "which so curiously starts in full bloom in the infant, and then unripens." Generally we are charmed by an infant's trustfulness and directness, and by its innocence and naiveté. But we must not mistake the charm of an infant for a discovery of its true nature or for a desirable or achievable analytic goal. For an adult to achieve a certain innocence might well be an attractive eventuality but it is certainly not a goal that is to be legislated, hoped for, or declared to represent health. That full bloom of manifest honesty is what some people do before or after analysis. They have it (or do not have it) for a host of conscious and unconscious reasons.

In a theory such as Winnicott has put forward, other truths about children—unpalatable truths—have been conveniently overlooked. Children are not only pure and honest, but are also brutal and sadistic. Each of us can remember the cruelty of our classmates toward children who were different, vulnerable, or plain. Such cruelties are unnerving to recall, even if one did not personally indulge in them—hence our preferred amnesia for such remembrances. I, personally, have no belief that there is value in the emergence of some idealized inner child. All of this may be even more disconcerting when one takes note of the close resemblance between the ostensibly pristine true self or inner child, and the "inner child" hypothesis of Alice Miller (1983), and so enthusiastically embraced by the North American recovery movement.

Against this theoretical corpus, I recount my usual case. I claim that psychoanalysis per se is not about development but, rather, is about the eternal state of moral dilemma in which desirous and guilty persons, young and old, find themselves. To advocate a return to the bloom of early infancy or the authenticity of a true self is, first, the pursuit of an illusion and, second, a behavioral goal unbecoming to analytic theorists and practitioners.

Winnicott is not alone in what, at first, seems like developmental theory gone mad—or, at least, turned upon its head. Marxist theories of psychoanalysis hold to a very similar formulation. Among such Marxist theorists I include Wilhelm Reich, Erich Fromm, Jürgen Habermas, Theodore Adorno, and other adherents of the Frankfurt School. To call these contributors Marxists is, perhaps, too strong. But all are certainly informed and influenced by Marxist thinking. Kinder, perhaps, to place them alongside Jean-Jacques Rousseau. Like Rousseau and Marx, these theorists believe that man in a state of nature is fine and good, and that the ills of man are due to corrupt social environments. Their analytic goals are often explicitly emancipatory.

I wish not to dismiss these theorists too lightly since, apart from Wilhelm Reich (and his bizarre pursuit of the liberating orgasm), they are highly sophisticated contributors. They are acutely aware of repression and the unconscious, but unfortunately have forgotten that Pandora's box—the unconscious—contains the good, the evil, and the mediocre alike. Be that as it may, their pursuit of an elusive good life makes their theories ultimately unacceptable as analytic theories of change.

Theories such as these, all of which assume an innate developmental schedule, would be perfectly suitable were they purely biological. As such, they would refer to developmental deviation only in those instances when the person under consideration is not biologically intact. To postulate a preprogrammed schedule of normal psychological development is quite another matter. All of us know, for example, about oral, anal, phallic, and oedipal forms of eroticism. But knowing this does not commit us to the sure belief that these modes of eroticism are hard-wired into the human species, that they ought to emerge in a particular sequence, or that these are the only available erotic modes. All of us are aware, of course, of a vast array of somatic arousal patterns, including many well-known perversions and vasovagal manifestations. Theories of developmental inevitability suffer from the same intellectual impoverishment as does the historicism that informs theories such as Marxism, that is to say, theories that anticipate an inevitable historical progression. None of the things that matter about a person are predictable. If I see an old friend after 30 years I may well be able to anticipate his laugh, his gestures, and his postures. However, it is highly unlikely that I will be able to predict whether he has married or divorced, whether he is sexually orthodox or unorthodox, what education and career he has pursued, or whether he has become a murderer, a saint, or an artist.

13

Preferred Metaphors
of Change

It is the greatest good for a human being to have discussions every day about virtue and other things you hear me talking about, examining myself and others, and that the unexamined life is not worth living for a human being.

Socrates

A proposal that claims that "the unexamined life is not worth living for a human being," is one that tempts analytic theorist and practitioner alike. Just the same, it is a temptation that is to be resisted. Although our lives as analytic practitioners are devoted to this proposition, and analytically attractive though it may be, Socrates' conclusion cannot be wholeheartedly embraced. It is, of course, true that we devote our professional energies to helping people to examine their lives, that is to say, to developing insight. At the very same time we are wary of absolute belief systems. Ultimately, we are only willing to say that Socrates is correct insofar as self-examination is highly important for some people but, as analytic theorists, we would also say that for many other people self-examination is uninteresting or is judged to be unimportant. Indeed, some would say that self-examination, at best, is self-indulgent and, at worst, disturbing or destructive.

It may well be that insight is the route to change for many people. Certainly it must be an important, if not the sole, vehicle of change during analytic treatment. The preceding chapters have been heavily biased toward an understanding of analytic treatment as an occasion of self-examination and self-knowledge. It must, however, be kept in mind that people change in many ways. I have already mentioned that there are some who believe that self-examination is disturbing and destructive and, for them, change for the better is to be accomplished by avoidance of the negative and the pursuit of the positive. Those of us with psychoanalytic biases typically react with distaste to such preferences but, in all fairness, we can only acknowledge that preferences vary and that only at our own analytic peril do we judge.

Nevertheless we do judge and, with regard to what is to count as analytic change, we are entitled to judge. Freud (1914a) once complained that he was the inventor or discoverer of psychoanalysis and that those who called themselves psychoanalysts had to adhere to its fundamental tenets. With regard to transference and resistance he stated that "anyone who takes up other sides of the problem while avoiding these two hypotheses will hardly escape a charge of misappropriation of property by attempted impersonation, if he persists in calling himself a psycho-analyst" (p. 16). But despite Freud's territorial claim, psychoanalytic theorists and practitioners alike seem all too often to have lost sight of its particular sphere of interest.

By now some readers may have become fed up with what has become a series of dissatisfied commentaries on well-known and well-respected analytic contributors. Many will have wondered what all the intellectual fuss is about and whether this is merely the scholastic quibbling of an enthusiast or an ideologue. But being fed up, I fear, is the required fate of those who deal with the psychoanalytic zealot—and zealots there are aplenty.

The reason for all the intellectual concern is that analytic theory is forever at risk of becoming reductionistically one sided. The true analytic theorist is never willing to acknowledge definitive truths about human affairs, that is to say, that there is a proper, a healthier, or a better way of life. She therefore views with skepticism all theories that claim to know the better way. She, the analytic theorist, is zealous on this score because she knows that any definition of what is better or healthier condemns the analyst to a form of behaviorism, that is to say, to an advocacy of particular behaviors. Although in principle she is skeptical and ironic about these matters, it must be acknowledged that in her practice the analytic therapist may well be cautiously liberal. Nevertheless, she shrinks from behavioristic intent on the grounds that, no matter how politely it is couched, any behavioral advocacy violates her determined stance of neutrality. To maintain that extraordinary and difficult neutral stance, she relies heavily on the support she receives from great critics and philosophers.

> In the end [Epicurus] proposes to seek not pleasure in its usual sense, but *ataraxia*—tranquillity, equanimity, repose of mind; all of which trembles on the verge of Zeno's "apathy." [Durant 1953, p. 77]

> The appeal of the text, of the work of art or music is, radically, *disinterested* . . . The dividends of the aesthetic are, precisely, those of *"disinterest,"* of a rebuke to opportunity. [Steiner 1989, p. 27]

The zealous analytic theorist therefore rules that the developmental theories of analytic change are out of order. Although she knows and shares in the public attitudes toward what is called mature behavior, she simultaneously maintains that—privately, theoretically, and analytically— she is uneasy about that attitude, even as she all too often discovers it in herself. As an analyst, she is convinced that she must shy away from advocacy of any institutionalization of, or predetermined certainty about, what constitutes health or maturity.

To avoid the problem of behavioral advocacy I have, in this book, used a very general term when I have referred to the elements of analytic change. The term I have chosen is *psychological shifts*. I derived that term from an earlier idea to which I have previously referred. This is the notion of analytic regression. This conceptualization is charmingly and convincingly described in Menninger and Holzman's (1973) book in a chapter devoted to that topic. What they have in mind is that the patient, when he begins treatment, is frozen into particular psychological configurations and that, in the analytic situation, these frozen positions melt. This metaphor certainly describes or illuminates what happens in most analytic psychotherapies. Patients, one realizes, begin to "emit" or "play with" or "experiment with" novel and previously nonexistent modes of thought and modes of being. Menninger and Holzman do not use the metaphors of "freezing," "melting," "diligent praxis," "playing around," "sealed off," or "emit," as I have. Instead they have chosen the metaphor of regression. There are historical reasons for their choice of metaphor but, had they opted to do so, they could have used any or all of my metaphors. Or they could have opted for any of a multitude of other metaphors. For example, they could have experimented with metaphors such as "lovemaking," "fighting," "fencing," "releasing," "letting go," "dancing," or "cleaning out cobwebs." The problem with the metaphors of "development" and of "regression" is that they are, first, too limited to capture the kaleidoscopic possibilities in change and, second, they are typically concretized and literalized so that they are viewed as a "real" or "nothing but" explanation.

The choice of regression as the metaphor of change is to choose a metaphor used by Freud in Chapter 7 of *The Interpretation of Dreams*. There Freud used a model of the mind that resembled an optical instrument in which light (or energy) can flow in one or another direction. If the flow of energy is reversed, Freud suggested, this could be referred to as a regressive direction of flow. And, if the apparatus is blocked from discharging its energetic flow, the direction of flow is necessarily reversed and regressive. This, Menninger and Holzman postulate, is what happens in the psychoanalytic situation. The frustration produced by the analyst's silence, and the analytic situation's relative sensory deprivation, lead to a regressive shift in the patient's behavior. In that regressive mode, novel or forgotten types of behavior tentatively make an appearance; in the later progressive reintegration period of the analysis, more enduring synthetic modes can become established.

This is a plausible theory (albeit, a minor theory) of change and, to its credit, it requires no assumption of particular preferred behaviors that are considered to be evidence of health. The theory suggests only that change takes place—without any advocacy of specified goals.

But this theory has its problems. First, the theory, by using the word *regression,* has an implication of negativity that leaves me a bit uneasy. Besides, the psychological shifts that one sees in analytic treatment could just as well be called progressive. One could then ask who it is that makes the ruling as to whether a novel idea or behavior is regressive or progressive. Certainly not the neutral analytic therapist. She characteristically shrinks from such judgments.

A second problem with the regression metaphor is that it, too, has become reified and institutionalized. Each of the metaphors that I used earlier suggests its own subtleties, angles, and perspectives on behavior that other metaphors fail to reveal. The phrase *psychological shifts* seems preferable because it is able to encompass a myriad of metaphors, each of which, from time to time, may further enlighten us with regard to what is going on. Freud thought it necessary to repeatedly remind his readers that his spatial model in *The Interpretation of Dreams* was a "fiction of a primitive psychical contraption" (Freud 1900, pp. 511, 533, 536, 564–568, 570–574, 599, 608 ff., 618. Quoted by Daniel Ornston 1985) and not to be understood as an anatomy of the mind. Note that "contraption" is a more accurate translation than is the "apparatus" rendition that has been bequeathed to us by Strachey, and that the differing translations make all the difference in the world. Regression, as an essential ingredient of that contraption model, must therefore be treated as just another nonprecious metaphor.

But the regression metaphor was certainly helpful to me. It suggested that stereotyped character behaviors can be unlocked, freed up, and dissolved into an abundance of previously unknown thoughts, feelings, and behaviors. Note here that, in attempting to convey to the reader how the notion of regression helped me, I have no recourse but to introduce more metaphors. And when one begins to note metaphors in this way, more metaphors spring from the page: "note," "convey," "help," "introduce," "spring"—and so on. Eventually I settled for yet another metaphor, the metaphor of "'psychological shifts."

Because of its generality, I will stick to the metaphor of psychological shifts and rely on it to be an encompassing term for many other ways of referring to psychological or analytic change. All of the metaphors to which I referred earlier are plausible ones and, although they were put forward playfully and provocatively, are also to count as serious contenders for explanatory power. Dancing, playing, fencing, love-making, flirting, working, melting, fragmenting, and exploding are all terms that enlighten us with regard to analytic change and they do so with not insignificant power. In fact, they seriously illuminate our understanding of how psychological shifts take place.

I would also remind the reader of another commonly used metaphor that is used to refer to psychological change. The term I have in mind is "creativity." It suggests that, in changing, the patient becomes, in a way, artistic. It is surely as valuable an idea as is the idea that the patient "falls apart" in the analytic situation. Both metaphors, and many others, are of value to us.

Curiously, the metaphor for change that I reject is probably the one that is currently most popular. It is, of course, the metaphor of developmental change—probably lambasted by me too often already.

Yet another metaphor that deserves attention is the one emphasized by Brenner (1976). In his section on change,

Brenner is intent on pointing out that defenses never disappear and that the aim of eliminating defenses is futile. Instead, he argues, one hopes for "shifts" in defenses. It is quite possible that my use of the word *shifts* was originally derived from Brenner. Its very generality is what makes it such a worthwhile theoretical term. Brenner's use of the word *defenses* is also very general. As he points out, any psychological event—thought, feeling, or behavior—can be used for defensive purposes. By using terms as broad as *defense* and *shifts,* Brenner has opted to use the same linguistic and theoretical tactics as have I.

One way or another, all such shifts are related to yet another metaphor, on this occasion the metaphor of the "superego." All defensive aspects of behavior are invoked on moral or moralistic grounds. "Do not do this" and "do not do that," says the superego, because it is wrong, or because it symbolically stands for one impropriety or another.

Any one of us is a certain kind of person because, all things considered, being that kind of person seems to us to be the only possible compromise considering the conscious and unconscious morality and justice of our personal life situation. Or, at least, so we decide when we submit ourselves to our value-assigning and value-enforcing superego. What we see in such a circumstance is that the patient, in his actions, attempts to do his worst. Any psychological shift or change necessarily is a shift in the balance of moral forces. A man who eternally defeats himself and who begins to do this less frequently, has made a moral shift. Earlier, self-punitive behavior of a particular intensity was required; later, that required intensity was decreased. Obviously a lessened moral judgment upon himself has occurred. All decreased suffering, according to analytic theory and the analytic theory of change, is due to superego amelioration. This position on analytic change is by no means new and has been extensively examined by Bibring many years ago (Bibring 1937). Bloom and Rosenberg (1990) make the same point this way:

> The Freudian superego just about *is* . . . Yahweh, and causes our unconscious sense of guilt, a "guilt" that is

neither remorse nor the consciousness of wrongdoing. Rather, Freudian guilt is a Yahwistic irony: it comes from the unfulfilled wish to murder our father the creator, Yahweh. We do not know this guilt as emotion; we know it as depression, anxiety, the failure of desire, the castration complex, as all of negativity taken together. [p. 305]

To Freud and to Shakespeare, character is one's fate and one's destiny and we are eternally subject to it. The analytic question is whether or not the superego (God, the law, the demand system) can relent a bit and thereby unleash a storm of changes—each tiny, but each impish and yet, at the very same time, profound. Impishness itself may be our rebellious squelching of ourselves when we are self-injurious fools or, in other words, a correction of our own character when we are self-defeating.

Every belief, every idea, and every dream are reflections of character. A change in any single element of mental functioning changes everything. Beliefs, for example, can only be held in the context of other beliefs. If I postulate a patient who reports that he has an intrusive, bullying mother and a kind, gentle father, I can only do so if I acknowledge that the beliefs—the narratives—about the parents exist in a context. In fact, the two parental images exist in the context of one another. Let us say that the analyst raises with the patient the question of why the father did not protect him from his aggressive and intrusive mother. If the patient takes this question seriously, he will find himself to be revising his laudatory ideas about his father. But one must remember that a kind father exists only in a context of ideas and beliefs about fathers in general, about mothers in general, and about his specific father and mother. Kind and gentle fathers, in general, must now be redefined. Such new ideas, either dramatically or subtly, will change, that is to say, *analytically* change, the whole context—the whole universe of discourse, the whole characterological balance—of the patient in question.

His intrusive mother, for example, will take on a new

coloration. She may now be understood to have a problematic husband. Just as the patient wonders why the father did
not intervene on his behalf, so the patient's mother can now
be seen as having to put up with a passive husband who
neglected his parental duties. The patient may, in such
circumstances, suspect that the mother was angry at her
husband's neglectfulness and that her ostensible brutality
was an element in a difficult marriage. A case of mine in
which I made a single remark about the father's failure to
protect the patient from the nastiness of his mother led to an
obvious and dramatic change in his perception of his mother.
Suddenly, the patient began to see his mother as being on the
brink of collapse, after a lifetime of seeing her exclusively as
a "bitch." She had, he realized, sacrificed all hope of a
personal career in order to raise her family and to cater to her
husband's passivity. Rather than being brutal, the mother
was, over a period of a few months, transformed into a fragile
victim.

I would not want the reader to believe that, in a sche-
matic example like the one I have just cited, the truth has
been discovered. The lesson is only that change always is a
redescription of something in a context, that is to say, when
one thing changes, everything changes. We, the analysts,
don't explain the real meaning of things any more than
literary critics explain the real meaning of texts. Nor do we
evaluate the worth of particular meaning interpretations
preferred (or adopted) by the patient. Instead, in analogy with
literary criticism—which also does not aim to evaluate the
texts that it examines—the goal is to contextualize, compare,
and, especially, to study the language games that are being
used by the patient, preferentially, dogmatically, and ideo-
logically.

Like a piece of art, we hope that our analytic work will be
comprehensible and yet be forever elusive; that its outcome
will be simple yet capable of supporting a rich and various
array of interpretations—even as it disavows particular interpretive positions. There will be plenty of food for thought to
keep the patient chewing and digesting—if he wants to—for
many a year to come.

Such changes are, of course, redescriptions. When we redescribe with a patient the meaning of what he says, we are not
necessarily granted a welcome reception. People do not want
to be redescribed and much prefer to be accepted as they are.
All of us want to be taken at face value. This may be less true
of our patients than it is in the general population since, by
and large, our patients come to us with the conscious idea
that they wish us to redescribe them. A word of caution is
warranted on this score. Those who pursue redescription, as
it turns out, may also be notoriously refractory to redescription. How, I might ask, does one redescribe the wish-
to-be-redescribed? If we naively redescribe such a man, are
we, perhaps, not redescribing him at all and simply con-
firming him in his conviction that he is the-man-who-
likes-to-be-redescribed? Must we, and can we, point out to
him that, after all, like all persons, he does not like to be
redescribed?

Shifts in psychological functioning do not take place in a
vacuum. The atmosphere of the analytic situation and the
behavior of the analytic therapist are vital ingredients in such
transformative events. The situation in which the patient
finds himself is designed to permit reflection. He is not
interrupted by the analyst nor is he enjoined to perform any
particular task. Indeed, the analytic therapist rarely speaks.
And certainly she never indulges in chitchat. When she does
speak, she interprets to the patient how he interprets the
world. Her particular angle on her interpretations is to point
out to her patient how he deceives himself, that is to say, how
he represses, avoids, and retreats from wonderfully disturbing inner worlds that he therefore knows little about. Further
detailed remarks about the analytic situation are to be found
in earlier chapters of this book. Suffice it to say here that any
new information that the patient obtains about himself
from the analyst leads to a modified view of himself. To view
oneself differently is a major event. For example, he who
treats himself as a criminal is very different from the man
who treats himself as the-man-who-treats-himself-as-a-

criminal. Such a change, although it takes place only incre-
mentally, is a profound change.

Upon reading *King Lear* or *As You Like It* one is struck by
the analytic perspicacity of Shakespeare's fools. Like the
analyst, they catch at and illuminate the self-deceptions that
they discover here, there, and everywhere.

> Like all Shakespeare's fools, Touchstone is a corrupter of
> words. Language is one of his main preoccupations, and he
> likes to bewilder simple souls like Corin by demonstrating
> the superiority of words over facts. What matters to him is
> the denial of the single, objective nature of reality. [Corin]
> and the fool simply represent antithetical ways of looking
> at the world. Neither perspective is advanced as a model.
> Corin's simplicity is obvious and he is thereby limited, but
> then so is Touchstone in his willful and perpetually com-
> plicated verbal kingdom. [Barton 1974, p. 367]

Such linguistic conundrums always incline us to seek
simpler, more explanatory solutions. For example, at times of
analytic ending we, the analysts, are tempted to comprehend
that ending by way of a model such as grief or mourning. Our
patients must, we say, mourn the passing of analysis and the
loss of their analyst. True enough. But the linguistic counsel
of Shakespeare's fools also awakens us to the fact that we
must give equal billing to other languages—languages that
have equivalent power to enlighten us and our patient about
ending and termination. Is not ending merely another of the
many *punctuations* that characterize a life? And is it also not
death, release, satiety, emptiness, a *sunset,* an *eclipse,* the
last *narrative* of the analysis, and (so that we do not forget the
self-deceiving intent of all persons) yet another game of
smoke and mirrors?

Our interpretations have had as their topic the patient's
preferred belief preoccupations, that is to say, psychological
constellations by way of which patients comfort and deceive
themselves. In our work we are inclined to suggest that such

self-deceiving solutions may cause more trouble than they are worth. Our skepticism about solutions of any kind leaves open the possibility that it may well be that life does not have a solution and, instead, has the quality of a puzzle. Despite all of the analyst's fussy worrying about privileging particular behaviors or beliefs, she cannot help thinking that there is something valuable in recognizing that life is a puzzle and a mystery.

A neighbor of mine mentioned to a group of friends that her 10-year-old son had stolen money from her purse and from her husband's wallet. She explained that they had decided on a number of punishments and restrictions that they intended to apply very consistently. They also intended to explain and emphasize to their son that such stealing was bad because they wanted him to be absolutely clear about what was right and what was wrong.

The next day my neighbor spoke again of these events but did so without other people present. This time she explicitly acknowledged that I was a psychiatrist. "What did you think yesterday when I told what has happened with my son?" My initial response was to say something noncommittal about the difficulties of child-rearing and of how hard it was to know just what one should do in such circumstances. But my neighbor persisted in asking for my opinion until I responded more in accord with what I really thought:

> "To tell you the truth, psychiatrists think a bit differently about such things. First of all I would say that you should be prepared for the possibility that your conscientious measures may not succeed. Life, after all, seems repeatedly to resolve into a muddle. In addition, I'm not as sure as you are that your son does not know what is right and what is wrong. What if, for example, he is feeling guilty about something, misbehaved so that he would get caught and punished, and you have cooperated with him by way of informing him so clearly that he is bad. Not that certain sanctions are not warranted. It's just that it might be of interest to point out to him that he knows perfectly well that his behavior is bad and to emphasize that this situation is not a simple matter of what is right and what is

wrong. Instead, the important thing may be that his stealing behavior is a puzzle."

The analytic therapist resonates with such a story by agreeing that, in analytic work as well, we are eternally turning things into puzzles. Does this metaphor about change enlighten us? If a patient comes to see life as a puzzle, is he a better person for it?

Although analytic therapists dread the idea that their therapeutic effects are due to suggestion, the idea must not be shrunk from. There is no doubt that some patients have what is called a transference cure. The magical linking up of himself with the wonderful analyst—the shaman-priest—becomes an enactment of one of the patient's preferred psychological postures. To apply a word used by Nietzsche, some patients use the analyst as a self-curative "intoxication." To a certain extent this must be true in all therapies, including all analytic therapies. Although self psychologists give the opposite counsel, I suggest that the analytic therapists should analyze idealizing transferences with the same quiet determination, and with the same resolute irony, as she analyzes anything else. But the fact that, to a certain extent, the patient inevitably has a transference cure is acceptable, even if not completely satisfying to the analytic zealot.

The transference cure is the method adopted by an Indian guru who was once described to me. Devotees, I was told, are expected to completely subject their lives to him and to unquestioningly obey his every command. If the guru asks it, the devotee explained to me, a follower is expected to leap to his death, leave behind his family, or end his career, and to do so without thought and without question. The guru is to be submitted to in this way because, in his spiritual life, he has achieved an exalted status that warrants such unquestioning obedience. One can see that the guru is conceived by his followers in an idealized image and, contrapuntally, his followers are understood to occupy a humble status, far beneath his. The followers discover contentment in this situation, a contentment analogous to what we call a transference cure.

In the Western world it is less common to explicitly seek such humble positions vis-à-vis an idealized figure such as a guru, although, in a far less explicit way, we too are prepared to seek and create hero figures. Analytic theorists and practitioners recognize the ubiquity of such idealizations, and have great interest in permitting—but not encouraging—the appearance of such idealizations in the analytic situation. However, analytic therapists do not (intentionally) promote or perpetrate such situations, and usually submit them to analytic scrutiny just as they submit to analytic scrutiny dreams, symptoms, and character style. It is doubtful that the improvement rate of our patients is any less than is the improvement rate of devotees of an Indian guru. Nor is it likely that our patients fare less well than do those of our colleagues who leave idealizing transferences unanalyzed.

The explicit promotion of a situation in which one party to the analytic enterprise is granted higher status than the other is, in the West, an uncomfortably distasteful circumstance. To us, this smacks of the improper, and is a neglect of the analytic goal.

Related to this are parallel idealizations of nature, political positions, ideologies, health propositions, and the like. For example, as I write these words, I find myself thrilled, after a bitter Canadian winter, by the excitement of an urgently anticipated spring. It is no surprise that we glory in such days and it is also no surprise that, today, nature is cast in the image of a special good. Today, many might be inclined to speak of "back to nature" as an ideal state to be longed for and idealized, and, given the proper circumstance, any of us may be intoxicated by such philosophical musings. We might even find ourselves voicing wistful or ideological thoughts on behalf of Rousseau's back-to-nature theme.

When in the sway of modern development and of progress we are just as liable to do the opposite, that is to say, we may blindly exploit that same natural world that we ourselves have only recently idealized. Psychoanalysis, its practitioners, and, sometimes, analysands want only to study such positions, to ponder them, and to contemplate counterpositions.

Identification with the analytic therapist is an inevitable consequence of the intense involvement between the analyst and her patient. On every occasion upon which the analyst speaks, the patient can do nothing with her words unless he identifies with her. He must, if he wants to grasp her view of him, become her. This he may do momentarily or eternally or, perhaps more accurately, he always identifies with her momentarily *and* eternally. But that is not all. He may also ward off, deny, and forget his identification with his analyst, just as do all people with all identifications.

Identification is a funny business. In a certain sense, every action, thought, or emotion is enacted in identification with someone else. As I sit here and write I identify with a thousand writers, a thousand teachers, and a thousand fathers. And, microcosmically, I identify with specific writers, teachers, and fathers—not to speak of a grandmother and an aunt—memories of whom suddenly press to be acknowledged. An enormous psychological tale about me could be constructed from the record of such identifications, not to speak of the tales that this record resolutely does *not* tell about me.

It must be remembered that when a patient identifies with his analyst, that identification is an interpretation of his analyst. That funny business—identification—is one of the most typical of human acts and, like any artistic performance, or any act of artistic criticism, is an interpretative act. Every such identificatory interpretation is a reinvention by the patient of who he is. Such reinventions are fundamental elements of change and can add complexity, simplify, reverse, or disguise who he is. Like a new performance of *Hamlet* or like an operatic version of a play, identifications create new meanings and new worlds of personal existence. Its centrality could lead us to a reinterpretation of my designation of psychoanalysis as the "ironic science." Instead it could—perhaps should—be called the "interpretive science."

In identifying with the analyst, the patient does what Shakespearean characters do so brilliantly. He, like Hamlet and Lady Macbeth, begins to talk to himself. He reflects and observes and interprets. What he interprets and how he interprets, is both an aping of his own analyst and a multi-determined resolve *not* to interpret as did his analyst. She, in turn, interprets her patient's way of interpreting the world and, in true Shakespearean fashion, the patient begins to interpret his own way of interpreting the world.

> Chaucer, rather than Marlowe or even the English Bible, was Shakespeare's central precursor in having given the dramatist the crucial hint that led to the greatest of his originalities: *the representation of change by showing people pondering their own speeches and being altered through that consideration.* We find this mode of representation commonplace and even natural, but it does not exist in Homer or in the Bible, in Euripides or in Dante [Bloom 1987, p. 54, my italics]

> This is Shakespeare's astonishing originality, founded upon the representation of impending change, *a change to be worked within Lear by his own listening to, and reflecting upon, what he himself speaks aloud in his increasing fury.* He goes into the storm scene on the heath still screaming in anger, goes mad with that anger, and comes out of the storm with crucial change deeply in process within him, full of paternal love for the fool and concern for the supposed madman, Edgar impersonating Poor Tom. Lear's constant changes from there until the terrible end remain the most remarkable representation of a human transformation anywhere in imaginative literature. [p. 71, my italics]

I will leave it to the reader to read from the soliloquy of Molly Bloom in Joyce's *Ulysses* for another literary rendition of change by way of self-reflection. Her reflectiveness is the very change that we seek to understand and to emulate, but which, for psychoanalytic theory, has no implication of maturity or health. Words like wisdom, or ironic wistfullness might do just as well.

Curiously, self-reflection is both the method and the goal of psychoanalysis. Ironically, it comes to pass that, by way of reflectiveness, we become more reflective. This is the peculiar, profound, and modest cure that we can offer to our patients.

Ludwig Wittgenstein explicitly compares his philosophical method to psychoanalysis and calls it a "therapy." What he has in mind is that philosophical problems, like all psychological problems, are due to linguistic conundrums—conundrums that are, in principle, resolvable, although resolvable only by way of a great effort of will.

> All that philosophy can do is destroy idols. And that means not making any new idols—say out of "the absence of idols." [Wittgenstein quoted by Suter, 1989, p. 5]

> [The task of philosophical work] is to remove particular misunderstandings; not to produce a real understanding for the first time. [Wittgenstein 1974, p. 115]

> [Wittgenstein] likes to compare his way of doing philosophy with therapy and talks of it "as in certain ways like psychoanalysis." [Suter 1989, p. 12]

Most impressive to me is that Wittgenstein recognizes the crucial role of motives, a recognition that is not characteristic of most nonanalytic thinkers. Indeed, it is a recognition from which we analytic thinkers, all too often, are liable to lapse. He does not, however, suggest that it might be worthwhile to discover what the motive for our befuddlement might be. The solution of philosophical problems, he says, takes place

> by looking into the workings of our language, and that in such a way as to make us recognize those workings: *in despite of* an urge to misunderstand them. [Wittgenstein 1958, p. 47ᵉ]

> What makes a subject hard to understand—if it's something significant and important—is not that before you can understand it you need to be specially trained in abstruse matters, but the contrast between understanding the subject and what most people *want* to see. Because of this the

very things which are most obvious may become the
hardest of all to understand. What has to be overcome is a
difficulty having to do with the will, rather than the intel-
lect. [Wittgenstein 1931, p. 17]

In other words, Wittgenstein has recognized the phenomenon of resistance. We must, he says, "persuade" people to
rethink what they have always taken for granted. I use
scare-quotes around the word persuade because it is liable to
make analytic thinkers uncomfortable. Yet persuasion is
very close to what we do. Typically we are liable to say that
change by way of suggestion (*suggestion* is the word we use
more often than persuasion) is not analytic change. I believe
that it is better not to get too precious about these matters.
Analytic change is a product of many things including increased self-reflection, modifications of problematic logical
patterns, the recognition of life as a puzzle, identifications
with the analyst, and linguistic shifts. Probably, despite the
uneasiness that I have about development as a model for
analytic change—especially when proposed to be the essence
of analytic transformation—I should concede a mutative
function to psychological development. But, for the reasons
that I have explicated in the previous chapter, I retain an
uneasiness on this point. Contrariwise, I nominate persuasion and suggestion to a more prominent role in change than
is usually conceded. Resistance is very real and does not yield
easily.
       Resistance is problematic in other ways as well. The
word itself—*resistance*—invites the analyst to counterresist
in a manner that has the quality of struggle. Although the
analyst's interventions may, indeed, be a heavy labor,
working with the resistance is just as often a task that is
playful, ironic, or matter-of-fact.

And so our patient comes to his analytic ending. As someone
said, he is now financially poorer but psychologically better,
or, perhaps, just psychologically different. He is at least
different. Perhaps sadder but wiser? To accomplish this he
must have done what literary and biblical critics nowadays
ask us to do:

to work back through three stages of varnish, plastered on by the rabbis, the Christian prelates, and the scholars . . . you need to clear away three sealings-off, three very formidable layers of redaction. But if you will do the work . . . you will give birth to your own father. Yahweh and Superego are after all versions of yourself, even if the authorities have taught you to believe otherwise . . . Yahweh and Freud's Superego are grand characters, as Lear is a grand character. [Bloom and Rosenberg 1990, p. 306]

References

Adorno, T. W. (1973). *Negative Dialectics*, trans. E. B. Ashton. New York: Seabury, 1966.

Atwood, M. (1979). *Life Before Man*. Toronto: Seal Books, McClelland-Bantam.

Barrett, B. (1984). *Psychic Reality and Psychoanalytic Knowing*. Hillsdale, NJ: Analytic Press.

Barton, A. (1974). Introduction to *As You Like It*. In *The Riverside Shakespeare*. Boston: Houghton Mifflin.

Bibring, E. (1937). On the theory of the results of psychoanalysis. *International Journal of Psycho-Analysis* 18:170–189.

Bloom, H. (1987). *Ruin the Sacred Truths*. Cambridge: Harvard University Press.

Bloom, H., and Rosenberg, D. (1990). *The Book of J*. New York: Grove Weidenfeld.

Bowie, M. (1991). *Lacan*. Glasgow: Fontana Press.

Bowlby, J. (1960). Grief and mourning in infancy and early childhood. *Psychoanalytic Study of the Child* 15:9. New York: International Universities Press.

_____ (1961). Notes on Max Schur's Comments on Grief and Mourning in Infancy and Early Childhood. *Psychoanalytic Study of the Child* 16:206. New York: International Universities Press.

_____ (1969–1980). *Attachment and Loss*, 3 vols. New York: Basic Books.

Brenner, C. (1976). *Psychoanalytic Technique and Psychic Conflict*. New York: International Universities Press.

_____ (1982). *The Mind in Conflict*. New York: International Universities Press.

Bynum, C. W. (1992). *Fragmentation and Redemption: Essays on Gender and the Human Body in Medieval Religion*. New York: Zone Press.

Cayley, D. (1992). *Ivan Illich in Conversation*. Toronto: House of Anansi Press.

Dare, C. (1976). Psychoanalytic theories. In *Child Psychiatry: Modern Approaches*, ed. M. Rutter and L. Hersov. Oxford: Blackwell.

Dennett, D. (1981). *Brainstorms*. Cambridge: MIT Press.

Dilthey, W. (1894). Ideen über eine Beschreibende und Zergliedernde Psychologies. In *Wilhelm Dilthey's Gesammelte Schriften*, vol. 5; pp. 139–240. Leipzig-Berlin: Teubner, 1921–1934.

Durant, W. (1953). *The Story of Philosophy*. New York: Simon and Shuster.

Eissler, K. (1953). The effect of the structure of the ego on psychoanalytic technique. *Journal of the American Psychoanalytic Association* 1:104–143.

Erikson, E. H. (1954). The dream specimen of psychoanalysis. *Journal of the American Psychoanalytic Association* 2:5–56.

_____ (1963). *Childhood and Society*. New York: Norton.

Ferenczi, S. (1929). *Final Contributions to the Problems and Methods of Psycho-analysis*. London: Hogarth, 1955.

Flaubert, G. (1857). *Madame Bovary*. New York: Rinehart, 1955.

Freud, A. (1960). Discussion of Dr. John Bowlby's paper. *Psychoanalytic Study of the Child* 15:53. New York: International Universities Press.

_____ (1981). Psychoanalytic psychology of normal development. In _The Writings of Anna Freud,_ vol. 8. New York: International Universities Press.

Freud, S. (1894). The neuropsychoses of defense. _Standard Edition_ 3.

_____ (1893–1895). Studies in hysteria. _Standard Edition_ 2.

_____ (1900). The interpretation of dreams. _Standard Edition_ 4 and 5.

_____ (1911). Letter to L. Binswanger May 28. In _Ludwig Binswanger, Sigmund Freud: Reminiscences of a Friendship,_ trans. N. Guterman, pp. 32–33. New York: Grune and Stratton, 1957.

_____ (1913). On beginning the treatment. _Standard Edition_ 12.

_____ (1914a). On the history of the psychoanalytic movement. _Standard Edition_ 14.

_____ (1914b). On narcissism. _Standard Edition_ 14.

_____ (1915). On transference love. _Standard Edition_ 12.

_____ (1916–1917). Introductory lectures on psycho-analysis. _Standard Edition_ 15.

_____ (1919). Lines of advance in psychoanalytic therapy. _Standard Edition_ 17.

_____ (1925). An autobiographical study. _Standard Edition_ 20.

_____ (1930). Civilization and its discontents. _Standard Edition_ 21.

_____ (1933). New introductory lectures on psycho-analysis. _Standard Edition_ 22.

Frye, N. (1991). _The Double Vision._ Toronto: University of Toronto Press.

Geertz, C. (1973). _The Interpretation of Culture._ New York: Basic Books.

Gill, M. (1954). Psychoanalysis and exploratory psychotherapy. _Journal of the American Psychoanalytic Association_ 2:771.

Greenson, R. (1967). _The Technique and Practice of Psychoanalysis._ New York: International Universities Press.

Grünbaum, A. (1984). _The Foundations of Psychoanalysis:_

A Philosophical Critique. Berkeley: University of California Press.

Hartmann, H. (1927). Understanding and explanation. In *Essays in Ego Psychology,* pp. 369–403. New York: International Universities Press, 1964.

Heller, E. (1958). *The Ironic German.* New York: Paul P. Appel.

Hendin, H. (1982). Psychotherapy and suicide. In *Suicide in America,* ed. H. Hendin. New York: Norton.

Hiley, D., Bohman, J., and Shusterman, R. (1991). *The Interpretive Turn.* Ithaca, NY: Cornell University Press.

Husserl, E. (1929). *Cartesian Meditations,* trans. D. Cairns. The Hague: Nijhoff, 1960.

Jacobs, T. (1993). The inner experiences of the analyst: their contribution to the analytic process. *International Journal of Psycho-Analysis* 74:7–14.

Jamison, K. R. (1993). *Touched with Fire: Manic Depressive Illness and the Artistic Temperament.* New York: Guilford.

Kaufmann, W. (1980). *Discovering the Mind,* vol. 3. New York: McGraw-Hill.

Kernberg, O., Selzer, M. A., Koenigsberg, H. W., Carr, A. C., and Applebaum, A. H. (1989). *Psychodynamic Psychotherapy of Borderline Patients.* New York: Basic Books.

Klein, M. (1946). Notes on some schizoid mechanisms. *International Journal of Psycho-Analysis* 27:99.

Klerman, G. (1984). *Interpersonal Therapy of Depression.* New York: Basic Books.

Kohut, H. (1977). *The Restoration of the Self.* New York: International Universities Press.

——— (1984). *How Does Analysis Cure?* Chicago: University of Chicago Press.

Lacan, J. (1953–1954). *The Seminar of Jacques Lacan. Book I. Freud's Papers on Technique,* Chapter 7. New York: Norton, 1988.

——— (1954–1955). The dream of Irma's injection. In *The Seminar of Jacques Lacan. Book II,* Chapter 8. New York: Norton, 1988.

Lawrence, D. H. (1971). *Fantasia of the Unconscious* and

Psychoanalysis and the Unconscious. New York: Penguin.

Liberman, R. P., and Eckman, T. (1981). Behavior therapy vs. insight oriented therapy for repeated suicide attempters. *Archives of General Psychiatry* 38:1126–1130.

Linehan, M., Armstrong, H., Suarez, A., et al. (1991). Cognitive-behavioral treatment of chronically parasuicidal borderline patients. *Archives of General Psychiatry* 48:1060–1064.

Loewald, H. (1960). On the therapeutic action of psychoanalysis. *International Journal of Psycho-Analysis* 41:16–33.

Luborsky, L., and de Rubeis, R. J. (1984). The use of psychotherapy training manuals: a small revolution in psychotherapy research style. *Clinical Psychology Review* 4:5.

Luborsky, L., Singer, B., and Luborsky, L. (1975). Comparative studies of the psychotherapies. *Archives of General Psychiatry* 32:995.

Ludwig, A. M. (1994). *The Price of Greatness.* New York: Guilford.

Mahler, M., Pine, F., and Bergman, A. (1975). *The Psychological Birth of the Human Infant: Symbiosis and Individuation.* New York: Basic Books.

Mann, T. (1929). *Mario and the Magician.* In *Stories of Three Decades.* New York: Random House, 1936.

———— (1941). *The Transposed Heads.* New York: Vintage Books, 1959.

Meissner, W. (1986). *Psychotherapy and the Paranoid Process.* Northvale, NJ: Jason Aronson.

Menninger, K., and Holzman, P. (1973). *Theory of Psychoanalytic Technique.* New York: Basic Books.

Miller, A. (1983). *For Your Own Good: Hidden Cruelty in Child-Rearing and the Roots of Violence,* trans. H. Hannum and H. Hannum. New York: Farrar, Straus & Giroux.

Nahmias, J. (1990). Selection criteria in short term dynamic psychotherapy: I. Overview. *International Journal of Short Term Dynamic Psychotherapy* 5:167–183.

Nietzsche, F. (1873). *Untimely Meditations: Schopenhauer*

as Educator, trans. R. J. Hollingdale. New York: Cambridge University Press, 1983.

―― (1878). *Human, All Too Human*, 2 vols., trans. R. J. Hollingdale. New York: Cambridge University Press, 1986.

―― (1882). *The Gay Science*, trans. W. Kaufmann. New York: Random House, 1974.

―― (1885–1886). Beyond good and evil: prelude to a philosophy of the future. In *Basic Writings of Neitzsche*, trans. W. Kaufmann. New York: Modern Library, 1968.

―― (1888). The twilight of the idols. In *The Portable Nietzsche*, trans. W. Kaufmann, p. 521. New York: Viking Press, 1954.

Ornston, D. (1978). On projection: a study of Freud's usage. *Psychoanalytic Study of the Child* 33:117–166. New Haven, CT: Yale University Press.

―― (1985). Freud's conception is different from Strachey's. *Journal of the American Psychoanalytic Association* 33:379.

Powys, J. C. (1962). Preface to "Homer and the Aelther." In *Homer: A Collection of Critical Essays*, ed. G. Steiner, and R. Fagles. Englewood Cliffs, NJ: Prentice Hall.

Rapaport, D. (1959). The structure of psychoanalytic theory—a systemizing attempt. In *Psychological Issues* 6. New York: International Universities Press, 1960.

Reich, W. (1949). *Character Analysis*. New York: Farrar, Straus & Giroux.

Reik, T. (1948). *Listening with the Third Ear*. New York: Farrar, Straus & Giroux.

Rieff, P. (1961). *Freud: The Mind of the Moralist*. New York: Harper and Row.

―― (1966). *The Triumph of the Therapeutic, The Uses of Faith After Freud*. New York: Harper and Row.

Robertson, J. M. (1922). *Voltaire*. London: Watts and Co.

Rorty, R. (1989). *Contingency, Irony and Solidarity*. New York: Cambridge University Press.

―― (1993). Centers of moral gravity: commentary on Donald Spence's "The Hermeneutic Turn." *Psychoanalytic Dialogues* 3(1):21–28.

Sartre, J. P. (1953). *Existential Psychoanalysis*, ed. Rollo May. Chicago: Philosophical Library.

Schafer, R. (1976). *A New Language for Psychoanalysis*. New Haven: Yale University Press.

_____ (1983). *The Analytic Attitude*. New York: Basic Books.

Schur, M. (1960). Discussion of Dr. John Bowlby's paper. *Psychoanalytic Study of the Child* 15:63. New York: International Universities Press.

Searles, H. (1967). The "dedicated physician" in the field of psychotherapy and psychoanalysis. In *Countertransference and Related Subjects*. Madison, CT: International Universities Press, 1979.

Sharpe, E. F. (1949). *Dream Analysis*. London: Hogarth Press.

Spence, D. P. (1982). *Narrative Truth and Historical Truth*. New York: Norton.

_____ (1993). The hermeneutic turn: soft science or loyal opposition? *Psychoanalytic Dialogues* 3(1):1–10.

Spitz, R. (1960). Discussion of Dr. John Bowlby's paper. *Psychoanalytic Study of the Child* 15:85. New York: International Universities Press.

Steiner, G. (1989). *Real Presences*. Chicago: University of Chicago Press.

Stern, D. (1985). *The Interpersonal World of the Infant*. New York: Basic Books.

Stone, L. (1961). *The Psychoanalytic Situation*. New York: International Universities Press.

Sulloway, F. (1979). *Freud, Biologist of the Mind*. New York: Basic Books.

Suter, R. (1989). *Interpreting Wittgenstein*. Philadelphia: Temple University Press.

Szajnberg, N. (1992). Psychoanalysis as an extension of the autobiographical genre: poetry and truth, fiction and reality. *International Review of Psycho-Analysis* 19:375.

Vizinczey, S. (1986). *Truth and Lies in Literature*. London: McClelland and Stewart.

Warme, G. (1987). The way of genius: psychological development in Thomas Mann's *The Magic Mountain*. *Psychoanalysis and Contemporary Thought* 10:4.

Winnicott, D. (1942). *The Child, The Family, and the Outside World.* London: Penguin Books, 1964.

Wittgenstein, L. (1931). *Culture and Value,* ed. G. H. von Wright, trans. P. Winch. Chicago: University of Chicago Press, 1980.

—— (1958). *Philosophical Investigations,* ed. G. E. M. Anscombe and R. Rhees, trans. G. E. M. Anscombe, 3rd ed. New York: Macmillan; 1958.

—— (1967). *Lectures and Conversations on Aesthetics, Psychology and Religious Belief,* ed. C. Barrett. Berkeley: University of California Press.

—— (1974). *Philosophical Grammar,* ed. R. Rhees, trans. A. Kenny. Berkeley: University of California Press, 1974.

Wright, L. (1993). Remembering Satan. *The New Yorker,* May 17 and May 24.

Zee, H. (1972). Blindspots in recognizing serious suicidal intentions. *Bulletin of the Menninger Clinic* 36:551–555.

Index